PENGUIN BOOKS

NOT JUST LUCKY

Jamila Rizvi is a writer, presenter and commentator. Previously, she worked as an adviser in the Rudd and Gillard governments and was Editor-in-Chief of the Mamamia Women's Network. Jamila has been named one of Australia's 100 Most Influential Women by the *Financial Review*. She lives in Melbourne with her husband, Jeremy, her son, Rafi, and a lot of clean but regrettably unfolded washing. It is not Jamila's hand on the cover of this book; her nails aren't that pretty.

JAMILA RIZVI

NOT JUST LUCKY

Why women do the work but don't take the credit

PENGUIN BOOKS

PENGUIN BOOKS

UK | USA | Canada | Ireland | Australia
India | New Zealand | South Africa | China

Penguin Books is part of the Penguin Random House group of companies
whose addresses can be found at global.penguinrandomhouse.com.

Penguin
Random House
Australia

First published by Penguin Random House Australia Pty Ltd, 2017
This edition published by Penguin Random House Australia Pty Ltd, 2018

Text copyright © Jamila Rizvi, 2017

The moral right of the author has been asserted.

Cover design by Adam Laszczuk © Penguin Random House Australia Pty Ltd
Cover photograph by Nilesh Patankar/Alamy Stock Photo
Typeset in Adobe Garamond by Adam Laszczuk, Penguin Random House Australia Pty Ltd
Printed and bound in Australia by Griffin Press, an accredited ISO AS/NZS 14001
Environmental Management Systems printer.

A catalogue record for this
book is available from the
National Library of Australia

NATIONAL
LIBRARY
OF AUSTRALIA

ISBN 978 0 14378 354 1

penguin.com.au

For Jeremy.
Thank you for loving and supporting me,
even when I am not very nice.

And for the women who became so much more
to me than colleagues, you know who you are
and none of you were 'just lucky'.

CONTENTS

AUTHOR'S NOTE

In this book there will be generalisations. I'm going to say a lot of 'women feel this' and 'women are expected to behave like that'. Generalisations are an intellectual necessity but also an imperfect tool – there are always exceptions. So what I say about women will not be the experience of every woman reading. Similarly, there will be men and non-binary people that pick up this book and see themselves in the experiences I describe. After first reading the introduction, my husband commented on how much he identified with the feelings of self-doubt that I wrote about. Lack of confidence isn't the exclusive domain of women.

An exploration of gender involves using terms like 'women' and 'men' to analyse the different roles and responsibilities society ascribes to us. I want to be clear that when I speak about women, I mean to do so as inclusively as possible. Gender is not biologically determined. Gender is a socially enforced identity, as well as a personal one, and affects how we present, how we understand and how we are treated in the workplace. Women's experiences at work are also shaped – and disadvantages amplified – by other aspects of their person, such as race, sexuality, disability, class and religion.

That is a long and complicated way of saying the entirety of this book might not apply to you. That's okay. Take from it what is helpful and applicable to your life, and leave the rest for someone else. Consider this book the non-fiction, feminist version of a breakfast buffet. Mmm. Buffet.

INTRODUCTION

Because women should buy more lottery tickets.

I'm on stage at the Australian National University in Canberra, dressed in full academic regalia and gazing out at a blur of expectant undergraduate faces. In front of me are notes that I've written, rewritten and rewritten again. They're still not quite right. My hands grip either side of the dark wooden lectern, feet planted shoulder-width apart. I read somewhere that this stance projects power and authority. I hope that's the case. Although I sincerely doubt I'm projecting anything other than my own self-consciousness.

Graduation speeches are a tricky business because there are so many people to please. Each group in the audience has different, often contradictory expectations of what the address should be. The administration wants something with an air of gravitas and a sense of occasion. This is a shame because it means all my best 'drunk at Orientation Week' stories are automatic nonstarters. Parents, who have spent significant time and sometimes money on their child's education, want to be assured of a return on investment. They want to be told that their baby done good. To feel secure in the knowledge that a suburban brick house, the latest model Lexus and a

Thermomix lie in their kid's future. The students themselves are the trickiest customers. They're craving advice and inspiration, but mostly they just want to have a laugh. They're anticipating you'll deliver none of the above.

Online are YouTube videos of great graduation speeches given by people like J.K. Rowling, Barack Obama, Jim Carrey and Steve Jobs. The many millions of views attest to the peak levels of inspirational-ness they delivered. Their words are tremendous. The speakers deftly weave a linguistic combination of encouragement, insight, laughter and poetry. So that's not intimidating at all. Add to this the fact that only four years earlier I'd been sitting in the same hall waiting to receive my own undergraduate degrees. A little bored and a lot uncomfortable, I remember that my hired gown smelled of stale sweat. I couldn't wait to take it off. The students here today are similarly over it. They want me to get on with my disappointing speech so they can go outside. They want to drink champagne and Instagram themselves throwing their caps in the air.

By now the audience has firmly reached the conclusion that I'm nervous. I've been silent at the lectern too long for it to be purposeful. Some audience members are looking at me intently, wondering if maybe this might be more interesting than they'd anticipated. Maybe I'm about to fall apart. My hands are vibrating so violently I'm sure it's visible from the back row. They'll all be assuming that I've got a severe case of the panics, and fair enough. Who am I to be giving a speech of this scale? Who am I to be standing in this grand place, telling people only a few years my junior how to succeed? What brilliant career advice could I possibly have? I still get anxious merging lanes in busy Sydney traffic. I bite my fingernails until they bleed, forget to pay the water bill and have never used an accountant. I don't remember which night is bin night. Who wants life advice from a person who eats Milo straight from the tin?

But I'm not actually shaking because of nerves. My anxiety about mispronouncing a word or tripping over the hem of my gown has been suddenly displaced. I feel overcome by something far more powerful. It's the sort of thing that my mates would tell me to stop being so bloody earnest and politically correct over. 'Not everything is about feminism *all* the time,' they'd say, rolling their eyes at my apparent melodrama. But I can't help it. My chest feels hot and heavy. I'm a mess of frustrated anger.

In front of me are hundreds of young people excited to enter the workforce, keen for their 'real' lives to begin. Their heads are full of possibilities. They're giddy with impatience. They envisage great, grand and dazzling careers. Between them there's a veritable abundance of ambition, idealism and cleverness. These are women and men who will go on to build cities, cure diseases, protect the planet, write the truth and create a fairer, more equal world. But those same women and men will be anything *but* equal in the years to come. Tomorrow the women in the room will embark on their working lives already one step behind the blokes sitting beside them.

Even the women who have topped their classes and scooped the awards pool will get starting salaries of $3000 a year less than their men peers. They've been told all their lives that girls can do anything, that girls can be anything and that they're just as good as boys. But that's only partially true. For those who haven't already experienced it, gender bias is about to rear its ugly, discriminatory head. This is a lesson that women who went directly from school to paid work learned years earlier. Women are consistently and systematically undervalued in Australian workplaces.

Well, unless they get lucky, that is . . .

Have you ever noticed that really successful women are always lucky? Lucky women have made it in every sphere of professional life, from courts of law to the bright lights of Hollywood, from the pointy end of corporate hierarchies to floodlit Olympic stadiums. Women who were given a chance. Women who were in the right place at the right time. Women who caught all the breaks. And also all the clichés.

Flagged down by *Access Hollywood* after her best actress win at the Academy Awards, Cate Blanchett said, 'Every single female performance was amazing, and the fact that they chose me? I'm lucky.' Television host and former magazine editor Lisa Wilkinson got her start in media because she was 'lucky enough to find that job in the paper, to be in the right place at the right time'. Just before Gail Kelly became CEO of Westpac Banking Corporation, the previous CEO was 'as luck would have it' looking to finish up. Nicola Roxon was Australia's first woman attorney-general, yet speaking about her first year in parliament Roxon recalled how uncomfortable she was receiving compliments from colleagues. 'Oh, I was just lucky,' she'd say, explaining away her achievements as chance.

This epidemic of women's luckiness isn't confined to the lucky country. Look across the seas and far away, and you'll find countless women kicking arse – all of whom just happened to get lucky. The formidable Lady Justice Brenda Hale said upon her appointment to the British Supreme Court that she 'was in the right place at the right time'. Reflecting on her career before writing *Lean In*, Facebook COO Sheryl Sandberg said that she 'was hugely lucky, and that explains most of my success'. The late Princess Diana described the influence she had through her humanitarian work as 'lucky enough in the fact that I have found my role'. PepsiCo CEO Indra Nooyi 'wouldn't be here today' if she hadn't been lucky to have mentors to guide her. Olympic judo champion Ronda Rousey said 'the Olympics is a once-in-a-lifetime thing. I was lucky to go twice, but most people only get one chance.' And what helped Ursula Burns, the first black American woman in charge of a Fortune 500 company, to progress from summer intern to full-time employee to the top job? You guessed it – luck.

Except not really.

Luck describes random occurrences, events that are outside our control. For an outcome to be considered 'lucky', success must be unlikely were it not for chance. By this measure, to be considered truly 'lucky', these women's successes must literally hinge on a particular chance event. And that's hardly believable. It's not like these women rolled the dice of life and plonked their tokens down on Mayfair while the rest of us landed on the $100 Super Tax space. Yes, luck inevitably had an impact on their lives and many of these women were born into privilege. However, the likely outcome for these women, regardless of any lucky event, would not have been failure. They would almost certainly have found some kind of career success. When women attribute their enormous achievements to luck, they discount other, far more relevant factors. Factors like hard work, honed skills and natural talent. This is the true source of their success. They weren't just lucky. They were really good at their jobs.

It's not only women at the peak of their careers who call themselves lucky, either. I've noticed the same word creeping into the conversations of my twenty- and thirty-something friends and colleagues. No doubt there are young women graduating from high schools, TAFEs and universities today who use it to describe themselves. *She was dux of her year and captain of the rowing team: lucky. She made partner in the law firm by age forty: lucky. Her hairdressing*

*business has an annual turnover of half a million dollars: lucky. She
wrote a bestselling novel: lucky. She's on the principal track and has
only been teaching seven years: lucky, lucky, lucky.*

So why are successful women quick to put their achievements
down to chance? After all, only a handful of women make it to
the very top of their fields. Why is it that those who do aren't able
to recognise the contribution of their own talents to what they've
achieved? Why are women so reluctant to claim credit for their
own success?

It's all about expectations. Expectations that society has about
what a woman should be and how she should behave. Expectations
that women themselves have internalised and made their own.
Expectations that, as a woman, your role is to make yourself likeable above all else.

If little girls are made of sugar and spice and all things nice,
then adult women are basically pavlova. Early in womanhood we
are taught to please others, whether that is our parents or our teachers or our peers. We're encouraged to behave nicely and follow all
the rules and are told that rewards will flow from that. By teenage-
hood, popularity is the northern star for girls, guiding their every
move. Those who achieve Peak Likeability reign supreme in the
schoolyard, Queen Bees each and every one of them.

As adults, women learn to put the emotional needs of others
ahead of their own. It is Mum, not Dad, who is expected to sac-
rifice her own fulfilment for that of her children. It is sister, not
brother, who is presumed will take care of elderly relatives and drop
the lasagne round when the next-door neighbour is sick.

Inevitably, the ugly shadow of these expectations infiltrates
workplaces too. In the office, women stand back and let others have
a turn rather than thrusting themselves forwards. We are polite,

deferential, helpful, and if we're not we face social repercussions. Modesty is a mandatory workplace requirement lest women appear intimidating, pushy or, *worst of all*, ambitious. Where men are bold and visionary, women are aggressive and overbearing. Falling over themselves to appear nice and non-threatening, even the highest-achieving women in the world attribute their success to chance.

'I was just lucky,' she says aloud.

Please don't hate me is her unspoken plea.

The negative ramifications of these unwritten rules of women's likeability are most apparent at work because workplaces reward precisely the opposite kind of behaviour to what is generally expected of women. This is particularly true of corporate structures. Traditional workplaces were built for, and by, men. Women are still relatively recent additions to these environments in the context of history. Women remain few and far between in the rooms where executive decisions are made and office culture is shaped. So workplaces continue to accommodate and reinforce typically masculine behaviour. Self-promotion remains the fastest path to actual promotion. Big deals are sealed through competition, not collaboration. Leadership opportunities are awarded to the dominant, not the deferential. More money is paid to those who ask for it, rather than those who worked hard for it.

Women are left with an impossible trade-off between being liked and being successful. It's a Sophie's Choice hard-coded into Microsoft Outlook and hidden between the lines of shift rosters and interdepartmental memos. The result is gender bias that's firmly taken root inside our own heads. A bias just as powerful and sinister as the one that sees women earn on average $1 million less than a man over the course of a lifetime. A bias that manifests itself as an inner voice that tells us we're not good enough. A voice that says we do not belong. A voice that warns us we might fail and nobody will like us if we do. A voice that slowly, surreptitiously, erodes a woman's belief in her own abilities.

I spent several years as the editor-in-chief of Australia's largest independent women's website. In that job, my boss was a woman, my team were women, my team's teams were women, and our readers were women. Management supplied tampons in the toilets. Too busy for lunch breaks, we ate cereal sprinkled with oestrogen at our desks (I'm kidding but only a little). The women I worked with were clever, curious and determined. They had every reason to feel buoyant about their futures, and yet when success did come their way it was always met with surprise and hesitation. An intern called Kahla was once so taken aback when I offered her a permanent job that she actually tried to talk me into hiring someone else. She wanted the role but, despite being an emerging writer of considerable talent, she couldn't wrap her head around why she had been chosen above others.

My experience working in federal politics was entirely different. The corridors of political power are dominated by two kinds of people: old men in suits and young men in suits. When I worked in Parliament House, my world was full of men: a legitimate sausage fest. The women tended to be employed in less senior roles and their voices rarely carried the weight of their men colleagues. When they did hold positions of power, women were treated differently and scrutinised more closely. Regardless of the actual gender breakdown in the building, it was decidedly a man's world. This remained the case even when Julia Gillard became Australia's first woman prime minister. While a brilliant woman occupied the main office, there were still men in the background and on the sidelines making her already difficult job all the more so.

My four years working predominantly with men in politics was immediately followed by those four years working almost exclusively with women in media. The most significant difference between my experiences was undoubtedly the confidence of the young people I worked with. The men tended to display the easy self-assurance of those who know they belong. They understood the rules of this game. I remember one occasion sitting in my office with a young bloke who reported to me. He had made what can only be described as a monumental cock-up. After I carefully explained the scale of the problem to him, he shrugged his shoulders and said, 'Shit, eh, that's some bad luck, isn't it?'

The men I came into contact with tended to feel very much in control of their careers. The world tells men they are masters of their own destinies and they believe it. They know how they want their working lives to go and take active steps to get there. They assume a high degree of influence over the world around them. Success is not a desire or a hope for them but the natural result of their hard work and skill. Their failures are treated as aberrations, mere tripping points on their way to the summit of Everest.

By contrast, the women I've worked with assumed that their success lay in the hands of others and that they had little control over outcomes. They put their heads down, their bums up and work bloody hard, waiting to be tapped on the shoulder for a promotion. They leave it to their colleagues or managers to determine their worth, rather than asserting it themselves. When success comes their way, they worry it's a mistake or that they didn't really earn it. Failure is something women feel deeply responsible for, and often take as evidence of a personal deficiency.

I suspect we have history to thank for the sense women have of being at the mercy of others. Until very recently the story of humanity was entirely controlled by men. Prior to the nineteenth century, most women had no financial and legal independence. Women were regarded as the property of their fathers and brothers until that ownership was transferred to a husband. In some parts of the world, this remains the case today. Historically, women were unable to own property under their name. The first record of women attaining university qualifications was the 1870s and even then a professional career wasn't available to them. Most countries didn't award women the vote until the twentieth century. For women of colour it took a whole lot longer. It wasn't until the 1960s that Australian women were able to control their own fertility with reliable contraceptives. Women's right to access safe, legal and affordable abortion remains contentious and is still a crime in some states. Equal pay is a myth. Large corporations control the vast majority of the world's wealth and men control the vast majority of those corporations.

So is it any wonder that women feel like the world is in control of them, rather than the other way around? Is it any wonder that we consider our success to be luck rather than something of our own making?

Think about the women you've worked with. Think about yourself. How many times have you scoffed at praise for your own work and instead credited the people around you? Have you ever been too nervous to ask what the salary was in a job interview, and then accepted the surprisingly low amount because you assumed you couldn't ask for more? Do you think twice about taking risks, worried that the universe might deliver an outcome you won't be able to handle? Have you ever wanted to ask for more Sunday shifts but didn't want to appear 'greedy'? How about looking at the selection criteria for a job you would love, but deciding not to apply? Was it because you didn't quite tick every box?

Have you ever had to give a big presentation at work and been embarrassed by the applause that came at its conclusion? Did you spend the next ten minutes telling anyone who would listen that you ran out of time to prepare, that your PowerPoint didn't work properly, that really it wasn't very good at all? Have you ever argued with the nagging internal voice of self-doubt? The voice that warns, *You don't deserve this, you're not up to it.* Do you sometimes feel like you're actually a fraud? A pretender? That unlike everyone else who earned their success, you just got lucky? Do you play down your past achievements because you fear you won't be able to replicate them in the future? Do you live with a stomach-churning sense of inevitability that eventually, one day, like some sort of awful bomb with a staccato-ticking cartoon timer, your good luck will run out?

Me too.

Young women today are entering the workforce well aware that gender bias exists. Thanks to the internet they are more cognisant of and articulate about these issues than any generation before them. They've heard about the pay gap and the old boys' club and the boardrooms full of men. They read in the newspaper on International Women's Day that even at the top, women managers earn on average $93 000 less per year than men. They understand that moving in and out of the workforce around childbirth and childrearing will bring challenges. They're expecting all of that stuff. What they're *not* expecting are the obstacles that have already been planted inside their own heads. Social conditioning tells them that women should behave one way, but career success requires them to behave entirely differently. They can't win.

As a measure of gender equality, the media often points to politics. We observe that there are more women in parliaments today than there were forty years ago and consider this a sign of progress.

But the question we ask far less often is: How many women never put up their hands to run for election in the first place? In other words, how many women would have liked to do the job but were made to feel that it wasn't for them? One famous piece of research showed how differently women and men make the decision to apply for a new job. When faced with an advertised role, women will only apply if they meet close to 100 per cent of the listed criteria. Women consider a company's description of the ideal candidate and think about all the ways they *don't* measure up to that. Men, on the other hand, will apply for a job when they meet just 60 per cent of the criteria. In politics and business, women are ruling themselves out of contention for jobs that they *really want* if they're anything less than perfect. Men are willing to have a shot regardless. This tells us that gender bias doesn't just affect the final outcome. It dictates women's decision to get in the game in the first place. Lack of confidence can hold women back before lack of opportunity even has a chance to take effect.

It's in vogue to label women's absence of confidence as the culprit for workplace inequality. My own experience tells me there is a lot of truth in that, but what I can't abide is the outrageous way women are blamed for it. Our society raises women to behave in a certain way and expect certain things, but when the workplace turns around and whacks them for doing exactly that, we tell them it's their own fault. Women are blamed for the lack of confidence that the world has given them. Even though that lack of confidence is entirely rational given the gender inequality they're up against.

. . . And this is why I am standing at the lectern mute. Still frustrated, still angry, and entirely unsure about how to begin my speech. The bright, eager young women in front of me share the hopeful and expectant expressions of their men peers. They don't,

however, share the same future. It feels phony to deliver them the
same speech. I am here charged with providing wisdom and all I've
got is a Hallmark card–style presentation full of empty platitudes.
The women deserve better than what I have to give them. Each of
them knows that the glass ceiling exists, but nobody has been brave
enough to tell them that there's one on every floor of the building,
and that they're double-glazed.

As it turns out, I'm not brave either.

I'm embarrassed to say that I delivered my speech as written.
Later that afternoon I clinked glasses with the students, effusively
thanked faculty members and congratulated proud parents, all
while wearing the smiling mask of a deceiver. Alone in my room
that evening I began writing a series of notes. They were notes
about what I wished I could have said. As my thoughts became
longer, messier and admittedly rather ranty, I realised that there
was a book emerging from the scribble. This book.

The ambition of this book is simple: to challenge and change
the way women think about their work, their careers and each
other. To help them realise that they're bigger, better and braver
than they thought and that their success is deeply and inextricably
intertwined with that of other women.

The book is an exploration of the deeply gendered nature of
Australian workplaces and how that affects the way women think
about success. It reveals truths about gender inequality that you
may not be able to name but that you've almost certainly encoun-
tered. It won't stop you experiencing sexual harassment or retiring
with less superannuation, or deliver affordable childcare – even
though I dearly wish it could. But it will assist you to navigate the
contents of your own mind a little better and restore your faith in
your own abilities.

Together we'll examine what confidence looks like, what it sounds like and what it feels like. We'll tackle some of the big personal workplace challenges, like applying for new jobs, managing people, dealing with imposter syndrome, coping with a bad boss and, yes, how to ask for more money. You will come to realise that confidence is mostly about conditioning. It's about what you've been told and what you've been taught. And while what has been put into your brain by a gender-biased world can't be removed, it can be countered with facts.

I want to help you understand why you think the way you do, what you can do to change it and why it's not your fault. This means grappling with the social, psychological and gender norms that contribute to women's confidence deficit. It means questioning expectations of how women 'should' behave and what makes them likeable and what doesn't. It means finding the courage to try in spite of all of that and, most importantly of all, helping pull other women up along with you.

The book is limited by my own experiences. I do not claim to speak to – or for – all women. Nor would I ever seek to. I have had the enormous advantage of a comfortable middle-class upbringing and a world-class education. This has meant I've enjoyed freedoms and opportunities denied to many women. It also means I will never fully comprehend the struggles of those who have been systemically disadvantaged in ways that I haven't, no matter how intensely I might try.

I should also warn you that this isn't a self-help book. Nor is it an instruction manual on how to 'get ahead' at work. It isn't a book about balancing work and family, because I am still utterly confused about how to do that. It isn't an academic book or an inspirational book. There will be no heartfelt quotes in cursive writing, set against a backdrop of snow-capped mountains. And it certainly isn't a book about how you can learn from my career (although I do hope you'll at least get a laugh from my rather spectacular failures).

What this book is, is a career book that is unashamedly feminist. One that will help you to help yourself, but also prepare you to help the woman sitting beside you and the woman who dreams of sitting beside you but thinks she never will. It's a book that will help you to feel more confident about work without blaming you for being less-than-confident to begin with. It's a book that will help you become brave enough to truly enjoy the success of others and to claim the credit for your own.

It's a book about being more than just lucky.

It's a book about being brilliant.

FORGET ABOUT NATURE VERSUS NURTURE

Because how brave you are isn't how you were born.

Let's get the biological stuff out of the way up front, shall we?

If you held them in your hands, a man's brain would be bigger than a woman's. Historically this difference was used to justify discrimination against women. Smaller brain equals less intelligence, concluded the (bloke) scientists of the nineteenth century. That hypothesis has since been proven, to use the technical terminology, as bullshit. Men's brains are bigger because their bodies are physically bigger, yes. However female and male brains actually have the same number of cells, it's just that the cells in a female brain are more densely packed together. Modern science has repeatedly determined that the difference in cognitive abilities between female and male brains is nil. We're the same amount of smart.

Some research indicates that hormonal differences cause equally intelligent women and men to reason their way to the same outcome using different parts of the brain to get there. A female's capacity to think is the same as a male's, but we do – biologically speaking – think ever so slightly differently. If you've ever read the cartoon-illustrated classic *What's Happening to Me?*, you already know that the main sex hormones are oestrogen and testosterone. Both sexes possess both hormones, but in varying amounts. Females generally have higher levels of oestrogen and males have higher levels of testosterone. The levels vary over the course of a lifetime. Oestrogen is connected to the area of the brain in charge of social interaction and observation. That's why baby girls tend to develop their verbal communication skills more rapidly than boys. Testosterone has been linked to risk-taking and aggressive behaviour. When testosterone levels are present at higher levels in the body, a person is more likely to press ahead in the face of objective danger. While baby boys do experience surges of testosterone in the womb, the hormone doesn't appear in high concentration until puberty. This means little girls and boys are more hormonally similar than adult women and men. By adulthood, testosterone is present in males at a rate ten times higher than in females.

Researchers have produced varying results and come to varying conclusions about the extent of the brain's impact on gender. This isn't physics, where the laws of gravity haven't been contested since the apple fell from Newton's tree. Not everyone agrees. The existence and impact of sex-based differences on the brain is contentious. For example, the hippocampus (which is the part of the brain that controls emotion and memory formation) was previously thought to be larger in women than men. Anecdotally, this makes sense, given the female inclination for communication, friendship and emotional connection that we observe day-to-day. However, that hypothesis has more recently been called into question. Male brains have been found to have larger amygdala, which is the section of the brain that registers fear and triggers a confident and aggressive response. The development of a male brain in this way seems logical, given the human species' hunter-gatherer origins. But, again, more recent studies suggest that if you correct for body size, the difference isn't actually that significant. Those scientists are clever but awfully quarrelsome. The cause of all the difficulty is separating the genetic from the environmental. That is, what differences are caused by how we are born and what differences are the result of how we are raised. More recently, researchers have also come to ask an additional question: how do these two components *interact*?

Biologically similar but socially poles apart

Given that I didn't exactly excel in science at school, this is as far as we'll take the brain stuff. You may have noticed that we've been operating at the *Play School* level thus far. The key takeaway here is this: neurologically speaking, the male and female brains are overwhelmingly similar. In fact, the *total* genomic difference between the sexes is all of about one per cent. While every human being is, of course, born with their own unique set of characteristics, the nature of our personalities is enormously influenced by the environment we grow up in. Environment is critical in determining a person's gender identity.

Many of the attributes we consider 'female' and 'male' aren't determined by a gendered brain but are the by-product of a gendered world. The emerging field of epigenetics explores the interaction of genetics and environment in determining personality, and developments in that space are worthy of attention. More and more though, academics are coming to view gender as something that is socially constructed. In other words, we raise and respond to children differently depending on the sex they are born with. That in turn interacts with a child's individual characteristics to help determine the kind of person they become and how they behave. Lise Eliot, associate professor at the Chicago Medical School, explains it like this:

> All the mounting evidence indicates these ideas about hard-wired differences between male and female brains are wrong. Yes, there are basic behavioural differences between the sexes, but we should note that these differences increase with age because our children's intellectual biases are being exaggerated and intensified by our gendered culture . . . They are a result of what we expect a boy or a girl to be.

This means that the confidence gap between women and men is not something we can pin on biology. The gap isn't caused by women being born inherently less confident than men. It's a result of how they're expected to behave.

Culturally, Western societies value very different traits in girls and boys. This gender bias begins in infancy and has ramifications far beyond the pink versus blue dichotomy. Girls learn quickly that attractiveness is their most powerful asset. Positive attention is correlated with how a girl looks rather than what she can do or how much she knows. This shapes her view of the world and her role within it. Society values her first as an object of men's desire, and subsequently as a vessel and nurturer of new life. Of course, women's other endeavours are gaining more attention and recognition, but progress is painfully slow. You only have to glance at tabloid coverage of human rights lawyer Amal Clooney – which always focuses on what she's wearing and who she's married to, not what she's saying – to see that. This mixture of belief and expectation about what makes a girl valuable has fostered all manner of negative consequences. Much has been written about girls being taught that their power comes from prettiness. (If you're looking for material on this, you can't go past Naomi Wolf's *The Beauty Myth* as your starting point.) However, this isn't the only gender-based difference that affects how children are raised.

Modern parents are well versed in the danger of teaching a girl that her value lies in her looks. In fact, many new parents – myself included – work actively against the most obvious gender stereotypes. We're trying to raise little people who aren't limited by a binary view of gender. So we pat ourselves on the back for buying our boy a doll or our girl a truck, and think job well done, bravo me, potential disaster avoided. But the problems run far deeper than that. Gender bias is embedded in our subconscious in ways that even the best-intentioned parents fall victim to. The impact of gender roles increases as children spend more time living in a gendered world. From the moment a child is born, parents unwittingly begin to shape the confidence levels their child will carry into the workplace. And we shape our boys and girls differently.

Worrying about getting it wrong

'You can go first,' I said, gesturing elegantly with my right arm like a stewardess giving the safety demonstration. Standing at the top of the waterslide, my seven-year-old self was benevolence personified. Most kids clamoured up the stairs, pushing each other out of the way in a rush to the summit. They'd hurl themselves into the plastic tube of chlorinated water, often headfirst, ignoring the warning signs that said not to, in their haste to get to the bottom so they could begin the whole process again. Waterslides have a high time-investment-to-payoff ratio. The more squelchy steps you climb on the way up, the longer and more exciting the slide experience on the way down. On busy summer days you faced a ten- or even fifteen-minute wait while you lined up, shivering in clingy wet swimmers and trying not to step on a left-behind bandaid. Letting even one kid go down ahead of you was a pretty nice thing to do. And me? I graciously permitted dozens and dozens to take my place.

I was scared. Slides of that kind fell into the category of Truly Horrific Experiences that Everyone Else But Me Seemed To Enjoy. Even worse, during that summer all the kids were doing this fancy slide-down-on-your-knees-then-stand-up-halfway trick. I had never done it. I didn't know how to do it, and I didn't want to try for the first time in front of everyone. The only thing scarier than being on that waterslide was other kids watching me attempt the trick and failing. It would be primary-school social suicide. So up those stairs I went, pretending to be cool but dreading the fact I would eventually have to come down again. Once at the top, my stalling tactic was to let every other kid go ahead of me. But after a quarter of an hour ushering other kids forward, the same ones were returning for their next slide. I was about to be found out. The ruse was up.

I was an incredibly cautious kid. I was genuinely scared of heights, but I was even more scared of looking foolish in front of peers. My parents were pretty understanding of their eldest daughter's nervousness. Adults generally were indulgent. Teachers would shrug their shoulders in gym when I flatly refused to take the balance beam. A friend's dad even called my fears 'cute'. It would have been a far tougher existence had I been born a boy. A boy wouldn't have had the luxury of gentle coaxing and kind encouragement. He would have suffered the ire of coaches, uncles and friends of the family who told him to 'man up'. Risk-taking is applauded and even expected in boys. The grazed knees and broken bones that come from physical exertion are simply part of being a boy. Injury is a badge of honour.

Dainty little girls and big tough boys

Did you know that mothers hug their girl babies more often and are willing to spend longer periods of time comforting them when they cry? Some studies show that a mother will lie in bed at night hoping a baby boy will settle himself for much longer than she will wait for a girl baby. Parents also think they see different strengths or personality traits in a newborn girl and boy. For example, baby boys are more likely to be oohed and aahed over for being strong or athletic. When my son was born, all the early visitors exclaimed over his height and long feet. 'He'll play footy for Carlton!' they crowed. The family took great pride in my son's supposedly brilliant hand–eye coordination even during those first few weeks of life when he didn't know he had hands or eyes. By contrast, girl babies are called 'sweet' or 'gentle'. Those descriptors follow them into toddlerhood despite the fact that all toddlers, irrespective of gender, are irrational monsters incapable of such qualities. These doting parental observations aren't actually observations. They're projections.

Even before the age of one, parents anticipate the development of children differently depending on gender. Parents of boys have higher expectations of their child's physical capabilities, and those expectations kick in earlier. One study asked mothers of eleven-month-old babies to describe their child's crawling competency. Mothers of sons routinely *over*estimated their child's ability, even though girl infants actually develop faster than boys. Parents of girls are also more ready to assist their children with difficult tasks rather than let them figure it out themselves. While girls and boys spend roughly the same amount of time engaged in physical play, girls tend to be asked more questions by their parents about what they're doing. Boys are left to get on with it.

Boy children are more actively encouraged to explore their physical limits independently of adults. In one study, researchers observed the different ways parents behaved when watching their kids play on a fireperson's pole. Both girls and boys were encouraged to have a go by their parents, but different attitudes became apparent when the child was struggling. Parents of boys would shout instructions from the comfortable park bench, often coupled with phrases of encouragement like, 'You can do it.' Parents of girls were more likely to caution their child against hurting themselves and intervene bodily to assist.

The underlying assumption here is that girls are physically fragile and less able. The use of value-laden phrases such as 'don't be such a girl' and 'man up' reveal how entrenched the assumption is. Biologically speaking, it's unfounded. The research I described above was all conducted before the children reached seven, so puberty had not yet created any meaningful difference in strength between girls and boys. Other than standing or sitting down to wee, kids are basically the same at that age. The assumption that girls are less physically able creates a self-fulfilling prophecy. Girls receive a subconscious message from adults that their physical limits are lesser than boys, so they become more cautious and tend to be less adventurous as a result.

Importantly, girls don't need to observe different treatment to come to this view. They aren't necessarily making an active comparison between how they and their brother are treated. Girls take the messages adults send them about their own physical abilities and internalise them. At a macro level that message is different to the message being sent to boys, and different messages will yield different results. Across the developed world, records show that teenage girls grow up to be substantially less physically active than their boy peers. Adult women participate less in organised sport when compared to men.

Another generation of brave boys and perfect girls

The effect of this differential treatment extends well beyond the physical. Girls' conditioned nervousness about trying new activities has ramifications for the more general development of new skills. Think about it like this: a parent shouts repeated words of caution to their daughter at the park. When she tries something new, the parent might even bodily correct her and make sure she doesn't get hurt. This happens again and again and again. The little girl puts together the pieces of a mental jigsaw and concludes two things. First, taking risks is dangerous and perhaps it's safer not to try unless she has help. Second, failing at a new activity is bad and should be avoided. Her confidence to navigate the world independently is affected, as is her confidence to take risks and be comfortable with getting something wrong before she eventually gets it right. She sucks up the unspoken information her parents are giving her about her own abilities and sets her expectations accordingly.

Reshma Saujani, the founder and CEO of Girls Who Code, describes this as teaching boys to be brave and girls to be perfect. She sees the evidence of how this childhood gender bias plays out in her work. Saujani says:

> Every Girls Who Code teacher tells me the same story. During the first week, when the girls are learning how to code, a student will call her over and she'll say, 'I don't know what code to write.' The teacher will look at her screen, and she'll see a blank text editor. If she didn't know any better, she'd think that her student

spent the past 20 minutes just staring at the screen. But if she presses undo a few times, she'll see that her student wrote code and then deleted it. She tried, she came close, but she didn't get it exactly right. Instead of showing the progress that she made, she'd rather show nothing at all.

It's worth noting that the divergent treatment of girls and boys doesn't only have social repercussions but biological ones. A whopping 90 per cent of human brain development happens in the first five years of life, and a big chunk of the rest happens in the next five. Babies are born with few synapses in their brains; these are mostly formed postnatally. A synapse is basically like a traffic light intersection for the central nervous system. Neurons have to pass through synapses as the brain sends messages to various parts of the body. Similar to driving the same route to work so many times that it becomes instinctive, when a child receives the same gendered messages again and again, their synapses are formed and refined in line with that. So when a parent repeatedly and consistently treats their daughter one way and their son another, it affects the neural pathways that are formed. These gendered messages are coming at kids from all directions and from the earliest years. The more they hear or observe them, the stronger the actual physical pathway that forms in their brain in response.

Everything parents say and do – and everything they don't say and do – sends a message to their children about how the world works, as well as hard-wiring their brain to respond in a certain way. What we learn during childhood shapes the adults we become and how we approach the world. Parents are a child's greatest influencers in those early years, and we are unconsciously teaching our girls they should be scared. We're telling them to avoid risks. We're telling them that mistakes are bad and that failure is something to be ashamed of. We're telling them to ask for help rather than back themselves, or, worse, we're teaching them not to have a go in the first place. It creates worry and caution that girls carry with them for life.

Kids think that the way things are is the way they should be.

Adults shape children's view of the world even when children aren't part of the equation. Take the election of Australia's first woman prime minister, Julia Gillard, as an example. Few people who voted for the Labor Party in 2010 did so solely because they wanted their children to see a woman running the country (although high five to you if you did). Issues like education, healthcare and the economy were bigger priorities for most voters. Nonetheless, Gillard's woman-ness almost certainly had an impact on how Australia's youngest citizens saw and approached the world. While adults who'd never seen a woman prime minister before thought Gillard a novelty, preschoolers who'd never experienced anything else set their future expectations accordingly.

As a political adviser in the Gillard government, I remember an occasion sitting on a miniature red plastic chair around a table that was roughly half the height of my knees. It was an uncomfortable but necessary posture. You can't rally a group of three- and four-year-olds to behave without being on their level. You have to look them in the eyes. Literally. Later that day, the prime minister would be holding a press conference in this childcare centre in outer-suburban Sydney. My task was to make sure the kids weren't totally mental when she arrived.

The Hollywood adage about never working with children or animals exists for a reason. Kids are the absolute worst when they see a television camera. They sense the anticipation of adults nearby and go out of their way to be ghastly. But little kids also make for adorable front-page-winning pictures – so I had to make it work. Unfortunately, I was faced that day with a particularly discerning bunch of preschoolers. I'd used all my standard warm-up material and gotten nothing in return. One little boy, the redheaded ringleader of the bunch, wasn't giving me any love. He provided expressionless stares in response to my animated questions and hilarious jokes. The other kids followed his lead. I had no choice but to shamelessly suck up to him.

'Now, what do you want to be when you grow up?' I asked my redheaded nemesis.

No response.

'You know, I bet you would be really good at being the boss of people.'

No response.

'So you'll need a job where you can be in charge of everybody. Even in charge of your parents. And your teachers!' I coaxed.

Arched single eyebrow followed by further silence.

'Maybe you could be in charge of the *whole* country. Would you like that? Would you like to be in charge of the whole country? Would you like to be the prime minister like Julia Gillard?'

'No,' he replied coolly.

'Why not?' I said, on the verge of breaking down.

'Because that's a girl's job.'

Too right, kiddo.

Kids are attentive observers of the adult world, but their understanding of what they observe is limited by their undeveloped brains. This means that their observation of how things are translates automatically to how they think things should be. For a child who had only ever known life with Julia Gillard occupying the prime minister's office, a woman running the country was simply the way it should be. This mental transition from observation-to-assumption happens constantly for children whose brains are working overtime to figure out how adulthood works. A child's brain begins to process gender roles around age two. This is well before they're able to speak in complete sentences. Children then set about trying to work out what constitutes 'maleness' and 'femaleness' – so they can copy.

Parents are a child's primary source for how women and men are expected to behave and what they are expected to become. Kids observe which of their parents is the first to back down in an argument. They notice who cries and who yells. When sitting down for dinner, children take note of who sits where at the table. They notice who cooks and they notice who serves. They take this information and store it away in their little heads. Then, when the time comes, they retrieve the information, add it together with other pieces of information and start to form patterns and draw conclusions. In families with two parents of different genders, children observe that it's mostly Mum doing the pick-ups and drop-offs from school, and that the same is true for their friends' mums. Then they notice that when the whole family goes on holiday together, Dad drives and Mum sits in the passenger seat. The mental check happens: *Driving is important. Mum can drive. Dad can drive. But when Mum and Dad are together, Dad does the driving. Dads are better at this important thing. Dads are more important.*

While developmentally parents are the biggest influencers on gender identity in early life, the influence of peers tends to take over as childhood progresses. We know from our own pre-teen years that the high opinion of our girlfriends meant more than anything else. The praise or censure of a child's peers can have a similar effect to that of a parent, and children's views also tend to favour conformity to gender stereotypes. The sanctioning of what is and isn't appropriate behaviour for girls and boys is often direct and explicit among young children. I remember overhearing a friend's four-year-old telling off a toddler he was playing with because the toy she was using was 'for boys only'. He was incredibly sure of himself and confident in laying down the laws of imaginary play. In fact, a child's understanding and knowledge of gender stereotypes is well established by age six. Gender-segregated play also begins in the early years but is carried through into young adulthood. Through the formation of cliques, girls further reinforce stereotypes to one another about the behaviour that is expected of their gender.

All of these actions from adults and their peers send children a message about power, roles, jobs and gender. The simplest of actions by parents, like who skips work to stay home when a child is sick, helps shape a child's perception of which parent's job is more important. Just like the little boy who thought he could never be prime minister, children assume that how things are is how they are supposed to be. These messages determine their expectations of how adults of their gender 'should' behave and what they are entitled to expect in return. Those messages stay with them for the rest of their lives, forming the basis of adult gender-identity stereotypes.

Don't believe me? Try this little riddle on for size:

A father and son are driving in their car down a busy highway. There is a terrible accident and, tragically, the father is killed. The boy is rushed to the nearest hospital, prepped for surgery and lies unconscious on the operating table. The surgeon enters the room and says immediately, 'I am sorry. I can't operate. That is my son.' *Who is the surgeon?*

I've put this riddle to dozens of people – women and men – being careful to avoid any explanatory context. The answers included everything from 'the surgeon is his biological father, the boy was adopted', 'the man who was killed is his step-dad', right through to 'the surgeon is God'. Test it out on your own friends and family. You'll be surprised by how many people don't see the simple, obvious answer. Unconscious gender bias, ingrained in us from the earliest years of childhood, is deeply held. That bias tells us that there are jobs for women and there are jobs for men. That there are things women normally do, and working in a demanding, high-powered job isn't one of them.

We rarely realise that the surgeon in the riddle is the boy's mother.

SUGAR, SPICE AND ALL THINGS NICE

Because that's what little girls are made of.

A girl is presented with two paper dolls.

The first doll wears a black miniskirt and platform heels. Her midriff is exposed. She appears to be headed for a night out on the town. If Doll Number One's mum is anything like mine, she'll be chasing her out the front door proffering a cardigan. The second doll is dressed in flared denim jeans, a cream and blue V-neck sweater, and sneakers. Doll Number Two is cool but relaxed. She could be meeting a girlfriend for coffee, going to the skate park or spending the afternoon at the library. The dolls are physically identical. Blue eyes, tan skin and orange-coloured hair. They're slim-bodied with sweet, smiling red mouths and friendly, open expressions. The only difference is how they are dressed.

The girl is asked a series of questions. Which of the dolls do you want to look like? Which of the dolls would you like to play with? Which of the dolls is the popular girl at school?

She chooses Doll Number One. Every time.

The girl leaves the room and another takes her place. She is presented with the same two dolls and asked the same series of questions.

She chooses Doll Number One. Every time.

Again and again the scenario is repeated. Girls enter the same room, are presented with the same paper dolls and asked the same questions. Again and again they choose Doll Number One. She is the pretty doll. The sexy doll. The *beautiful* doll. By the end of the experiment, a whopping 72 per cent of girls have identified the 'beautiful' doll as being more popular, and 68 per cent would like to look like her if they could. She's the doll you want to hang out with.

Why? Because 'everybody likes her'.

There is a very precise pressure on Australian girls to look and behave in a certain way. The approval of parents, teachers, other adults and even their peers is contingent on conforming to feminine stereotypes. Those stereotypes are overwhelming for a girl of only six or seven years old, the age of the children in the experiment, so she conflates them. She looks at how adults around her interact and, with the crystal clarity of child logic, she draws her own conclusions. *Special clothes make you beautiful. Being beautiful makes you popular. Being popular means everyone likes you.* So that's the doll you choose. There is little room for shades of grey in the world of a primary school student. A little girl projects all the positive 'feminine' qualities she's been told to aspire to onto the same doll. Physical beauty, being dressed up and being liked are all parts of a single all-purpose equation for being a woman. We even have a word for it: ladylike.

Teacher says, 'Look nice, behave nicely and everyone will like you.'

Girls learn quickly that being ladylike requires a certain standard of behaviour. This lesson begins at home and is furthered at school and when she interacts with peers. Girls are socialised to be more egalitarian, and learn to take turns playing with the toy. They have to share. They have to be nice. Research shows that parents and early childhood educators have higher and earlier expectations for sharing from girls compared to boys. Teachers also tend to be more tolerant of misbehaviour by boys in the classroom because they expect it. The presumption that boys are predisposed to be disruptive gives them a far wider berth for what's considered appropriate behaviour. Girls are judged more harshly. They are expected to sit quietly and follow instructions rather than play up and be physical. Behaving in this so-called 'ladylike' manner remains a central component of girls' education. The explicit teaching of decorum is part of the curriculum in some all-girl schools. Mates of mine recall not being allowed to eat in public while wearing their school uniforms because something about the consumption of food is apparently not feminine.

These different standards for boys and girls in the classroom aren't part of some grand academic conspiracy. Teachers have been socialised in the same context as everyone else. They're not immune from the realities of a gendered world. In fact, their job requires them to prepare students for that world. When teachers place higher expectations on girls to behave, it's an unconscious recognition of what will be expected from those girls as adults. A girl's behaviour will dictate her future social status in a way it won't for her boy peers. How much a boy is valued by the world is generally determined by strength and wealth, whereas a girl's value is usually dictated by her looks and relationships. So if a little boy is naughty and smashes over a tower of blocks or rams a truck into another kid's shins, it doesn't matter because the stakes aren't as high. Let's all sing it aloud, shall we? *Boys will be boys.*

Behaving nicely requires girls to be deferential to the needs of others. They're expected to be less demanding and more

accommodating than their boy peers. The lack of women protag-
onists in children's literature is a case in point. Boys are far more
gender-specific in their consumption of books than girls and often
aren't engaged by a book with a woman lead. Conversely, girls tend
to show content-based preference in literature rather than bothering about the protagonist's gender. Publishers know this, and so
accept more children and young-adult manuscripts with men pro-
tagonists. Teachers know it too. They go out of their way to find
characters the boys will relate too, safe in the knowledge that girls
will be engaged as long as the story is a good one. The result? Boys
are accustomed to consuming literature that places someone of
their gender at the centre of the story. Girls, however, are required
to cross-gender empathise with the experiences of men.

By the teenage years, 'niceness' is the prevalent dictator of girls'
social interactions. Stand near a group of schoolgirls at a shopping
mall and you'll hear them verbally tripping over one another to
achieve Peak Nice Status. 'Oh, your hair is super cute', 'No, your
hair is way cuter, I hate my hair' and so on and so forth. 'Oh, she's
so nice' is the ultimate girl-on-girl compliment. Of course, teenage
girls can be horrendously cruel to one another, but this behaviour
is usually concealed from view. It's a covert operation. In public,
under the watchful gaze of friends, adults and teachers, girls smear
on the niceness like strawberry jam. Critically, niceness among girls
tends to be defined more by what it isn't than what it is. Nice girls
aren't up themselves. Nice girls don't 'dob'. Nice girls aren't atten-
tion-seekers. Nice girls don't suck up to teachers. Nice girls don't
sleep around. Nice girls don't steal other people's boyfriends. The
very worst thing a teenage girl can call another is a bitch.

Girls from diverse cultural backgrounds can suffer the effects of
the 'niceness' expectation more profoundly. For girls from Indian

or Japanese backgrounds, for example, the expectation that they be demure and deferential may be even stronger at home than it is in school. For girls of colour, meeting the 'niceness' expectation requires overcoming racially discriminatory barriers to acceptance. The doll experiment I described earlier was based on an earlier study where black and white dolls were used. Children – including children of colour – would consistently attribute positive qualities to the white doll and negative ones to the black doll. Girls of colour have to navigate additional unfair and sometimes conflicting stereotypes that arise from their race and their gender.

LGBTIQ students suffer doubly at the hands of the niceness expectation because it's so intertwined with stereotypes of femininity. One study found this to be a causal factor in teenage girls' anxiety about presenting as a lesbian. In the minds of the teenage girls in that study, lesbianism was akin to being unfeminine and therefore neither nice nor popular. As a result – and especially in all-girl school environments – it was important not to be called gay. Young women may choose to actively deny their sexual identity in pursuit of social acceptance.

It's not my fault! The television made me do it.

Society mirrors the requirement of niceness back to girls through popular culture. It serves to reinforce messages they're getting from parents, teachers and peers that there is only one path to a woman's likeability. It starts early. Brands produce clothing for baby boys that label them a 'Tiny Terror' or proclaim, 'I wreck things!' as if it's something to be proud of. The slogans on baby girls' clothes take a different tone. They are 'Princess' or 'Sweetie-Pie!' There is even the vomit-inducing 'Daddy says I'm a good girl' slogan that's regularly plastered on baby-girl onesies. A study of toy catalogues found that in the 1970s less than two per cent of toys were branded as specifically for girls or boys. Today, every toyshop sports a wholly pink aisle, dictating to kids the kind of fun that is or isn't designed for them. The games and toys marketed at girls still focus on tasks like baking, shopping, craft and make-up, each associated with either looking nice or making something nice for others.

Organisations like Girl Guides, which historically emphasised girls' abilities to survive in the outdoors, propagate the 'girls are good' stereotype. Scouts, which began as an organisation for boys, teaches kids to 'be prepared', while Girl Guides are instructed to 'lend a hand'. This is not to say that either message is a bad one – on the contrary, they're both positive lessons for children. But why is it that girls and boys traditionally receive such different instructions?

Reality television loves stereotypes too. Shows like *Australian Princess* and *Ladette to Lady* take 'bogan' women and miraculously transform them into respectable ladies. The contestants are taught about the importance of manners, of not being outspoken or crass, and of deferring to the needs of others. There is no men's equivalent of these shows despite the overwhelming need for a program to teach teenage boys that Lynx body spray is not an effective antiperspirant.

Individually these examples might not seem like much, but they're the tip of the iceberg. Their effect is both well documented and substantial – there's a whole book to be written on that topic alone. Let's take a closer look at film and television to demonstrate the point. The Geena Davis Institute, which was founded by the actress of the same name, conducted the largest ever study of how girls and women are depicted in children's programming. They've looked at how girls and women are portrayed onscreen, how much talk time they have, what jobs they do and how much power they wield. Then they've examined how that affects the gender perceptions of the children who consume those programs. The results are staggering.

In family films – those made and intended to be watched by children – the ratio of men to women characters is 3:1. That ratio hasn't improved since the earliest days of motion-picture technology. There are fewer women characters in crowd scenes, fewer women characters with dialogue, and women characters speak for less time overall. Critically, of the characters in movies who have paid employment? Only 19 per cent are women. That's less than one in five. For every working woman a child sees onscreen, they see four working men. Here in Australia the workforce gender split is approaching 50/50, with women making up 46 per cent of all paid employees. So we're painting our children a seriously warped picture of what workplaces are. When this study was replicated on a global scale, the results were similar and sometimes more stark when professions were considered individually. Less than 10 per cent of the politicians depicted in family films were women, along with only 14 per cent of corporate executives. For characters in science, technology, engineering and maths (STEM) fields, men dominated at a ratio of 7:1. Judges and lawyer characters were 13 times more likely to be men. Geena Davis says:

> Images have a profound effect on how we see the world and our role in it. For every hour of television a girl watches, the fewer opportunities she thinks she has in life . . . That psychological ceiling, installed at an early age, continues to influence her decisions as an adult.

Creative and storytelling industries have tremendous power and opportunity. They can help show children our society as it *should be*, rather than simply how it is. By depicting women onscreen in powerful jobs for an audience of children, assumptions could be challenged and stereotypes overcome. Instead, little girls grow up seeing a screen world where men dominate, men control and men make the decisions. Children's media portrays women as quiet, silent or non-existent characters. When girls see characters that look like them, they're defined by their kindness, their sweetness or their love affairs – not the work that they do. These characters exist to serve others, never themselves. They don't interrupt or assert themselves nearly as much as the men. If they do, they're usually the cruel-hearted boss or the evil queen and it's a rare little kid who wants to grow up and be puppy-killing Cruella de Vil. Actress Emily Blunt says agents have always encouraged her to take on 'likeable' film roles because it's critical to maintaining her adoring – mostly women – fan base. She maintains that the less 'likeable' characters tend to be more interesting but, commercially, the choice to play them doesn't add up.

What's so wrong with being nice?

Maybe you think this 'niceness is the root of all evil' caper is overblown. Maybe you're sure there's nothing wrong with being nice. After all, niceness is – well, it's nice. And if niceness is an established part of the woman stereotype then surely that ought to be celebrated, not decried, right? The world would be a kinder, more peaceful place if everyone were a little nicer to one another. Surely we need parents and teachers who are raising children to be empathetic and loving human beings . . .

I agree with you wholeheartedly. I'm not trying to start a war on niceness. I'm really not.

My concern lies in the fact that niceness is valued in girls in a way that it isn't in boys. We're not talking about kindness, a positive trait that is respected in all human beings. We're talking about niceness, a standard of behaviour that is overloaded with value judgements. Our society values niceness in girls *above and beyond* other positive characteristics. Anea Bogue, creator of the REALgirl empowerment workshops, cautions that 'we teach our girls in a variety of ways that being nice, avoiding conflict, not upsetting others and not challenging the status quo are all part of being a likeable, desirable, successful girl – and one day woman.'

Unfortunately there isn't a lot of space between the stereotype of a nice, well-behaved girl and teaching our daughters to be pushovers. Little girls easily mistake a message about niceness for something quite different. Society values niceness in girls to such an extreme degree that it can become something that holds girls back. A girl wants to look nice, but the expectations about her appearance require spending a fortune in both time and money on 'maintenance'. A girl wants to behave nicely for her teachers, but this means never questioning what's being taught. A girl wants her parents to see her playing nicely, so she gives her brother yet another turn on the bike. A girl wants to be sensitive to the needs of her boyfriend, so she puts up with emotional abuse. A girl wants to run for school captain, but doesn't want her mates to think she has tickets on herself.

Girls are conditioned to please others, and that can come at the cost of pleasing themselves. It limits their happiness, their confidence and their willingness to be themselves.

Listen more.

Talk less.

Be agreeable.

Keep the peace.

Don't be difficult.

Stop causing a fuss.

It's not all about you.

You're just showing off.

'Jamila, you need to stop being so *bossy* all the time.'

As a kid (oh, okay, and as an adult too) I preferred to be in charge, whether it was rallying cousins to write, rehearse and perform concerts at Christmas time, or organising the games my peers would play at lunch. I liked to enter lots of competitions and participate in any available activities after class. I was wildly enthusiastic about pretty much everything, and had a suite of opinions to match. I liked to tell people what I thought. Loudly. I had a tendency to get carried away with my own ideas. I liked to test my abilities, to find the boundaries of debate and potential child dictatorship. At school, the teachers who liked me would praise my 'leadership qualities'. The teachers who didn't called me bossy.

By Grade Six I'd finally cottoned on to where my social behaviours were going awry. When I asserted myself in the classroom the teachers didn't appreciate it. Nor did my peers. I wasn't one of the popular kids. Oh, and I badly wanted to be one of the popular kids. So in the summer before I started high school I decided to make a change. I would throw everything I had into being the kind of girl everyone liked, the nice girl who was everyone's friend. I commenced the most important years of my schooling focused not on academic achievement but on being liked. I stopped trying so hard on my assignments because other kids didn't like the girl who got the top grades – she was up herself. I pulled back from being in charge, from raising my hand or drawing attention to myself. Pleasing others became my modus operandi and wholly replaced my previous goals. I would no longer be the bossy one.

'Bossy' is such a loaded term. It's brimming with negative implications. Being called 'bossy' tells a girl her assertiveness isn't appropriate or welcome. It's a word that's rarely applied to boys. When a girl is called bossy, it's usually for the same sort of behaviour that would mark a boy out as a future leader. By being negative about girls' leadership skills, we teach them that the inverse of bossy is what is good. We teach girls that being demure and deferential is what's expected. We teach them that they should be quiet about and diminish their achievements. We teach them that by making themselves small, they make themselves more feminine. We teach them that taking up less verbal, physical and emotional space in the world is a good thing. 'Bossy' teaches girls that deferring to the wishes of others, pleasing others, living their *lives for others* – rather than for themselves – is how nice girls behave.

And that, my friends, is precisely how niceness becomes dangerous.

DEFINING THE DOUBLE STANDARD

Because you're damned if you do and damned if you don't.

The Day the Interns Took Over became part of company folklore.

Each working day at women's website Mamamia began with a stand-up morning meeting of the editorial staff. We would gather in a circle to discuss which stories were shaping the zeitgeist. Writers would throw a small rubber breast to one another, signalling whose turn it was to contribute next. Whoever had the boob had the floor. The image dominates my recollections of that job: a ring of clever women, takeaway coffees in hand, enthusiastically tossing around a boob and talking about feminism.

After the stand-up meeting our senior editorial team would move to the boardroom for a more strategic discussion. On this particular day, the editors' chat had barely gotten underway when our boss, Mia Freedman, burst into the room. Mia is petite but formidable. She dominates every space she walks into. Standing at the head of the table, she directed her question to no one in particular: 'Ah, what exactly just happened? How is it that the interns ended up setting the day?'

'Setting the day' referred to our publication plan. It was a moveable feast, depending on how the news cycle unfolded, but acted as our guide for the 24 hours ahead. Setting the day was the single most important editorial responsibility. The combination of the stories and angles to be taken was what dictated how many people would click on, read and share our content. It was crucial we got it right, and that morning the key decision-makers had been three university student interns. They had utterly dominated the morning conversation, with the boob tossed exclusively between them like a childhood game of keepings-off. Inadvertently, the senior staff had handed custody of our beloved brand to the most inexperienced people in the room.

'It's Type-A Personality Thursday,' piped up one of the team, by way of explanation.

'It's what we call the Thursday interns,' added another. 'They're really . . . confident.'

'Well, more confident than any of us,' finished up someone else before the room broke into uncomfortable, embarrassed laughter.

The Thursday interns were supremely self-assured. They possessed an unabashed confidence that the more experienced women around them didn't. It was the confidence that flows from having the system worked out and knowing how to make it work for you. These young women had come straight from thirteen years of formal schooling, a period of time in which they'd always been the highest performers. They were used to working hard and reaping the rewards that come from that. They were used to being called on in classroom discussions, having their ideas valued by teachers and scoring highly in exams. The interns were simply doing what they'd always done – behaving nicely and meeting expectations. The supportive all-woman environment of Mamamia did nothing to stem their confidence either.

Nothing beats beating the boys . . .

Socialising girls to be nice pays off for them at school because educational environments favour students who display stereotypically feminine traits. If you follow the rules, if you're willing to sit quietly, be well behaved and study hard? Then *tick, tick, tick* – that's A plus–worthy, teacher-approved behaviour. Typically masculine traits – like aggression and bravado – run contrary to the quiet formality and discipline of school. Psychologist Carol Dweck says, 'If life were one long grade school, women would be the undisputed rulers of the world.'

Historically, Australian girls and boys have performed strongly in different subjects. Girls dominated in the humanities and social sciences, whereas boys produced better mathematics and science results. That changed during the period when millennials – people born in the late eighties and nineties – were at school. During the last 15 years, girls have extended their lead in subjects they previously excelled at and have begun to outperform boys in other areas, too. NAPLAN results show that girl students achieved a higher percentage over the national minimum standard than boys for reading and numeracy, in every assessable year, through both primary and high school.

Australian girls are graduating from school in greater numbers and with more academic success than boys. In 2015, more than 90 per cent of women aged 20–24 had achieved a Year 12 certificate or Certificate II TAFE equivalent, compared with 86 per cent of men. Average university admission index scores were around four per cent higher for women students. Women are responsible for three in every five applications to university, and a higher percentage of women are offered places than men. Trying to understand these differences, researcher Margaret Vickers interviewed hundreds of hopeful Australian high school graduates. She found that 'the biggest factor . . . is the marked difference between the aspirations of the two sexes. Successive studies have shown that no matter if a family is wealthy or poor, well educated or illiterate, many more of their female offspring hope to go to university than the male – and they do.'

Similar patterns are being observed across the English-speaking world, including in Canada, New Zealand and the United States. This is why more educational theorists are looking for alternative learning approaches to use with boys. Young men don't respond as well as girls do to the structured nature of a classroom environment. The way boys are socialised doesn't match the values of the institutions in which they're learning, and it's holding them back. Add into the mix that the majority of classroom teachers are women, who are more likely to teach in a way that they personally would have responded to. Schooling structures have become increasingly feminised, and the education system isn't necessarily working for boys in the way that it should.

But it's sure as hell working for the girls.

School shields girls from the full effects of a gendered world. At school rewards *do* flow from niceness. Being kind to your peers and respectful of adults *is* highly valued by teachers and parents. Good grades are the logical result of hard work, dedication and attention to detail. There are rules, tests and objective merit-based rewards, which make achievement straightforward. Success is linear and predictable. School is a place where girls are permitted to shine and there is a kind, cushioned, supportive little cocoon around them for when they don't. By separating girls and boys entirely, gender-segregated schools produce this same result, in an even more acute way. Girls emerge from schooling optimistic that their good behaviour, hard work and natural talents will earn them a living and bring a successful future.

For girls who pursue further education, the cocoon can remain intact for a little longer. The achievement gap between the genders widens during this time, with women building on the dominance they acquired at school. For example, women are more likely to win places at high-ranking universities and more likely to study high-status courses like law or medicine. There were almost 80 000 more Australian university graduates in 2015 than there were in 1999, and women account for a whopping 63 per cent of that increase. Of students graduating with honours, women dominate the first-class and upper second-class results. Men dominate the lower second- and third-class results. Beyoncé says girls run the world. That might not be quite true (yet), but they definitely run the classroom.

Set against the backdrop of this revealing data, it's hardly surprising that the interns behaved the way they did. Their confidence in their right to take up space in the world was, as yet, unshaken. At university they were still operating in an environment that played to their strengths. They had *only* ever operated in environments that played to their strengths. If asked, the interns probably wouldn't have been able to remember a time when they weren't at the top of the class, outstripping the boys. The natural optimism that accompanies youth, combined with their track records of academic success, had turbo-charged their confidence. It was a kind of confidence that the senior editorial team – women who had been in the workforce for a while – had lost.

What happened to our confident 22-year-old selves?

I was twenty-two years old when I landed my first full-time job working for the prime minister. I was halfway through my university studies and about to conclude a term as student body president. I'd thrown myself into student politics like a woman possessed. Judging by how seriously I took my position, you might have thought I was running the United Nations, not a student union. Nonetheless, that position had opened me up to a whole new grown-up world of boards and meetings and staff and speeches and budgets. I was very important, I reasoned to myself. My pomposity was embarrassing. Starting a new academic year with only essays and take-home exams to occupy my mind wasn't an option. I needed something to fill the gap. I needed a new challenge.

Over drinks one Saturday, my friend Maggie told me about a job that was about to become available: media assistant to Australia's then new prime minister, Kevin Rudd. We were at an Irish pub in the city, surrounded by dozens of political types. It was one of those delicious spring days with a cloudless sky and a beaming sun, a cold bite to the breeze. My hair had blown simultaneously into my eyes and my pint of cider. I was gracefully trying to extract it as I nodded along at Maggie's description of the role. She was doing an excellent but unnecessary sales job. I'd met Rudd at his 2020 Summit a few months back. I'd campaigned for him the previous year and been swept up by the possibility of the Kevin07 promise. I wanted that job. I would do whatever it took to get it.

And I did.

I'm thirty-one years old now. I'm a mother and a wife, with nine years more experience and nine years more knowledge than I had back then. I know that I will never again have that kind of confidence. The young woman in that story – the one who cold-called the prime minister's office to make sure they'd *definitely* seen her resumé – is a stranger to me now. She's cocky. She's arrogant. She's naïve. The wisdom of hindsight leaves me in equal parts horrified and impressed by her audacity. Unqualified and inexperienced, it was incredibly presumptive to apply for that job. But, annoying self-importance aside, you have to admit that 22-year-old me had serious chutzpah.

The workforce values different qualities to educational institutions. Being nice and behaving nicely doesn't correlate with success at work. In fact, merit and effort don't always correlate with success at work. Workplaces are inherently competitive and masculine structures, which require a different set of attributes to get ahead. Risk-taking, boldness and assertiveness get rewarded. They're the qualities that help move employees up the hierarchy. Getting to the top requires employees to compete against one another to win. There isn't a participation ribbon to recognise everyone who worked hard. There are no pats on the back for effort or good behaviour. You either get the job or you don't. You win the client or you don't. You get promoted or you don't. It's a win–lose tournament-style situation that was designed with men's success in mind. As you would have thought, it also means that women tend to struggle.

Competing to win isn't something girls are socialised to do well. While girls are good at competing to *excel*, competing to be victorious isn't something many feel comfortable doing. Being overtly competitive is considered unladylike. The schoolgirl who wins everything all the time isn't the most popular. In fact, she can be a social outcast. Some research suggests that competing to win is linked to depression and loneliness among teenage girls. It's why you'll often overhear women saying things like, 'I'm just not a competitive person', while men rarely make similar comments. Boys are encouraged to be comfortable with competing to win and to exhibit competitiveness openly. Former Harvard Medical School psychologist Lynn Margolies puts it like this:

> Men are typically comfortable with competition and see winning as an essential part of the game, rarely feeling bad for others after a victory, and maintaining camaraderie with their buddies. Because women learn that they are not supposed to be competitive and win at others' expense, their natural competitive spirit cannot be shared openly, happily, or even jokingly with other women . . . What could have been healthy competition becomes a secret feeling of envy and desire for the other to fail – laced with guilt and shame.

In the workplace women are thrust into an environment where they are expected to compete and this throws them off course. They're unsure of how to navigate such unfamiliar terrain. This is particularly the case with some corporate office environments, which tend to be not just competitive but downright combative. Negotiating a pay rise requires you to assert your own financial worth. Being promoted comes at the expense of someone else's progression. If you want to be recognised for your contribution to a group project, you have to make sure your boss notices and gives you the credit. Assertiveness. Competitiveness. Attention-seeking behaviour. They're personality traits expected – if not required – of employees who want to reach the top of their field. And they're exactly what we praise boys for being – and encourage girls to avoid – during school.

Socially damned if we do.
Professionally damned when we don't.

Sometimes women feel pressure to behave in a way they're not comfortable with in order to advance at work. This includes adopting typically 'masculine' behaviours that may run contrary to their skill set. Leadership opportunities are generally awarded to those who appear resilient, independent, determined, competitive and even aggressive. Promotions go to employees who actively and loudly advertise work they've done, rather than those who patiently wait to be noticed. It's why a litany of books and articles exist instructing women how to stop sabotaging their own careers by behaving *like they have been socialised to behave*. These books instruct career-focused women how to abandon their pathetic, girly approach to the workplace and just be More Like Men.

In order to be taken more seriously, women are variously instructed to lower their voices, keep personal information private, create boundaries and avoid displaying overtly feminine behaviours like decorating their desks with personal effects. Other supposedly problematic behaviours of women include helping too much, sharing personal information with colleagues and – prepare to gasp – *baking* for colleagues' birthdays. These books and articles tend to be written by men who are confused by the behaviour of women who have worked for them, or they're written by women who have had to fight damn hard to make it in a man's world. Their advice to young women hoping to be successful at work is to make their femininity a non-issue – by trying to eliminate it.

I have a lot of admiration for women who hold this view and give this advice. They are generally alpha women, self-assured, no-bullshit firecrackers. They're personally comfortable operating in a traditionally 'masculine' way. In some respects, I think I'm one of them. Nonetheless, the advice to eliminate all signs of femininity in order to succeed doesn't sit well with me. Surely the workplace is big enough and bad enough to accommodate an individual's preferred approach to work. Women shouldn't be expected to pretend they're something they're not in order to progress. That is an awfully narrow formula for success. While a preoccupation with being liked can hold women back, that doesn't make it their fault. Nor should it mean women have to abandon nice behaviour entirely.

It doesn't serve our society well for people to be deliberately cold or rude to their colleagues. Indeed, becoming friends with workmates has been one of the great joys of my working life. I can't bake at all, but I very much enjoy and appreciate it when someone else in the office does. And when it comes to decorating your workspace? Well, I'll defend the desk presence of miniature cacti and photos of adorable offspring to anyone who will listen. Furthermore, the evidence shows that deliberately employing masculine traits doesn't work for women, anyway. It's not as if women whose personalities tend to the more masculine end of the spectrum are free from gendered stereotyping. These women face the same expectations as other women, and when they don't conform, they're punished.

The social penalty for women who display traditionally masculine traits at work can be severe. In one study, researchers compared the experiences of woman candidates for senior jobs with those of men. In that experiment, candidates who spoke without apology about their achievements and abilities were all judged to be highly capable by the interviewers. However, the women candidates were judged to be *other things* as well. Specifically, they were considered less socially attractive. The interviewers deemed these women to be competent, but not 'nice', and perhaps not a good 'cultural' fit for the job. The same kind of self-promotion didn't affect the interviewers' social perceptions of how 'nice' the men candidates were. Men who talk about their achievements are fine. Women? Not so much. Owning your success and vocalising that violates expectations of women's likeability. Self-promotion does not a demure and modest woman make.

Taking all this advice and evidence into account, what have we got? Well, some women display typically masculine traits in order to advance professionally because that is what works for the blokes. Yet when they do, it jars with people's expectations about how women should behave – so they're penalised socially. They're less popular. Less *likeable*. These negative stereotypes are even more pronounced – and kick in earlier in the hierarchy – for women who work in men-dominated industries like science, engineering, construction and technology. Just like the schoolgirl who is told to stop being so 'bossy', women in senior jobs face a catch-22 situation. They must make a choice. Do they want to be successful? Or do they want to be liked? They can't possibly be both.

You can see why women lose confidence when they enter the workforce. They are at a loss about how to tackle structures that reward behaviour contrary to what they've been taught is valuable. It causes confusion and self-doubt. Remember, women are already more likely to feel they have a limited ability to impact on the world around them. So when the world around them – school – supported them and played to their strengths, they felt confident. And later, when the world around them – work – had completely different rules, their confidence evaporated.

Gender inequality is about more than who births the babies.

When we talk about gender disparities in workplaces, we tend to focus on the biological realities of who grows and births babies. While it's true that the birth and care of children is a major contributor to gender inequality, it is not the sole source of discrimination against women at work. Women are paid less than men from the very beginning of their careers, when babies are often the furthest thing from their minds. Women university graduates are paid base

salaries of up to 10 per cent less than their men counterparts. While men's salary earnings reach their peak at age 39, women peak eight years earlier, at 31 – and at a much lower dollar figure. Research conducted by the Equal Opportunity for Women in the Workplace Agency found that 'two of the most common reasons for women to leave a job were difficulty in progressing and a lack of clear career development'. Leaving a job to have children or in pursuit of better work-life balance did not even enter the top *five*.

The increasing casualisation of the Australian workforce is having a greater effect on women than men. It means less certain employment arrangements and reduced job security for the women who can least afford it. As the overwhelming majority of the country's part-time workforce, women spend more time worrying about being underemployed or unemployed. This leaves them stressed and anxious at work, less focused on attaining the next job because they're so worried about keeping the one they have. Women are more likely to be earning the minimum award wage and so are most at risk when penalty rates are cut or when lower-end wage growth is stagnant.

Through the course of their lives women also do more unpaid work and men do more paid work. For example, housework disparity is a real issue for many heterosexual couples. The work is rarely distributed evenly and can be a source of ongoing conflict. In households where women are working as much as men partners – and even when women are the sole breadwinners – women *still* do more housework. In 2012, women were responsible for 1.8 times more housework than men, compared to twice as much in 1992. In 20 years there was only a marginal shift. Things are changing too slowly, and I've cleaned that damn toilet enough for this lifetime, thanks very much. When duties around the home are combined with childcare responsibilities and paid employment, working mothers are contributing 93 hours of total labour each week, compared with an average of 71 hours for partnered men.

As we plod slowly towards gender equality, women are increasingly contributing to the household income. Feminism has helped get women into workplaces and made an economic contribution to our country and to family incomes. However, men aren't boosting their childcare or domestic duties in the same way, and certainly not to the same degree. It means that the distribution of total work between the sexes is more unequal today than ever before. Our society assumes women will work, care and clean, but men just get to work. Whenever I travel interstate for my job, I'm hit with a barrage of queries about where my son is and who is looking after him. Everyone seems very worried about who is picking up the caring duties in my absence. My husband sometimes travels for work as well and never gets asked the same thing. Why would he be? He's a man.

The achievement and earnings gap between women and men begins early and grows over time. It becomes most apparent at the very top – in that women rarely get there. Ninety per cent of senior leaders in major corporations are men, despite both genders being hired in roughly equal numbers at the graduate level. This means men are nine times more likely to reach executive level than women. The 'stupid curve' refers to the phenomenon of companies looking for leadership candidates only among the men within their talent pool. It's called a stupid curve because that's exactly what it is: stupid. Ignoring half your potential talent is not just discriminatory, it's poor business practice. Yet you don't see the treasurer on the evening news holding a press conference to discuss that particular economic problem.

Women are missing from key leadership roles both in Australia and globally. Holding just 20 jobs between them, women make up only four per cent of CEO positions in the top 500 global companies. Here at home, women do a little better, holding 15.4 per cent of CEO positions and 14.2 per cent of board chair positions. But, still, there are more CEOs named John than there are women CEOs among Australia's top 200 companies. Australian women hold 23.6 per cent of directorships and make up 27.4 per cent of all key management personnel. Our best performance indicator when it comes to high achievement in the corporate sphere is woeful, at best. More than 25 per cent of top Australian companies have *no* women in management positions. Women are also significantly under-represented in Australian parliaments, winning around 30 per cent of seats. Our country has only had one woman prime minister in 116 years, and we all know what happened to her.

As the late actress Carrie Fisher said when asked why Princess Leia never got her own lightsaber in the *Star Wars* films: 'Even in space there's a double standard.'

The reason that Australian women and their sisters around the world are failing to reach the highest levels of workplace success is about so much more than who bears children. Anyone who tells you that gender inequality is impossible to achieve because of biology simply isn't paying attention. The assumption that women's careers stagnate only because of structural barriers around motherhood is false. Motherhood is simply one of several significant factors inhibiting women's success at work.

The odds never have been (and may never be) in our favour.

Feminism and the women's liberation movement have brought us a tremendously long way. There is no question that life for mothers today is better than it was 100, 50 or even 30 years ago. Mothers in Western democracies like Australia have more choice and independence and autonomy than we've had at any other time in history. That is something to cherish and to celebrate, but it doesn't mean the work is done yet. Parenthood still negatively impacts women's careers and their income earning potential in a way it simply does not affect men. I'm yet to observe one of my girlfriends have a child and return to work without substantial hiccups. From impolite questioning of their choices to unfair expectations around workload to downright illegal workplace discrimination, being a working mother can be pretty rough. Most Australian workplaces lack the necessary support, understanding and flexibility to meet the needs of new parents. Mothers of young children take a hit – both to their confidence and their bank accounts – as a result.

When paid parental leave was introduced in Australia in 2011, it was a historic occasion. The government scheme provides 18 weeks of paid leave for mothers at the minimum wage. The World Health Organization says a new mother should have at least six months off work to bond with her baby, which is a lot more than 18 weeks. The idea is that employers will also provide some paid parental leave, and that, together with the government allowance, will make up at least six months. Sounds great in theory, but it rarely works in practice. Many Australian employers provide no paid leave at all. Casual and part-time employees are even less likely to be eligible for employer-funded maternity leave, despite the bulk of this workforce being women. For mothers whose physical and mental health necessitates a longer period of leave, there are no contingencies available. There have also been successive government attempts to make these schemes *less* generous. The scheme isn't gender-specific, which means fathers can take it up instead of mothers. Again, that sounds great in theory, but in practice only a handful of Australian men decide to stay at home full-time with their newborns.

If you don't have children but are planning to, then I have some rather alarming news for you: Australia's childcare system is broken. Parents reading this are nodding their heads sagely. They know firsthand how hard it is for women to participate fully in the workforce in the years before their children start school. The truth of it is in the data.

Australian women with young children have lower rates of workforce participation than women in comparable OECD economies. Accessing childcare is the first hurdle. Horror stories of being unable to find places, even after putting a child's name on waiting lists before they were born, are commonplace. For shift-workers or employees with hours outside the standard nine-to-five, access is even more difficult.

Even if you manage to find a childcare place, the struggle is just beginning. For many families, having both parents working – even part-time – doesn't add up financially because childcare is so expensive. Costs exceeding $130-per-day aren't unusual in the major cities and they're rising all the time. Childcare costs rose 8.3 per cent on average between 2015 and 2016. In fact, surveys have shown that the number of Australian women in the workforce would increase dramatically if childcare fees were more affordable. Most families still 'weigh up' the cost of childcare against the mother's income, rather than against the family's income as a whole. The 'choice' we construct is between the income Mum brings in and the price of childcare, and that choice rarely comes down on the side of Mum returning to work full-time. The lack of affordable and accessible childcare is the single largest contributing factor to why part-time working mothers aren't working more. Single parents rarely have the privilege of this evaluation process. Full-time work is a necessity for the family to survive, so Mum heads back to work no matter how small the margin between her salary and the cost of childcare.

'Childcare isn't *just* a women's issue!' I hear you say. And I agree – but the statistics don't. The birth of children dispro-portionately affects the way women organise their work when compared with the family unit as a whole. This continues well beyond the initial 12 months when a woman might be recover-ing from childbirth and is more likely to be breastfeeding. Having a family changes how women work, but it barely has an impact on how and when men work. Labour participation rates for women drop from 70.8 per cent average to just 51 per cent for those with children under the age of four. Yet the presence of children in a household has little to no bearing on men's participation rates. Women spend twice as much time as men each day caring for chil-dren. Even when children are of school age and both parents are working, women still spend an average of five hours a day caring for them compared to 2.5 for men. It's true for me, as well: my hus-band and I split work and care fairly evenly between us, but when our toddler is sick, the assumption is that I'll be the one taking the day off.

For women who face multiple forms of discrimination these challenges are compounded further. In 2011, only 51.2 per cent of Indigenous women were able to contribute to the labour force compared to 70.9 per cent of non-Indigenous women. The unem-ployment rate for Indigenous women in the same year was almost three times higher than for non-Indigenous women. Annette Vickery from the Aboriginal Legal Services says the nature of work-place discrimination against Indigenous people means it can be hard to define with precision. 'It is debilitating to people experiencing it, because it is like fighting shadows; always there, but hard to prove,' she explains.

Women with disabilities are more likely than men to have informal or vulnerable employment arrangements. The unemployment rate among women with disabilities has remained steady over the past decade, while it has improved significantly for disabled men. My friend, the late-and-so-unbelievably-great Stella Young, wrote extensively about how difficult it is for women with disabilities to get into the paid workforce. Even physically attending job interviews was tough, she said:

> My favourites were the ones where I couldn't even get into
> the building. I quickly learned that asking if an interview space
> was wheelchair accessible was a bad idea; it gave a potential
> employer an immediate bad impression. It was either a black
> mark against my name, or a straight up discussion of why
> I wouldn't be able to work there because they had no wheelchair
> access. Then again, not mentioning it sometimes meant that
> I had to be interviewed outside. Damned if you do, damned
> if you don't.

If you're a woman – particularly a woman with children – there are some real hurdles to moving in and out of the workforce. If you're also Indigenous, a person of colour or living with a disability, you're (at least) doubly disadvantaged.

Women are overwhelmingly more likely to have to leave the workforce early to become a primary carer for an elderly parent or someone with a disability. Over 70 per cent of primary carers are women, and this has an ongoing effect on the level and nature of their employment throughout their working life. Twenty-three per cent of primary carers reported their income decreasing as a result of their caring role, while 30 per cent state that their responsibilities incurred additional expenses. The way women from culturally diverse backgrounds experience this effect is more pronounced. For example, there are deeply held cultural expectations that Chinese women will be the primary carers for elderly parents as well as young children. For many, caring requirements are simply incompatible with pursuing a demanding career. You have to pick one.

These factors, coupled with the outrageous fact that women still face a gender pay gap of 17 cents in the dollar compared with men, combine to deliver a particularly dire result: the feminisation of later-life poverty. If you're an older woman in Australia, the chances are you're struggling financially. Typically, an Australian woman holds just $35 200 in superannuation, while men hold an average of $62 900. This is an enormous disparity, which is even more significant when you consider that women live longer than men. It's the reason that more and more Australian women are relying solely on the aged pension and falling into poverty later in life. A massive 40 per cent of retired single Australian women live below the poverty line. We live in one of the most prosperous countries in the world, but women's share of that prosperity is markedly less than men's.

Ladies (but not gentlemen), please mind the gap.

There is no single answer to why the gap between women and men's workplace achievements remains as wide as it does, just as there is no single solution. Academic and writer Anne-Marie Slaughter says society undervalues caregiving and overvalues breadwinning. She wants to start having conversations with boys and men about work-life balance the same way that girls and women already do.

Facebook's COO Sheryl Sandberg claimed in her manifesto, *Lean In*, that women begin leaning 'out' of their careers in anticipation of having children, preparing for a juggle that doesn't even exist yet. This, she explains, automatically lowers women's expectations of achievement and holds them back.

The American Association of University Women goes straight for the jugular and blames deep-seated sexism in the workplace. In a recent report it found that sexual harassment in workplaces is a far greater problem than many of us may have realised, and that sexist stereotypes inhibit women's achievement. Australian journalist and author Annabel Crabb argues that women are struggling to break through because they don't have a 'wife' at home taking care of domestic and caring duties. Men are five times more likely to have someone at home who looks after their kids and tidies the living room, Crabb explains. This gives men more time to devote to networking, overtime or whatever else will propel them up the corporate ladder.

I gobbled up the theories of these tremendous women like Nutella on toast. I dog-eared pages of their books, highlighted quotes and nodded along so vigorously that my neck got sore. But still I felt like there was another unidentified factor at play. A factor contributing not just to why women are prevented from workplace success but why they *feel* less capable of it. The way workplaces are structured and the very nature of how they operate makes women feel like they don't belong. The consequence is a lack of confidence that begins in the earliest years of women's working lives. Maybe, just maybe, addressing that might be the missing piece of the gender-equality puzzle.

THE CONFIDENCE DEFICIT

Because that damn glass ceiling is double-glazed.

There was a hugely unfortunate occasion when I was tricked into playing golf. The event was a charity fundraiser where media personalities were paired up with rich business people for a round of nine holes. My friend Airini worked for the charity and needed some extra media people to make up the numbers. Airini convinced me to participate by describing the event as 'like a fun run'. Now, I love Airini, but she is a dirty, dirty liar. This was not 'fun' in the slightest. It was a stuffy, full-on, collared shirt, shorts with creases down the front and cream lace-up brogues kind of event. Ready to go jogging, I arrived in my not-at-all-golf-appropriate active wear. The organisers looked at me with deep disdain and I was promptly shuffled off to the pro shop to be fitted for more suitable attire. Then I was assigned to the 'limited' golf experience group. Fair.

Luckily, my fellow golfers were similarly unskilled. Two of them were lawyers from top-tier firms, who specialised in mergers and acquisitions for the financial industry. This gave us precisely nothing in common about which to chat. The bloke lawyer was probably in his early forties and, despite being a pretty piss-poor

golfer, was carrying a set of the best clubs money could buy. I knew
they were the best clubs money could buy because he informed me
several times over that they were the best clubs money could buy.
His woman colleague was younger, with a severe blonde bob and
the intensely anxious expression of someone whose expensive man-
icure was about to be ruined. The third member of our group was
a 25-year-old guy with more swagger than Bart Simpson. He was
rather handsome and more than a little bit flirty. I asked him what
he did. Swagger Guy replied with a long rambling sentence that
included words like 'innovation', 'synergies' and 'ideation'. I concluded that he was unsure.

Our group was allowed to tee off last so as to avoid holding
up teams with more golfing expertise. Swagger Guy and Mr Best
Clubs Money Can Buy became instant but highly competitive
buddies. Over the next four hours they made up in bravado what
they lacked in talent. Every time they sunk a putt there was much
back-slapping and celebration. They compared themselves to Tiger
Woods, Greg Norman – all of the great golfers (but none of the
women). Their confidence was unabashed even in the face of objectively poor play. When Swagger Guy hit a bad putt, he'd cheerfully
say, 'Take two!' before picking up the ball and having a second go,
as if the first attempt never happened. If either man played a particularly bad hole, it was because the clubs were 'bloody useless' or
the sun was in their eyes. If they played well, it was because of their
immense skill and ability.

The behaviour of the woman lawyer stood in stark contrast to
the cocky, confident men. So did my own. We both underestimated
our success from the outset. We assumed we'd be terrible. I did my
usual thing and made sure everyone knew that I knew I was bad at
golf. Self-deprecation prevents embarrassment. My companion was

paralysed by nerves and kept repeating random phrases from a 'how to play golf' website she'd been studying in the lead-up. Otherwise she hardly spoke, except to berate herself for letting the team down. She took each bad shot to heart and became easily discouraged. The funny thing was, she was probably the best of us all. After she sank an amazing chip shot that went over a sand trap, onto the green and directly into the tiny hole, she spent the long walk to the next hole explaining away her success. It was a fluke. It was the wind. She'd never be able to recreate it.

There's a glass ceiling on every floor, and it's double-glazed.

There is a clear correlation between success at work and competence. Workplace achievement and being good at your job go hand-in-hand. But did you know that there's an *even more* pronounced correlation between success and confidence? Confident people project a sense of assurance to those around them and are perceived as both more successful and more likely to succeed in the future. You've no doubt experienced this in your own life. I know I have. We all know those supremely confident, good-looking, suavely dressed young guys who sweep into a room. They dish out compliments like they're going out of fashion and tell complex jokes with great aplomb. There is an air about them. An air of 'I can do anything, I can be anything, and if you're lucky I might let you watch.' Basically, they're Swagger Guy from the golf tournament.

These men carry a confidence in their own abilities that they have been conditioned for since birth. They are comfortable in a combative, competitive work environment because it's what they've trained for their whole lives. And while these men are the extreme example, their behaviour is reflective of the whole. A man is more likely to declare that he can do something and then just get on with it. He assumes that he will land on his feet because millions of men like him have done so before. History tells him he's going to be a success. So why shouldn't he be?

Of course there are men who lack confidence. Just like women, men suffer from self-doubt and experience anxiety in their working lives. But at a general level, it doesn't seem to happen to the same degree. Katty Kay and Claire Shipman put it succinctly in their *Atlantic* essay, 'The Confidence Gap', when they said:

> Do men doubt themselves sometimes? Of course. But not with such exacting and repetitive zeal, and they don't let their doubts stop them as often as women do. If anything, men tilt toward overconfidence – and we were surprised to learn that they come by that state quite naturally. They aren't *consciously trying* to fool anyone.

Confidence also has positive internal effects. People who are confident in their own abilities are more likely to produce successful outcomes than less confident people of the same ability. There's a reason that elite athletes are told to visualise kicking the winning goal or sinking a basket from outside the circle. Doing an action and visualising yourself doing an action stimulate the same parts of your brain. If you believe you can do it, it actually works. Expecting success is a predictor of actual success.

Women routinely underestimate their own abilities because that's what the world has taught them to do. Exhibit A: my woman companion at the golf tournament. Research shows women tend to exhibit less confidence in their own competence when compared with men of the same level of ability. This damages women's perception of likely future success and also impacts the perceptions of others.

That is, when we think we're not going to be any good at something and we act accordingly, other people pick up on our lack of confidence and assume it's a reflection of the truth. Amy Giddon, the director of corporate leadership at Barnard College's Athena Centre for Leadership, says:

> There is a disconnect between women's confidence in their skills and abilities – which is often high – and their confidence in their ability to navigate the system to achieve the recognition and advancement they feel they deserve. Self-advocacy is a big part of this, and identified by many women . . . as the biggest barrier to their advancement.

It's the system, not our abilities, that causes women's lack of confidence.

I've had more angst-filled conversations with friends and colleagues about this stuff than I care to remember. They are clever, capable women who routinely underestimate their potential for success. It drives me crazy that they can't see in themselves what I can see so clearly: That they're really good at what they do. I bet you've experienced this with your own mates. Even when they're at the top of their game and kicking goals at work and winning all the awards, women assume it is down to luck. And so they suggest someone else for a special assignment. They don't apply for a job because they know a friend might be going for it. They won't stick up their hand in a meeting in case someone laughs at them or they accidentally say something silly. They couldn't possibly do something so *rude* as to ask for more money, even though they deserve it.

My women friends and colleagues have found and sometimes slammed into the ceiling of their career far too early. While their talents and abilities mean they could and should be thriving at work, this rarely eventuates. Women were fooled into thinking the glass ceiling only exists at the top, when really the invisible barriers to women's progression are at every level. It's a recurring glass ceiling built from the raw, malleable material of discrimination. And it's double-glazed by women's own lack of confidence.

Ping my inbox the next time confidence goes on sale.

Researchers at Columbia Business School have proven that women are much less likely than men to be selected as leaders, and have linked this explicitly to confidence levels. In one study, women were chosen to lead a group 33 per cent less often than men, including when their abilities were comparable. It was confidence that dictated how the group perceived different candidates' readiness to lead. The more confident candidates appeared, the more leadership potential the group decided they had. Women were less confident about their own capabilities and so generally defaulted to the men. The men 'seemed to know what they were talking about'. Or, at least, that's how they acted.

The researchers concluded that this has both meaningful and worrying ramifications for the real world. In the study, the success of the whole group was compromised by leadership choices that were based on confidence rather than competence. By exaggerating their own abilities, men are likely to oversell their actual capabilities and create unnecessary risk. By preferencing men over women, the group picked from a smaller pool of potential leaders and was therefore statistically less likely to pick the best person for the job. The flipside of this is that by discounting their own abilities, women actually contribute to worse outcomes for the organisations that they are a part of. By assuming the most confident person in the room knows best, we count ourselves out when we have so much to offer. This robs workplaces of the full potential of our brains, our expertise and our skills, in the same way the workplace denies women opportunities to learn, earn and lead. When women lose out, society does as well.

So what can we do about it?

First and foremost, policy makers have to deal with entrenched gender discrimination. They need to legislate for workplaces that don't penalise women for having children and don't burden them with unfair expectations. Corporate Australia needs to come to the party too, and pay more than just lip service to the idea of gender equality. This means more robust sexual harassment and gender-discrimination laws so a woman whose boss sticks his hand up her skirt doesn't have to choose between her livelihood and her personal safety. It means closing the gender pay gap once and for all, and building a fairer system of superannuation so women don't fall into poverty later in life. It means recognising that women of colour, LGBTIQ women and women with disabilities face overlapping and intersectional barriers to workplace equality, which must be dismantled. It means addressing the challenges faced by women in entry-level roles and middle management, rather than concentrating our concern on the lack of representation of women at executive levels. It means making workplaces more flexible for carers of all kinds and parents of both genders.

But government and business alone can't solve women's lack of confidence. That is a societal and cultural problem, which is embedded into how we've been raised, how we've been schooled and how we're expected to behave. For the next generation of women, perhaps we can stop this lack of confidence developing in the first place. But for those of us who are in the early or middle stages of our careers, unfortunately the damage is already done. We did not create and we certainly are not to blame for this confidence deficit. Nevertheless, it is something we're going to have to fix for ourselves.

My inner voice is a bitch.

My inner voice likes to begin with the cosmetic. On the day of a public lecture, when I know hundreds of pairs of eyes will be looking at me, she'll wonder why I look so fat. She'll point out the lack of definition around my jawline, the unmistakeable belly of a woman who's given birth. Next she moves to the substantive, and here she is less direct. Her meanness cloaked as empathy. Her intention? To sow the seeds of crippling doubt that will cause me to frantically question myself.

'Is that joke on page 11 of your notes really going to land with this audience?' my inner voice wonders. 'Are you sure you want to include that particular story? It makes you sound up yourself.' Her concern continues, unrelenting. Sometimes she seems almost sweet: 'Those other speakers are really good. You should be proud to be among the group!' But it's short-lived: 'Hopefully the audience don't compare you to them . . .' Then she'll top it off with a seemingly unrelated, totally devastating childhood anecdote: 'Remember that day in Grade Seven when Popular Melissa told you that nobody would like you if you didn't stop wearing blue mascara and trying so hard?'

Ouch.

My inner voice began as a series of outer ones. She channels various people I've met over the course of my life who have been critical of me – or who I've perceived to be critical. Most of the critiques were probably offhand comments or observations that the speaker thought little of at the time. But they stung and I absorbed them. I tucked them away in the back of my brain, mulling them over on those hot summer nights when the bedsheets are wet with sweat and no position is comfortable. They'll live there forever. My inner voice says things that no polite human being would ever say aloud to someone else. Like the comments section of an online news site, she is trying to get a reaction. And she always does.

We all have an inner voice. A voice born of the society we've been raised in, and shaped by our conditioning. For women, this inner voice is far more likely to wreak havoc on our confidence in the workplace. At work, women can still feel like they're encroaching in a place they don't quite belong. We've accepted as true the constant barrage of messages that tell women the workplace isn't necessarily somewhere they should be, let alone somewhere they can thrive. It's fertile ground for our inner voice. Over time we've stopped questioning whether the voice is right to doubt our abilities or not. We just let her do her thing . . . unchallenged.

But what if we did challenge her? What if women made a deliberate and sustained effort to question our inner voices? What if instead of assuming our lack of confidence is a reflection of our lack of ability, we tried to properly understand the cause of it? What if by understanding how the gender-biased work environment affects our confidence, we were able to push back against it? What if we stopped worrying about being liked all the time and got on with it? I, for one, think we might just be unstoppable.

So let's begin.

WHAT CONFIDENCE SOUNDS LIKE

Because we don't say sorry for doing our jobs.

I was on the train, and my ride coincided with the end of school. Office workers, identifiable by our sensible shoes, BlackBerries and vacant expressions, populated one end of the carriage. Up the other end was a group of teenage girls. Aged around 17, they were dressed in school uniforms. The frenetic, swirling energy of their conversation was exhausting. While the hum of the train meant I couldn't make out the exact detail of their discussion, snatches of dialogue caught my ear. There were repeated shrieking mentions of balloons and 'bros', and someone's outfit was resoundingly pronounced to be 'babein'. One of the girls was imitating someone who wasn't present, performing a repetitive and elaborate hand-movement mime around her hairline. Every time she did, her friends responded with squeals of laughter, followed by a unanimous exclamation of 'his *hair*!'

The suit-wearing man sitting opposite me smiled and rolled his eyes in solidarity. Both of us had headphones in, trying to concentrate on other things; he a phone call and me a podcast about the US Democratic Party's national convention. It was a useless exercise. I could barely hear myself think, let alone the podcast. The girls' chatter was constant and they kept shouting over one another. I couldn't imagine that anyone was actually listening to the substance of what anyone else in the group had to say. Vapid fools, I thought unkindly to myself.

Minutes later, the girls reached their stop and assembled at the door next to me. I could now hear their conversation clearly and distinctly.

'No competition from the Republicans. The Dems had *all* the celebrities. Who did the Republicans have? Trump. Blergh.'

'Michelle stole the show but. How about that thing she said, you know, how the White House was built by slaves?'

'A-*maz*-ing!'

The earlier mention of balloons should have tipped me off. It was the US Democratic Party's national convention. They'd been discussing the very topic of the podcast I'd been struggling to hear. The 'bros' weren't some cute boys the teens had been checking out in maths class but the famous followers of Bernie Sanders. It was the First Lady of the United States, Michelle Obama, who was 'babein'. The much-discussed hair belonged to none other than Donald Trump.

Without realising it, those girls had put me firmly in my place. I'd made the standard stereotypical assumptions adults tend to about teenagers, and I'd been totally off base. Those assumptions were made on nothing more than the fact that the girls were young, their voices shrill and the pitch high. I'd dismissed their conversation as inane, when it was anything but. There aren't many teenagers who would voluntarily spend their leisure time talking about the electoral politics of another country. Those girls were remarkable. Judgey-wudgey was a bear, and on that day, the bear was me.

Why the voice matters

It takes a grand total of 0.2 seconds for the brain to detect and make an assessment about another person's voice. Our brains gather audible clues the same way they do visual ones. While you might not be conscious of it, you use sound to form a judgement about someone the very first time you hear them speak. Even if it's on the telephone. Try it and see. Next time you get an unsolicited phone call from a marketing company wanting to sell you funeral insurance, don't make an excuse to hang up. Give yourself 30 seconds (or however long you can bear to stay on the line), and unpack the assumptions your brain is making about the person on the other end of the call. You'll be surprised by how many conclusions your subconscious draws.

Without seeing what a person looks like, sound allows us to make assumptions about age, gender, race and even cultural background. We also make sound-based judgements about other things, like I did on the train. The brain assesses voices to make determinations about a person's intelligence, maturity, humour, sincerity and even their confidence. Quiet, light or breathy voices tend to be perceived as passive or weak – think of the delicate, almost fragile-sounding voice of the late Princess Diana. On the other hand, deep, smooth voices, like that of actress and rapper Queen Latifah, are considered capable, sexy and smart. In one study, researchers found that the sound of a person's voice matters *twice* as much as the content of their message. Some overzealous human resource departments even use voice screening as part of the interview process. These are truly terrifying organisations at which I will never apply for a job.

You won't be surprised to learn that the vocal qualities our brains associate most closely with confidence are masculine – or, at least, they're traditionally masculine-sounding. Linguists and speech analysts use the terms 'authoritative' and 'masculine' almost interchangeably. This betrays our unconscious acceptance that deeper voices are more effective at conveying a message. Historically men's voices have been associated with power and influence. After all, back in the day, men were the only people who had any power. While modern women are challenging men in this respect, the stereotype that a strong voice is a masculine voice remains. In fact, women's voices are criticised not just for being higher (which is a biological quality) but for other characteristics too.

Talking: sorry, girls, but you're doing it wrong.

Women's voices have adapted to match expectations of how we *should* sound. It's happened so many times over that women now collectively rival contestants on *The Voice* in the vocal acrobatics stakes. Let's run through a few of the more recent evolutions. 'Upspeak' refers to the high-rising intonation at the end of a sentence, creating a speech pattern of constant questions. 'Upspeak' or 'Valley Girl' speech was observed as far back as the late nineteenth century in Northern Ireland and Scotland. Nobody is really sure how it gained modern popularity, first among American women before spreading across the Western world.

Alicia Silverstone's character Cher in the film *Clueless* best personifies the style of speech and the stereotype of immaturity that goes along with it. Famous socialites and influencers like Paris Hilton, Nicole Richie and Lindsay Lohan are all upspeakers or Valley Girls. These women – whose fame-worthiness has been questioned in the press – have perpetuated the speech pattern's 'ditsy airhead' association. But because upspeak has so profoundly permeated popular culture, it's actually far less noticeable to most of us today than it would have been 20 years ago. The upward inflection has been incorporated into most English-speaking women's everyday speaking patterns. It's a normal part of how we talk.

So *why* did we start speaking like this in the first place? Well, we know by now that women are more likely to be punished at work for asserting themselves because it goes against the nice-girl stereotype. The same behaviour that is called 'decisive' in men is criticised for being 'aggressive' in women. Researchers suggest that upspeak may be an unconscious feminine reaction to this. By retaining a sense of uncertainty in their voices, women are able to engage and put forward ideas without appearing too forceful. Expressing a statement as if it were a question means a woman appears to be merely offering a suggestion, rather than making a demand. It's like she is asking permission to speak as she is doing so. Upspeak is a tool women have subconsciously developed to maintain their likeability.

Unfortunately, upspeak can do more harm than good to women's reputation at work. It diminishes women's power. Research indicates that women who employ the speech pattern are perceived as submissive and overly deferential. Upspeak can undercut a woman's credibility at work even if the actual *content* of what she is saying is highly persuasive. One study of 700 bosses (both women and men) revealed that 85 per cent consider upspeak to be an indicator of an employee's insecurity and emotional weakness. A further 70 per cent found the speech pattern annoying and 44 per cent would mark down an applicant for a job because of upspeak.

I suspect that right now you're sinking deeper and deeper into your chair, probably reaching for something calorie-laden and delicious. That inner voice of yours is saying, 'Great, here's another thing for me to be worried about. Another thing to make me self-conscious?' See? Even the voice in your head is a Valley Girl.

I don't like the sound of my own voice, either. Actually, scratch that. I quite like my own voice as it sounds *to me*. It's the version of my voice that the rest of the world hears – the one I'm only ever exposed to via radio or television or a podcast – that is truly horrendous. Early in my media career I'd go to extreme lengths to avoid hearing recordings of myself speaking. When my voice would come on the radio, I'd shout, 'Turn her off!' only half-jokingly, and theatrically run out of the room. Alternatively, I'd make a big show of covering my face with my palms and sticking fingers in my ears.

I wanted to make out like I couldn't bear to listen.

The truth was, I couldn't bear to watch.

I felt embarrassed and uncomfortable watching the expressions of my colleagues while they listened to me. It was as if by watching them listen, the truth that my voice *actually sounded like that* became irrefutable. No doubt my colleagues were in their own worlds, barely paying attention. But in my deluded, self-centred mind, they were all inwardly flinching at my damn-awful voice. I'd read negative judgement into the natural movement of their faces. My fears would play on repeat inside my head: *I sound immature. I sound nervous. I sound confused. I sound stupid. I sound like a little girl . . .*

I'd been an upspeaker for as long as I could remember, until my mid-20s when I decided to try to do something about it. I was appearing on television regularly by that point and was determined to sound more grown-up. I began deliberately lowering my voice at the end of each thought. Instead of concentrating on the sub-stance of my comments, my brain became consumed with altering my tone. I gave several interviews where I performed well below my best. My anti-upspeak campaign interfered with performance. It confused the articulation of my points and caused another vocal casualty. I began to develop vocal fry.

Keeping up with the Kardashian Konversation

Vocal fry or glottalisation is the low, creaking vibration caused by a fluttering of the vocal cords. (Aside: glottalisation has to be the world's most disgusting word.) Your celebrity references for this voice pattern are singer Katy Perry and *New Girl* actress Zooey Deschanel. While the prevalence of vocal fry fluctuates between genders depending on language, studies from English-speaking countries suggest it's more common among women.

Over the past two decades vocal fry has massively increased in the Western world. One 2011 study found that more than two-thirds of college-aged American women now utilise this method of speech. Interestingly, millennials don't have the same negative reaction to vocal fry that the rest of the population does. In fact, among younger people, women who speak this way are perceived to be more intelligent and to possess high social status. Among older people of both genders, however, vocal fry induces an intensely negative reaction. And for now, at least, it's those older people who are more likely to be the ones giving you – or not giving you – a job.

The widespread adoption of vocal fry by young English-speaking women has generated considerable media attention. While men's vocal fry passes largely unnoticed, its use by women has become a cultural phenomenon. 'Drop the vocal fry immediately!' instruct the click-bait headlines, warning of career suicide for women who use it. Vocal fry has been labelled 'annoying' and 'grating' by major corporate employers, some of whom have given public interviews urging young women to avoid it. Like with upspeak, it betrays a lack of confidence on the part of the speaker.

Ira Glass, the host of podcast *This American Life*, is a heavy, heavy fryer. He has expressed confusion that it's only on occasions when a woman colleague fills in for him that the company gets letters of complaint about how 'annoying' vocal fry is. He's on air every week, but nobody is bothered by his vocal fryage. Ira's experience isn't unique. Vocal fry is a trait that occurs naturally in both genders, but women are much more likely to be criticised for it. Studies show that when a person is asked to preference a statement spoken by both genders, first in vocal fry and second in the more usual modal tone, the normal voice is overwhelmingly more likely to be hired. However, the negative perceptions of women using vocal fry are much stronger – particularly when the *listener* is a woman. Put another way: women don't like women who vocal-fry.

The problem isn't the way women talk, it's that we're talking at all.

Let's briefly recap this confusing circle of noise, prejudice and awareness, shall we? Power has been vested in men for most of history, and, biologically, women's voices are higher than men's. These two facts have combined to mean that human beings perceive higher voices as less commanding and less authoritative. As women gain more power in the workplace, they may be adopting habits to help them avoid the negative consequences that come with that power. This includes an upward inflection at the end of their sentences. This style of speech is read as a lack of confidence and an indicator of women's uncertainty and immaturity, and consequently affects credibility. Perhaps to combat *this* prejudice, young women have begun to lower their voices and developed vocal fry.

This, in turn, makes them croaky, annoying and unemployable. If you're a woman for whom English is a second language, your plight is even worse. Studies show that when English speakers hear non-native speakers talk, they're more likely to doubt the veracity of what is said. So there's that.

Excuse me while I go and step barefoot on Lego for some light relief.

The problem isn't actually women's voices. Women's voices are *symptoms* of the problem. By focusing on the different ways women talk, we ignore the real issue of *why* women and girls alter their voices in the first place. Why is it that women feel – subconsciously or otherwise – they have to express factual statements as questions? Why do we consider women's voices to be weak? Why are we teaching women that the sound of their voice is more important than what they have to say? After all, constant criticism isn't going to make anyone *sound* more confident. Criticism only serves to send a resounding message that it would be easier for women if they just exited the conversation all together. As Professor Robin Lakoff, linguist at the University of California, puts it, 'this stuff is just one more way of telling powerful women to *shut up, you bitch.*'

Learning from the world's leading ladies: how to speak with confidence

I find it comforting and maddening in equal measure to know that the anxieties I have about my voice are a by-product of gender discrimination. However, as someone who wants to sound and present confidently, it doesn't actually help me very much. While it's nice to know that judgements about the voices of women are mostly invalid and unfair, that doesn't stop me being judged, or you or anyone else. Being able to blame the patriarchy for your uncertain speech pattern won't keep you warm at night and it's unlikely to calm your nerves before that big presentation at work.

So how do we learn to speak more confidently?

Communicating with confidence is like anything else: it takes practice. Even the most naturally impressive speakers weren't born expert communicators. And that's a fact I will stand by until someone introduces me to a toddler who can hold an audience like Turia Pitt. Speaking in front of a group or making your point effectively during a meeting are skills like any others. They have to be developed and practised before we can become accomplished at them. For most people, deliberately trying to alter your speech pattern will only make you more self-conscious. If the actual *sound* of your voice is integral to success in your chosen field – like singing, acting or presenting – then seeking out formal training isn't a bad idea. For everyone else, here are some simpler suggestions that might help.

1. **Identify how you talk when you're at your most comfortable.**
   We speak differently in different contexts. The voice you use when you're asking your partner to pass the broccoli isn't the same one you used on the first date. The next time you're speaking to a group, but in a setting where you feel relaxed and confident, examine how your voice sounds. You'll find that your choice of words has changed to match the setting (more sweary, fewer 'synergy's). The sound of your voice in that moment is pretty much directly transferrable to the work context. The *tone* you use when telling a story to your girlfriends at book club is the exact version of your voice that you should try to employ when giving a presentation or speaking in a meeting at work.

2. **Accept and celebrate the natural quirks of your own voice.**
    Confident voices come in many forms, and there is no formula
    for the perfect voice. Hollywood's best actresses are testament
    to that. Open YouTube and listen to Cate Blanchett in the
    film *Elizabeth*. She's powerful and poised, with a soothing,
    mysterious quality to her voice, like she's telling you a secret.
    Now compare that to Carey Mulligan in *An Education*. Her
    voice is delicate, euphonious and almost melancholy, but still
    manages to capture the viewer's undivided attention. Finally,
    search for videos of Viola Davis playing lawyer Annalise
    Keating in the courtroom for *How to Get Away with Murder*.
    Her voice is authoritative, rousing, firm and no-nonsense.
    She speaks with the hardened edge of someone who has seen
    and survived difficult times. Each of these women's voices is
    powerful in its own way. Yours can be too. Don't feel like you
    have to deny the natural quirks of how you speak.

3. **Steady your voice the same way a singer does.**
    Speaking in public is the same as singing but without the
    hassle of having to carry a tune. If you get nervous about
    public speaking, it's worth looking to singing teachers for
    guidance. This means speaking a little bit louder than normal
    to mask that you're feeling under-confident. Focusing on your
    breathing will help to steady your voice. Taking time to pause
    and gather yourself will ensure you don't rush ahead, babbling
    so you're impossible to understand. Clare Bowditch, who has
    one of Australia's most beautiful singing voices and the ARIA
    to prove it, says the trick to sounding confident is accepting
    your nerves. Recognise that they're there and say it out loud,
    she advises me. Say: 'I am nervous! I can hear it in my voice!
    See?' Clare explains that as you speak loudly and proudly,

you can push the nerves away with the sound. Focus on making the sound come from deep inside you, not just 'up in your throat'.

Are you a woman in a meeting?

Did you know that I'm bilingual? In addition to my native tongue, I'm fluent in 'Woman in a Meeting'. I'm proficient in reading and writing in my second language and, considering I'm entirely self-taught, you'll agree it's a mighty impressive feat. Woman in a Meeting is a specialised dialect that has been employed by working women for more than half a century. Wide adoption of the language is proof that gender stereotypes don't only affect the sound of women's voices. They affect the words we choose to use.

In the same way women use upspeak to disguise an assertion as a question, many of us insert additional unnecessary words into our sentences. Woman in a Meeting allows us to communicate our point while simultaneously offering an avalanche of hidden apologies for having the audacity to speak in the first place. It's perfect for occasions where you wish to appear non-threatening to the group (of men, usually) you're speaking to.

Comedian and writer Sarah Cooper has helpfully translated some plain English sentences into Woman in a Meeting. Let's say you want to instruct an employee about a deadline. In English, you would say, 'This document is due by 5 p.m. on Monday,' but in Woman in a Meeting it becomes, 'What do you think about maybe getting this done by Monday?' Shall we try another? This time, you've had a really great idea for how to improve a business process and want to share it with your colleagues. In English, you'd introduce your point by saying, 'I have an idea!' The Woman in a Meeting translation begins with, 'I'm just thinking out loud here . . .'

There are countless variations of this apology tactic. The most common is an actual apology. Hillary Clinton was the first US presidential candidate in history to apologise in a televised concession speech. I don't think it's any coincidence that Clinton was also the first woman to be a genuine competitor for the job. That one word – 'sorry' – seemed to envelop so much that she couldn't otherwise articulate. It spoke to the things Clinton wanted to do for others but would never get the chance to. It betrayed her fears about a future that was unwritten, one that would likely see a proven misogynist and sexual predator stem the progress of gender equality worldwide. There was a sense of Clinton's responsibility to other women in falling short of shattering the highest glass ceiling of them all. She said 'sorry' for the loss of faith that this might happen in her lifetime . . . or in ours. 'Sorry' encapsulated the inevitable public blame Clinton would personally shoulder for Donald Trump's triumph.

Sorry, she said. *Sorry that I wasn't enough.*

When I worked with lots of women, there was a regular chorus of 'sorry' that echoed around the office. We were sorry for interrupting. Sorry for going on annual leave. Sorry for not chatting when we were working on something urgent. Sorry for being in the bathroom and not at our desks. Sorry for wanting a pay rise. Sorry for asking why a task hadn't been completed. Sorry for needing someone to take notes in a meeting. Sorry for not knowing the answer to something we couldn't possibly be expected to know. My friend Alys used to counsel members of her team with the instruction that 'we are *not* sorry for doing our jobs'.

The issue extends beyond words of apology to phrases that actually undermine the substance of what a woman is saying. Have you ever started a sentence with 'I'm not an expert, but . . .' or 'This is probably stupid, but . . .'? How about adding a simple 'You know?'

at the end of a thought? These are all deliberately softening phrases that help women contribute to a conversation without appearing authoritative or confrontational. Their effect is to immediately weaken the argument we're about to make. They make us sound less sure of ourselves. Our point is lost in a sea of explanations as to why it's not valid.

My apologetic word of choice is 'just'. Just is just so simple and just so easy to just insert unwittingly into just about any sentence. At first 'just' doesn't seem like an apology. However, 'just' does contain a subtle message of deference. It places the person using the word – me – in an immediate position of subordination to the person I'm speaking or writing to. Consider these sentences: 'I'm just checking the document over once more before I send it', 'Could I just have a minute of your time?', 'I just work part-time'. Each sentence would be considerably stronger if the word 'just' were removed. The word is not required. 'Just' is a simpering addition that makes the statements less direct and lowers the status of the speaker.

I didn't realise how extreme my reliance on 'just' had become until it was literally accounted for. One of those 'Your Year on Facebook' links appeared in my social media feed, offering to create a word cloud that represented the past year of my life. A word cloud is a clump of words in different sizes and boldness. The larger words, towards the centre of the group, are those that pop up most frequently. The smaller words around the edges are the less popular choices. Programs like Channel 10's *The Project* will populate word clouds on the screen to show what's being discussed in the Twittersphere. Thinking it would be fun, I clicked to generate my word cloud for 2015. It was my first year of marriage and the year that my son was born. Unsurprisingly, 'baby' occupied primary position. And there, slightly left of centre – nestled between my husband's name and the word 'love' – was my third most utilised word, 'just'.

The boys made me do it.

Tara Mohr, author of *Playing Big*, says that 'most women are unconsciously using these speech habits to soften our communications, to avoid being labelled – as women so often do – as bitchy, aggressive, or abrasive.' She's right. These words and phrases have become so normalised that they're part of women's everyday vernacular. It means we rarely question why we use them or how they're perceived. The reason for their existence in women's speech patterns is rooted in sexism. Of course, there are men who also use apologetic language at work, but it doesn't happen nearly as much. Research has shown that these self-denigrating speech habits are most commonly observed among lower-status groups. We're deliberately trying to be less threatening. The effect, however, is to undercut our own contribution. By apologising as we speak, we render ourselves less effective.

But what happens when a woman does eliminate apologetic words from her vocabulary? It isn't always pretty. Actress Jennifer Lawrence wrote for Lena Dunham's *Lenny Letter* about what happened when she used plain-spoken, direct language during meetings.

I spoke my mind and gave my opinion in a clear and no-BS way; no aggression, just blunt. The man I was working with – actually, he was working for me – said, 'Whoa! We're all on the same team here!' As if I was yelling at him. I was so shocked because nothing that I said was personal, offensive, or, to be honest, wrong. All I hear and see all day are men speaking their opinions,

and I give mine in the same exact manner, and you would have
thought I had said something offensive.

Lawrence's experience reveals that abandoning our reliance on
'Woman in a Meeting' speech won't necessarily be met by rapturous
applause. And she is a powerful, wealthy, privileged white woman
with celebrity status. Imagine how taken aback people might be if a
black woman who worked for minimum wage in aged care did the
same thing? In some contexts people find women being authoritative or assertive downright confronting. A former colleague of mine
took it one step further when she embarked on a month of 'radical
honesty' without telling any of her friends, family or workmates.
When she concluded her month and revealed what had been going
on, the reactions were mixed. Several people had found it refresh-
ing. Others said they were relieved because they'd assumed she was
mad at them. Most agreed that she'd been pretty rude.

Accentuate the positives. Eliminate the negatives. (And then put some back in.)

I'm not advocating that we do away with niceties in the workplace.
Being a pleasant, cordial and supportive colleague is a worthy
aim. Moreover, the purpose of language is not always to make a
strong, declarative argument. Woman in a Meeting can be valuable, particularly in building meaningful and trusting workplace
relationships. Ann Friedman explains in *New York* magazine:

> Language is . . . about making yourself understood and trying
> to understand someone else. As anyone who's ever shared
> an inside joke knows, it's *fun*. This can be true even at work
> or in public – places where women are most likely to be

dismissed because of the way they speak . . . Maybe women *are* undermining themselves a bit when they, like, speak in a way they find more natural. But only in the sense that they are seeking to articulate their thoughts more authentically and connect more directly with the people listening to them.

I do think it's worth taking the time to examine your own use of language. Begin by studying your email correspondence rather than trying to alter your manner of speaking aloud. As I've explained, trying to actively amend your speech *while* you're talking is a recipe for saying something stupid. Reversing a habit takes time and practice. So start small. Start with your emails. Write your email, review it and then remove all of the apologetic language. It will suddenly seem very blunt. So much so that you might want to re-insert some of the pleasantries before you feel comfortable pressing send. That's fine. The purpose of this exercise isn't to commence being awful to your colleagues. The purpose is to eliminate words from your vocabulary that are there merely to please other people or indicate your subservience. These are words or phrases that actually undermine your ability to do your job. Removing them will improve your confidence as well as the clarity of your communication.

Debunking the 'women talk too much' myth

Oh, haven't you heard? In addition to talking the wrong way, women also talk *too much*. That women don't know when to stop talking is yet another stereotype that holds us back at work. Imagine this: you're sitting around the boardroom table or in a meeting with clients and you think of something to add. Instead of speaking, though, you hold your tongue. 'You've already talked way too much today,' that inner voice cautions. 'You don't want to dominate the conversation. Let somebody else have a go. People are going to think you're annoying.' As we've learned already, when it comes to women's voices, our perception rarely matches reality.

The often bandied-about claim that women speak 20 000 words a day compared to men's 7000 has been thoroughly debunked. While there is a persistent perception held by both genders that women are more talkative, research shows that at work the opposite is true. Take the legal profession as an example. An Australian study co-authored by Professor George Williams found that only 22 per cent of barristers appearing in person before the High Court are women. In more than half of the cases put before our nation's highest court, there is not a single woman barrister on the team. This in itself is appalling, but consider further – to what extent the women barristers who did appear were permitted to talk. Records show that women rarely speak. Most play supporting roles to a man barrister. In fact, a woman barrister in the High Court has only a 25 per cent chance of playing a speaking role, compared to a man barrister with a 63 per cent chance.

The myth that women speak more than men has arisen not because of women's actual behaviour but because of their *perceived* behaviour. Feminist writer Sady Doyle explains:

> Women actually tend to talk *less* than men in classroom discussions, professional contexts and even romantic relationships; one study found that a mixed-gender group needed to be between 60 and 80 percent female before women and men occupied equal time in the conversation.

This mismatch between the perception of how much women talk and how much they actually talk became a subject of public debate recently. A review was conducted of Australian current affairs program *Q&A*, which revealed that women were consistently under-represented. The review explained that 'there were fewer female panelists and those that were selected were asked fewer questions and permitted far less time to speak.' The review went on to note that both the panel moderator and the producers weren't actively anti-woman. Quite the opposite: they welcomed and encouraged women's participation. The lesser contributions of women were the result of an unconscious bias, where women were perceived to have spoken in the debate more often than was actually the case.

This bias is problematic for women because human beings make so many judgements about one another based on verbal behaviours. How much an individual speaks is a key determinant of status. It's central to establishing an informal hierarchy within a group of people. The more a person participates in discussion, the more 'power' others assume they have. In a Yale School of Management study, Victoria L. Brescoll discovered a strong positive relationship between a man's actual power and how long he felt entitled to speak in a group setting. There was no such positive correlation found for women, even those with the same degree of power or influence. Brescoll's research team discovered that high-powered women intuitively reduced their talking time to match that of low-powered men and women. In other words, men bosses talk more simply because they're the boss, but women bosses don't do the same.

Brescoll's study concluded that high-powered women mostly speak less because they fear backlash for talking too much. Sadly, her study also concluded that this fear of backlash was justified. A woman CEO who spoke for longer than average was rated significantly less suitable for leadership than a man CEO who matched her word for word. Interestingly, high-powered men who voluntarily chose to speak less were considered as *incompetent* as high-powered women who spoke too much. Brescoll says that society expects powerful men to display their power openly, whereas powerful women should not. Our expectations about the gender roles women and men should play in the workplace are firmly entrenched, to our collective detriment.

WHAT CONFIDENCE LOOKS LIKE

Because what you wear is entirely up to you.

With my first magazine column came a professional photo shoot. A photograph of yours truly would appear monthly in *Cosmopolitan*, next to a short collection of words. It would be a 'cowboy' shot, which meant I'd be photographed from mid-thigh upwards. Sitting in the passenger seat of a taxi, this was what dominated my thoughts on the way to the studio. I dislike my body about as much as the next woman who doesn't resemble Samantha Harris. So that's a lot. In a completely original and not at all clichéd way, I particularly dislike my thighs. While they would have come in handy had I been destined for a professional cycling career, they're not ideally suited to glossy magazine shoots.

Three hours, two pairs of Spanx, a mug full of make-up and a tonne of hairspray later, I was in the studio. It was a spacious all-white room with big glass windows. There was white furniture, decorated with white furnishings, set on white floorboards, with white walls and a white ceiling. I hoped nobody would offer me a Dorito. Standing in front of the whitest of the white walls, I smiled weakly at the camera. The photographer began coaxing me through different positions, as I stiffly moved my arms around. It was like I'd never had arms before. They were ineffectual slabs of skin and bone that hung uselessly by my sides or in strange tense, angular positions across my body. *WHAT THE HELL ARE THESE?* I yelled inside my head. *HOW IS IT POSSIBLE I'VE HAD ARMS MY WHOLE LIFE AND YET HAVE ABSOLUTELY NO IDEA WHAT TO DO WITH THEM?*

In my panic, I began to talk. I talked and I talked some more. Fixing my gaze on the photographer's assistant, the make-up artist and the stylist in turn, I tried in earnest to win each of them over. 'I promise I'm smart' was the not-so-subtle subtext of my banter. 'I promise I have something to offer that isn't my appearance. I know I don't look right. Please like me.' I told longwinded, elaborate jokes. I engaged in detailed sarcastic analysis of random current events. I worked that room like a stand-up comedian.

And then the photographer told me to shut up. 'You see, it's just really hard to take a picture when your mouth is moving all the time, babe. The photo is all blurry,' he explained. Quite.

How we look matters. Unfortunately.

My photo shoot anxiety wasn't entirely misplaced. The people in that room *were* making judgements about me based on my appearance. My error was in assuming that this kind of judgement only happens in the confines of a photographer's studio. The truth is we make appearance-based judgements about one another every single time we interact. How we physically present ourselves to the world has enormous bearing on how we're perceived, including at work. For women, historically valued for the ornamental over the practical, this perception matters even more. Aesthetics and presentation have been linked to everything from the likelihood of a woman getting hired to her chances for promotion and even what kind of salary she attracts.

Researchers have uncovered some pretty perverse – and downright discriminatory – results about the link between women's appearance and their work. One study found that women who wear make-up earn up to 30 per cent more than those who don't. Another discovered that people who are overweight or obese are more likely to be paid less. Women with observable disabilities are less likely to be in paid employment than men with the same disability. On average, a woman who is five feet seven inches will earn $5250 more over the course of a year than a woman who is five feet two inches. Chief executives are usually taller than their lower-ranking employees. One American study found that women with 'lesbian indicators' on their resumes were 30 per cent less likely to be called back for a job interview. Another study of 13 000 Caucasian women employees found that blonde-haired women earn more money than brunettes or redheads. In fact, the blonde-hair salary bump is comparable to an entire additional year of formal education. So study hard, ladies, or alternatively save yourself some time and effort by heading to the hairdresser for a permanent bleach job.

Economists Daniel S. Hamermesh and Jeff Biddle have identified something they call the 'plainness penalty'. Their research suggests that if you're less attractive than average, you're punished financially. While the exact figures vary between industries, women with less than average attractiveness generally took home seven per cent less in total earnings than women of average attractiveness. There is contradictory evidence, however, regarding the earnings of beautiful women. Some studies suggest beautiful women are paid more (although not to the same degree as beautiful men). And other studies conclude that beautiful women are more likely to be dismissed as stupid or unqualified, particularly during the hiring process.

I worked for several years in the political office of Federal Minister Kate Ellis. Kate was the youngest woman ever elected to Australia's House of Representatives. She is clever, warm, a great communicator and was an extremely capable minister. Kate also happens to look like a supermodel. When Kate would approach the despatch box to address the parliament, there would be crowing from the Opposition benches. 'Here comes the weather girl' was one of their favourite phrases, implying the minister was all fluff and no substance. Those jeers were disrespectful, their implication untrue and the assumption underpinning them deeply sexist. The world is populated by a substantial number of shallow, cosmetic arseholes, and our elected representatives are no exception.

There is a wealth of material available on the discrimination women experience based on physical attributes beyond their control. Unless you're a tall, slim, white, able-bodied, femme-presenting blonde who can magically shift between average and high levels of attractiveness depending on the situation, there's not really an upside to be found. Exploring that content here is unlikely to make you more confident. It will mostly make you want to stab yourself in the eye with a fork. Or run into the backyard, shaking your fist at the sky and screaming, 'Damn you, patriarchy!' (I really need to stop doing that. The neighbour's cat has become increasingly concerned.) So rather than traversing all that nonsense, in this chapter I'd like to focus on the elements of physical confidence that are actually *within* your control and worthy of your consideration.

Sit up straight when I'm talking to you, please.

How you comport yourself, how long you hold someone's gaze, what you wear and how you wear it all affect how you communicate with others. Author Leonard Mlodinow explains:

> In our perception of people, and their perceptions of us, the hidden, subliminal mind takes limited data, and creates a picture that seems clear and real, but is actually built largely on unconscious inferences that are made employing factors such as a person's body language, voice, clothing, appearance, and social category.

We see one thing and we assume another. Sometimes our brains make logical assumptions. For example, a candidate for a job saunters past with a designer handbag and we presume she's wealthy. And sometimes our brains rely on stereotypes to categorise the visual image in front of us, making it easier to comprehend. A man with grey hair stands at the front of the room surrounded by seated younger people, and we presume he's in charge. However, our reliance on visual clues can steer us in the wrong direction. The woman with the handbag might be a struggling single mum who borrowed the handbag from a wealthy friend. The gentleman in the boardroom might be a junior employee who has made a late-in-life career change and is preparing to take notes on the whiteboard at the request of his boss. Visual messages conveyed by body language and clothing are part of how we communicate, but they aren't always accurate.

There's argument between psychologists about precisely how much of human communication is non-verbal. The percentage varies from study to study. It's estimated to be somewhere between

55 per cent and a whopping 93 per cent. The academic community *does* agree that more than half of human communication with others is based on how we look and sound, rather than the actual content of what we say. So no matter how strong your idea is, the way you look when presenting that idea to your colleagues is equally, if not more, important. The positive flipside of this is how much stronger your communication will be when you have a good idea *and* you take control of the visual message you're sending your colleagues. I should note here the double disadvantage faced by women with physical disabilities who may be unable to exercise the same deliberate control over the messages their body language sends to those around them.

Women often betray our lack of confidence through non-verbal cues. While our confidence in the substance of what we're communicating might be enormous, our body language can give our uneasiness away. Management books will advise you to change roughly four or five million different things about your body language to improve confidence. I don't like management books. I find them scary and intimidating. I also know from experience that when you take yourself too far outside your physical comfort zone, you tend to look *less* confident, not more. Exhibit A: me kicking an imaginary football while wearing five-inch heels and a floral dress for *Cosmopolitan*. So let me share two suggestions that will help you communicate more effectively at work and feel more confident while doing it.

Status, hierarchies and the Big Scary Meeting

Within five minutes of meeting one another, a group of three strangers will have established a power hierarchy according to appearance and body language. Women are almost always at the bottom of those hierarchies. This might seem logical given women tend to have less positional power in the workplace. They're less likely to be CEOs or board directors, for example. However, these unspoken social hierarchies aren't based on actual power but *perceived* power. This is about the appearance of power, not the reality of who actually wields it. And a key contributing factor that places women at the bottom of a hierarchy is their body language. The very way in which women stand, sit or even move their hands can send a signal that the bottom of the hierarchy is where they belong. It's not women's fault that we do this. We're subconsciously reacting to where we expect to be placed.

Our alternative course of action is to *consciously* choose to be placed somewhere else.

Change where you sit in the hierarchy in five seconds.

When I was working in politics, I was given the chance to act as chief of staff for several months. I loved everything about the job, which exposed me to the highest policy-making structures of the federal government. The one exception was the regular chiefs of staff meetings, which I was required to attend. Those meetings were held in the boardroom adjacent to the prime minister's office. There was an enormous polished wooden table that would have taken several elephants to lift in the centre of the room. The window had a view of the prime minister's courtyard, so you would occasionally see a very official-looking car with a flag on the bonnet pull up while our meetings were in progress. The prime minister's chief of staff was in charge of the proceedings, and all the most senior advisers in the government would attend.

Being a complete nerd and perennially early person, I was usually the first to arrive. On the occasion of my first meeting,

I surveyed the enormous room and considered carefully where to sit. I counted the fancy high-backed leather chairs and quickly established that there were fewer chairs than there would be meeting attendees. Along the perimeter of the room were a bunch of extra chairs. They were the standard, office-furniture, metal-spokes-and-padded-seat variety of chair. I sat down in one of those. I specifically took the one furthest from the head of the table and out of the meeting chair's eye line. I then pulled out my BlackBerry and attempted to look busy and important and like I wasn't completely out of my depth and needing to wee.

As the rest of the senior staff filed in, chatting and at ease with one another, I watched the unspoken hierarchy being established. The more high-ranking the politician you worked for, the more likely you were to sit at the main table. The blokes were shouting across the room to one another. There was much backslapping. Several of the younger guys were rocking back on the rear legs of their chairs, like my toddler does when he's being deliberately naughty. Their hands were clasped behind their heads, legs extended and lazily crossed at the ankle. There were 24 carbon-copy Don Drapers and barely any women in the room. Maybe four, at most. Each of those women, regardless of the relative importance of her boss, took her place in the cheap seats alongside me.

I wish I'd known then what I know now. That the very act of sitting at the main table can help you feel like you belong there. It has the added bonus of making others think you belong there too.

When we're nervous, we try to take up as little space as possible. We make ourselves physically small. If you've ever watched people sitting front row at a stand-up comedy gig, you'll know what I mean. They're in prime position for cringe-worthy audience participation and they're desperate not to be noticed. So they hunch their shoulders, bring their knees close together and look determinedly at anything *but* the action. By trying to make themselves inconspicuous, they often achieve the opposite. Their actions speak louder than words ever could.

By avoiding a visually dominant chair in the chiefs of staff meeting, I was doing much the same thing. I was making myself small. I was making sure I didn't take up space in a room where I perceived myself as far less important than others. I sent a message to everyone in the room about my status. I was actively communicating my unimportance, while the men in the room were conveying authority. Have you ever been looking for a seat on the bus and the only spare one is beside a man with a swimming pool of space between his knees? That's called manspreading, and it is an unconscious expression of power. That bloke possesses a seemingly divine right to take up two seats instead of one. He's supremely confident about his position on that bus and his right to take up space in the world. There isn't a *better* seat to choose on the bus and yet he still subconsciously manages to communicate his power, so he conveys his status by taking *two* of them.

Imagine a long, rectangular boardroom table. The most powerful seats at that table are the most visible. First there's the head and foot of the table, where the king and queen might have sat in ye olde days. There are also those in the exact middle of the table, where the bride and groom are seated at a wedding. It's recognition that they're the most important people in the room. It's also where Jesus is sitting in Leonardo da Vinci's painting, the *Last Supper*. The son of God was in the power seat. Now imagine a circular table. In that scenario, every seat is of equal visibility and therefore projects power equally. A round table is often called a King Arthur's table after the famous leader who believed himself equal to and not above his advisers.

Tata Chemicals is an American company that deliberately changed the way it organised seating at conferences. It wanted to create a more egalitarian environment, where low- and middle-level staff felt comfortable being honest with their managers. To do this, it rearranged the chairs. Instead of theatre-style seating (with everyone facing a stage), it ran its conference in 'the round'. Chairs were arranged in concentric circles, like the audience at a circus. Like King Arthur's table. The results were tangible: lower-level employees' participation in discussion increased.

The inverse of this lesson can be applied in your own life. By changing where you sit in a meeting you can influence how much power you're perceived to have. While there is likely to be protocol about where the boss sits, at least one or two of the other powerful seats will likely be available. I'd wager that those power seats tend to be occupied by men. Next time you're in an intimidating meeting with a client or a manager or stakeholder, why not try claiming a power spot? It won't change your status overnight, but in time you might notice a subtle shift in how you're perceived and how you feel.

Power posing. Yes, seriously.

Body language affects how confident other people think you are and also how confident *you* think you are. Social psychologist Amy Cuddy says that non-verbal behaviour is a language and should be employed deliberately in the same way verbal language is. After all, we prepare for a presentation by writing notes on what we'd like to say. Why not prepare our bodies to communicate more effectively too? One way of doing this is through something called 'power

posing', which is just as ridiculous as it sounds, but also kind of genius.

Power posing is based on the idea that humans and animals use their physicality to convey status. For example, a gorilla in the wild will puff up its chest and raise its arms out wide to intimidate another gorilla. A male peacock extends his tail feathers to display his magnificence and win the interest of a female. Beyoncé stands with her hand on one hip, a sideways knee and a merciless stare because she's the most splendid creature of all. These physical displays of power and influence aren't just learned. They're innate. The 'pride' gesture – holding your hands above your head in victory – has been observed in people who were born blind and have never seen another human being do the same. It's an instinctual physical response to winning; an inbuilt reaction to victory.

Humans and animals also use physicality to show powerlessness. When we're being attacked, we instinctively make our bodies smaller to reduce the size of the target and to indicate submission. Women may adopt a kind of powerless positioning at work. We feel out of our league in a meeting and anxious not to be called on to answer a question, so we keep our head down and shoulders hunched. Our bodies recreate our internal desire not to be noticed. Sometimes we do it intentionally, to appear vulnerable or less intimidating or more 'likeable'. Interestingly, non-threatening body posturing is deliberately adopted in some Asian cultures where business introductions begin with a bow rather than the more assertive Western handshake. Most of the time, though, our body language is unconscious – which means we can *choose* to change it.

Cuddy claims that by altering your physical stance for just two minutes, you can have a profound effect on your own confidence and your projection of confidence. In Cuddy's experiment, a group of people had saliva samples taken before and after gambling. Half the group adopted power poses prior to hitting the casino and half the group didn't. By the end of that experiment power-pose participants were found to have a 20 per cent increase in testosterone and a 25 per cent decrease in cortisol (that's the chemical that regulates stress). Of the power posers, 86 per cent chose to participate in high-risk gambling games. By contrast, the participants who didn't adopt power poses exhibited a 10 per cent decrease in testosterone and a 15 per cent increase in cortisol. Only 60 per cent of them chose to participate in gambling games at all.

While this is only one experiment, Cuddy's research does mirror that of others in showing how interconnected human brains and bodies are. When you physically pretend to be confident it causes a chemical change in your brain that makes you feel more confident. So the next time you need to feel more confident, the next time you have a Big Scary Thing at work, you're going to try a two-minute power pose immediately beforehand. You are going to feel like a dufus when you first do it. You need to push through that feeling to get to the good stuff. Believe me.

Here are my favourites:

1. **The Silverback Gorilla**
   Stand at the end of the table with your feet shoulder-width apart, leaning slightly forward towards your audience, hands and fingers spread on the table so that they're wider than your body.
2. **The Wonder Woman**
   Have your feet shoulder-width apart, your shoulders back and chest open, your hands on your hips. A simple and effective power stance, named after an iconic made-up feminist.

3. **The Facebook CEO**

   A very expansive pose, where one or both arms are draped across an adjacent chair as you lean back slightly with legs widely spread. Grey hoodie, jeans and a multi-billion-dollar empire are optional.

How to get a job like Kim Kardashian (where you get paid just for living).

I once interviewed Kim Kardashian. At the time, Kim was in her post-sex-tape phase. *Keeping Up with the Kardashians* was definitely a thing, but this was before she and her family had achieved the total world domination they have today. My eight-minute interview with Kim wasn't until 3.55 p.m., but I was told to arrive by 3.40 p.m. to ensure her schedule wasn't disturbed by any unforeseen events. I was greeted by a public relations duo who appeared to be the world's happiest women. They were filled with unicorn-like joy simply because they were breathing recycled Kardashian air. I was bemused.

The PR types were making casual chitchat when Kim herself appeared. I went through the following thought process: first, Kim was the most exquisitely beautiful woman. Jaw-droppingly beautiful. Second, she was teeny-tiny and almost childlike in stature. I felt like the BFG in comparison. Third, she had phenomenal eye contact. Kim has these big intense brown eyes and she didn't shift them from mine. Fourth, she was extremely sweet and, despite being a multimillionaire, pretended to be genuinely interested in the bargain boots I'd bought for $25 at Rubi Shoes. Fifth, she was *still* making unbroken, unblinking eye contact, several minutes after we'd been introduced.

Kim's gaze was electric. I felt like we were the only two people in the world. It was as if we were real friends and I'd been invited into her secret confidences. Well it would have been, if real friends only discussed topics for which prior permission was given by Kim's minders (these included Kim's latest diet product endorsements and her 'keen interest' in fashion). The interview was admittedly kind of dull, but Kim's phenomenal eye contact transformed her listless conversation into a Dan Brown thriller. The woman was a magnificent, unflappable, unrelenting, unblinking miracle. No wonder she's so famous.

Human beings can read each other's emotions fairly accurately through eye contact. We subconsciously attach high emotional significance to the eye movements of those we interact with. Our eyes are the most expressive means of non-verbal communication. Eye contact produces powerful connections, even when people are not communicating in person. Simply looking at a photograph or drawing of someone's face can prompt an emotional reaction because of the expression we interpret from the eyes. Test it out when you're next in an art gallery or watching a cute baby riding on a robot vacuum cleaner (YouTube it). You will unconsciously be attributing various emotions to the portrait subject or baby. Research shows that men are better at holding eye contact in group contexts or when presenting to a large number of people, whereas women tend to be better at maintaining eye contact in one-on-one situations. Women are generally more comfortable with the intimacy that eye contact brings because they engage in intimate conversations more often. It's why a group of girlfriends who catch up for coffee will sit themselves around a circular table. They each want to be able to see one another. By contrast, men are often more comfortable chatting to a mate while sitting side-by-side on the couch watching TV. Sometimes there is no eye contact at all. They're strange beasts, men.

Eye contact can be an invitation for closeness between strangers. Its absence is usually a rejection. (A key exception is in some cultural groups, including the Japanese and the Finnish, where direct eye contact in a business context may be considered disrespectful.) Lack of eye contact can indicate embarrassment, depression, sadness or disgust whereas steady eye contact is a strong indicator of trust, confidence and competence. It can also help you attract and retain the attention of others. When initiating conversation people use significant eye contact 75 per cent of the time, compared to 40 per cent when listening to someone. So if you're in a group situation and feel that your point isn't being heard, focus your attention on capturing the eye contact of each person individually. When you're giving a speech or presentation, make sure you know your material well enough so that you can look out at the audience rather than at your notes. Looking at the audience will mean you're perceived as more confident and intelligent. Win–win.

What women want and what women wear

What we wear is deeply intertwined with both the projection and perception of confidence. Wearing an outfit that I know I look good in alters my mood. Some of my best days have been particularly good hair days. (I know that feels anti-feminist, but it's also true.) As women, what we wear has the power to bring us confidence. It is also the subject of constant discussion and critique. Our society pays attention and reads into what women wear to a far greater degree than we do for men. The consequences of this can be pretty appalling.

In her superb 2013 Andrew Olle Media Lecture, journalist Lisa Wilkinson laid forth some uncomfortable truths about the Australian media industry. She spoke eloquently about the many forms of sexism women in the media have experienced and shared a letter from a viewer. It read:

> Who the heck is Lisa's stylist? Whoever it is has Lisa in some shocking clothes. Today's outfit is particularly jarring and awful. Just my 2 cents worth. Get Some Style.

The letter, Wilkinson explained, wasn't particularly remarkable. Of the 200+ carefully chosen outfits the *Today* host wears each year, none had ever won universal praise. Wilkinson's appearance, rather than her effectiveness as a host and interviewer, is the thing most likely to draw comment from viewers. Contrast this with the experiment conducted by Wilkinson's co-host Karl Stefanovic one year later. Stefanovic wore the same navy blue suit on television, five days a week, for an entire year, wondering if anyone would notice. Nobody did. 'No one gives a shit,' Stefanovic told Fairfax Media. 'Women, they wear the wrong colour and they get pulled up.' Men in the media have their worth measured by their words. Women are measured by their outfits.

If the Emperor had been an Empress, her new skirt would have been too short.

The politics of women's clothing has a long and deeply sexist history. In some cultures it was men who traditionally wore flashier, attention-seeking attire and the women would be simply dressed or covered up. This acted to make the women invisible, reinforcing their status as people of lesser relevance. In other cultures, women's dress has historically favoured fashion over function – think bustles, corsets and hoop skirts. Women were meant to be ornamental and decorative rather than equal contributors to society and the economy.

It wasn't until the end of World War I that Western women began wearing clothes that enabled them to move more freely. However, women changed their clothing faster than society changed its attitude. Those who rejected more feminine silhouettes, like flappers in the 1920s, were considered shallow and promiscuous. The resurgence of ultra-feminine dresses in the 1940s and '50s coincided with regressing social norms of the era and a return to the belief that a woman's place was in the home. While the sexual revolution of the 1960s and '70s brought women more personal and sartorial autonomy, their clothing remained a matter of public debate and concern.

Even today, women can't win when it comes to what we wear. Expose too much skin and you're a slut. Too little and you're a prude. Wear a dress and heels to work – you're sleeping your way to the top. Wear a suit with pants and you're a dyke. Wear a hijab and you're subjected to judgement on a totally different scale of awfulness.

Journalist Hadley Freeman explained in *The Guardian* how then Democratic nominee for president Hillary Clinton should dress if she were elected. The firmly tongue-in-cheek description reveals how intense the pressures on women in public life really are:

She just needs to be perfectly groomed at all times, but not look high-maintenance; she must wear gorgeous clothes, but they must not cost any money; she should look relatable but never 'mumsy'; she must be feminine but not girly; she needs to look tough, but not like a bitch; she has to have perfect hair but spend no money on it; also her hair must not be too long (witchy) or too short; she must never have plastic surgery, but nor can she look old; she must think about her appearance at all times and simultaneously never think about such a frivolous issue;

she has to look reassuringly presidential, which means looking
like past male presidents, but she must never look masculine;
she can't wear dresses (too girly), but she also can't wear trousers
(too butch); she can't wear makeup, but she must also always
look as good as if she was wearing makeup; she should dress
age-appropriate, but she must also never look like a 68-year-old
woman; she should celebrate being a woman, but she also must
not remind any men of their mother/ex-wife/any woman in
their life who once made them feel sad.

Can't be that hard, right?

What the hell am I supposed to be wearing then?

Caitlin Moran explains in *How to Be a Woman* that 'when a woman
says, "I have nothing to wear!" what she really means is, "There's
nothing here for who I'm supposed to be today."' Moran is right.
There's so much pressure, expectation, judgement and stereotype
about what women wear that the simple act of getting dressed for the
day becomes a complex series of decisions. Clothes play a significant
role in how women communicate, and choosing an outfit becomes
conflated with 'what do I need to tell the world today?' When you're
getting dressed for an ordinary day at work, it's hard enough. When
your day involves meeting new people or giving a presentation or
going to an interview, then it's a Rubik's Cube of difficulty.

So here are some very simple suggestions (*not* rules) that might
make you feel more confident about what you wear at work:

1. **Stop clicking on internet articles that contain rules on 'what
   to wear'.** These articles are stupid. They are not based on any
   method or scientific approach or even what works

for one person. They're usually someone's hastily thrown-together opinion combined with a bunch of meaningless clichés and paid-for mentions by advertisers. Trust me. I used to write them.

2. **Avoid making radical outfit or appearance changes immediately before a Big Scary Thing.** Moments where you're lacking in confidence or searching for a confidence boost are no time for fashion experiments. The first time I ever wore a suit and sucky-inny underwear was for a job interview with the prime minister's office. I felt awkward, quite unlike myself, and struggled to breathe throughout the whole thing.

3. **If you have to force it? Let it go. Wear what you're comfortable in.** Don't use fashion to be something or someone you're not. The result is almost always uncomfortable, expensive and silly-looking. If you would like to see a lived example of this, please visit my social media and evaluate the photos of me during my 'I'm watching too much *Nashville*' phase. I was not born for peasant skirts and boot socks.

4. **Draw the line at your daggiest tracksuit pants.** If you wear clothes you're comfortable in, then your posture and body language is more likely to be relaxed. But this does not mean you should wear a dressing gown or tracksuit pants to an interview. Your clothes don't need to be expensive; however, being generally well presented and tidy is an important sign of respect for the people you're working with.

5. **If you dress a certain way for cultural or religious reasons then (please!) don't feel pressured to abandon that.** If that's part of who you are and an important element of your sense of self, then you do not need to change it for the workplace. Even employers who require that you wear a uniform are

legally required to offer you a variation that is in keeping with your beliefs. Don't be afraid to make that request or seek assistance from someone you trust to make that request on your behalf. It is your right.

6. **Choose clothes that help you feel excited about the task ahead.** This is the equivalent of putting your game face (or power pose!) on. We've all met a toddler who refuses to change out of her Princess Elsa costume for a trip to Coles. That kid knows how to dress for an occasion. Be like her. Remember when American senator Wendy Davis gave an 11-hour filibuster speech in the Texas state parliament to defend a woman's right to choose? She wore a power suit and highlighter-pink joggers for the occasion. Practical *and* empowering.

7. **Clothes don't give you power, but they give you confidence.** When my dad worked in the public service, he occasionally met with stakeholders who weren't very accepting of his dark skin. On the days he knew he'd be meeting with those individuals, he'd always wear the same tie. It was bright red, covered with white cartoon sheep, with a single black sheep dead in the centre. The chances are nobody except Dad ever actually noticed the gesture, but that didn't matter. It was enough for him to know it.

8. **If you're unemployed and don't own clothes that make you feel confident, ask for help.** There are some great organisations that support women who have been locked out of the workforce for whatever reason. They can provide you with clothes to wear at interviews that will help you feel polished, self-assured and like you belong. Clothes might seem like a minor consideration, but if they're messing with your confidence they're worth paying attention to.

WHAT CONFIDENCE FEELS LIKE

Because crying in front of the boss is pretty normal.

When I returned to work after my son was born, everything was different. The job had changed dramatically in my short absence and barely resembled the role I used to fill. To be honest, I'd changed a lot too. There was no real place for me in the business any more and that rattled my confidence massively. For the first time, I dreaded going to the office each day and job offers from other companies were becoming increasingly attractive. Something had to give. So after six confused weeks, I requested a meeting with my bosses. With me in Melbourne and management in Sydney, the meeting took place over Skype. I'm not sure how it could possibly have gone worse.

I'd prepared for the chat by jotting down some notes, a list of the points I wanted to make. I thought I had a compelling case, but as the conversation progressed, my mind started whirring ahead of the words coming out of my mouth. I was planning my response to their response before I'd even given my bosses anything to respond to. My adrenaline was pumping. The hairs on my arms were standing on end. In my chest I felt the warm, heavy pressure that comes with the fight or flight reflex. The arguments I'd made so eloquently in my head the night before wouldn't come out right. I grasped for examples that I knew were there but that I frustratingly couldn't recall in the moment. As each point came out wrong, again and again, I began to panic.

I felt the tears long before they actually appeared. If my body were a car backing out of the driveway, the beeps of the reversing sensor had been growing ever more urgent. By the time my tear ducts were as overwhelmed as my emotions, the warning sound had become a single, sustained, painful beep.

'You are going to crash,' said the car's emergency system.

And I did.

Can you ever come back from crying at work?

There are few events that match crying at work as a confidence killer. This overt display of vulnerability doesn't accord with our expectations about how to behave in the work environment. However, crying at work is quite common. Forty per cent of women admit to having cried at work on at least one occasion. Having lied in response to that very question myself, I suspect the *actual* number is higher than the data records. It's common among my girlfriends to describe these sorts of moments while peeking out from behind intertwined fingers of embarrassment. The phrase 'I cried in front of my boss' is usually followed by a faux howl of shame. While the actual crying event may be long gone by the time it's discussed, the mortification remains.

I've been on the other side of it too. I've been the boss faced with a sobbing employee, and it isn't the more comfortable place to be. Nobody likes seeing someone else cry. (Unless you're the kind of person who eats KitKats by biting into multiple biscuit fingers simultaneously. You sickos probably do like seeing people cry.) Humans are programmed to care for and comfort one another in times of distress. So when you're the boss and you see your employee crying, you want to help console them. Regardless of how the employee is actually performing or how unreasonable they're being, the in-the-moment reaction of a boss tends to be empathetic.

Crying in the workplace is considered a 'female' conundrum, and the research backs this. The number of men who admit to crying at work is in the single-digit percentages. This variance between women and men's tears isn't confined to the workplace, either. The average woman cries almost four times as often as a man – 5.3 times per month compared with 1.4 times. I don't know about you, but there have definitely been months where I've well and truly exceeded the statistical average. The reason women cry more than men do is not because women are weaker. It's not because we feel things more deeply. It's partly biological. Testosterone inhibits crying. There is a hormone called prolactin that promotes crying, and this occurs at higher levels in women. Men also have larger tear ducts, which means they can hold tears in their eye sockets for longer before they overflow onto their cheeks.

Social conditioning is another part of the gendered crying equation. While things are slowly changing, crying still doesn't fit with Australian society's view of being 'male'. There's pressure placed on boys to control their tears from an early age. So by the time men reach adulthood, they are socially conditioned – as well as biologically reinforced – to hold back their tears. Those social deterrents don't exist to the same extent for little girls. The incentive for girls to master the art of controlling their tears during childhood isn't as strong.

When a woman cries she's weak.
When a man cries it's serious.

I know women who cry when a puppy is reunited with its owner at the end of kitschy local news broadcasts. One of my girlfriends has a five-year-old who insists on watching *Bambi* every weekend, and she always cries when Bambi's mum dies – this is my adult friend, not the five-year-old. Personally, I've been known to shed a tear during particularly moving Qantas commercials. (Shut up, they're really, really good.) These kinds of tears are silly, even sweet, but they're inconsequential. They're not a reflection of gravity, of how deeply moved or distressed someone is. When a man cries it's different. Even if he's just tearing up during a soppy movie, those tears are generally awarded greater weight by those around him. The rarity of men's tears makes them *seem* more important. The unusual is noteworthy.

It may have been the boy who cried wolf, but it's the woman who suffers. The considerable weight society awards to men's tears is carried into the workforce, where women are penalised. At work the assumption that women's tears aren't 'a big deal' hurts women. In fact, there is an overwhelmingly negative perception of women who cry in the office – even if crying is atypical for them person-ally. Women who cry at work may be considered weak or unable to cope with difficult, stressful tasks. Crying is seen as an expression of inability rather than a natural part of processing distressing infor-mation. This is especially the case for women who cry regularly.

Dr Kim Elsbach, from the University of California, studies the repercussions of crying at work. She has discovered that there are certain situations where crying is 'acceptable' for both men and women in the workplace – namely following the death of a loved one or post-divorce. The expression of overt emotion by men in these situations can actually have a positive impact on their careers. When men cry, colleagues assume that something *truly horrible* has happened. This prompts responsive feelings of 'humanisation' and 'closeness' with the crying man. Crying women are rarely viewed positively, regardless of the cause. Even in the event of a socially legitimate reason for crying, like a death, a woman who cries is viewed neutrally, at best, according to Elsbach's research.

Women who cry excessively, repeatedly or in a prolonged way are at risk of being considered weak – or even unstable – by colleagues. Crying in response to looming deadlines, disagreements with co-workers or other work stresses prompts the strongest negative responses from others. In some cases, the repeated tears of women are considered purposeful or manipulative. Interestingly, it's women themselves who are the harshest judges of women's tears, with 43 per cent saying people who cry at work are 'unstable', compared with only 34 per cent of men.

So working women should never cry, right? Wrong. The answer is never simple in a gendered world. Women who are particularly stoic or fail to actively display emotion at work are also victims of criticism. Ardent Leisure CEO Deborah Thomas was panned in the media for not appearing 'upset enough' following four tragic deaths at a Queensland theme park owned by her company. When Thomas fought back tears at a press conference later that week she was then labelled overly 'emotional' and not on top of the pressures of the job.

Pennsylvania State University professor of psychology Stephanie Shields says:

> Women are not making it up when they say they're damned
> if they do, damned if they don't . . . If you don't express any

emotion, you're seen as not human, like Mr. Spock on *Star Trek*. But too much crying, or the wrong kind, and you're labeled as overemotional, out of control, and possibly irrational.

There are many managers who are adamant that the office is no place for emotions. However, there is an emerging school of thought that says injecting some emotion into the workplace might not be a bad thing.

Why are you crying? It's just a job.

We're generally expected to hide personal vulnerabilities in the office. At work, we are professional people who are paid to do a job, not to have feelings. At work, we should be calm and confident and in control. And crying? Crying is the opposite of control. Therefore, we reason, there must be consequences for those people who reveal too much of their feelings. Negative consequences. The problem with this reasoning is that it doesn't account for the reason behind the tears. That reason is important. In my experience, two factors influence why women cry at work. Both are reflections of how much women care about their work and how determined they are to do a good job.

Firstly, women cry at work because our professional and personal lives are deeply intertwined. Modern human beings spend more time working than we do on any other single activity. For many of us, the eight-hour day and five-day working week have been relegated to the history books. Australians work longer hours today than we ever have. Five million of Australia's 7.7 million full-time workers put in more than 40 hours a week. Of those, 1.4 million regularly work more than 50 hours per week and around 270 000 will work for more than 70 hours. Computers, smart phones and internal messaging systems mean the lines between home and office are increasingly blurred. It makes it harder for us to 'switch off'. Many of us spend weeknights at home on the couch, clearing emails so that we're better prepared for the next workday.

The interconnectedness of our work identities and our personal identities means that career has become a determinative part of *who we are*. One reason that women find maternity leave confronting is because you start to question what your identity is when you don't work. No matter your job – whether you're a banker, a farmer, a social worker, a university professor or working in marketing – it is more than just how you get paid, it's part of *who you are*. This fusion of identities makes it hard to separate your sense of self from your performance at work. It makes holding back your feelings all the more difficult. Women cry at work because their self-worth is integrally linked to their career and reputation. The professional and the personal aren't separate. The professional *is* the personal. So we feel strongly about it.

The second reason women cry at work is because they are angry or frustrated. Where boys are encouraged to hide emotional fragility as children, girls are actively discouraged from showing anger, especially in the form of aggression. For little girls who were not allowed to hit or throw things, the only socially acceptable outlet for negative emotions was to cry. This behaviour continues into adulthood. I've cried in front of a boss on two occasions and both times it was because I was frustrated, not because I was feeling sad. In the story at the start of this chapter, I was crying because I was angry. Angry at the situation. Angry at being misunderstood. Angry that I couldn't get my points across. Crying was my body's natural, instinctive reaction to those feelings.

Academic research confirms that women's tears are often an expression of rage or frustration. Ad Vingerhoets, author of *Why Only Humans Weep*, explains:

> Powerless anger is an important elicitor of female crying, whereas it is only quite exceptionally an elicitor of crying in men. Women also more often cite feeling rejected or insulted as a reason for crying than do men.

In one American study, 51 per cent of women were discovered to have cried as a result of feeling angry, whereas only two per cent of men said that they would shed a tear in anger. This is a response to women and men's different conditioning. Women have been taught that overt expressions of anger (for example, shouting) are inappropriate. They aren't *nice*. So when you've got all this anger inside you but no way to convey it, it causes frustration, which bubbles over into tears. Women aren't sad or distressed by work more than men, just as men aren't angrier at work more than women. We feel the same stuff, but we've been socialised to express or repress those emotions differently.

Being vulnerable can sometimes help you get ahead.

Pretending that we're not emotional, feeling beings at work isn't working. For anyone. Keeping up the charade that you're not emotionally invested in what happens at work is exhausting. It's a waste of time and energy that could be better spent. So why do we keep doing it? And why do we judge others harshly when they do? Why do we think that we'll be better, more effective employees if we dedicate a shit-tonne of energy to hiding our feelings? Surely that energy could be spent actually doing our jobs. After all, if we openly showed emotion in the workplace – and accepted that this was a natural, normal part of being human – would it really be so bad?

Brené Brown, an expert on social connection and all-round rad lady, says that expressing vulnerability is the single most effective tool in bringing people together. Vulnerability, she explains, does not mean weakness or submission. Being vulnerable is simply having the courage to be yourself and engage on a more personal level with those around you. It has long been thought that work is the last place where you should display vulnerability. However, Brown argues that vulnerability is critical to developing an authentic relationship with your co-workers: one that fosters trust, respect and cooperation.

If you're reading the above but quietly thinking, *Yeah, sure, I'm going to go into work on Monday, unload on the CEO about my traumatic childhood, snotty-cry and get a promotion . . . Bullshit,* then fair enough. This sort of magic woo-hoo, 'show your real self to the world and the goodness will be returned' isn't normally my cup of turmeric latte, either. But here's what you need to realise about vulnerability: it's not a weakness, it's a strength. The benefits of being honest about your own vulnerabilities are demonstrated and proven. Brené Brown isn't a mystic, Tarot-reading magician. She's a researcher. She deals with data and science, not the divine. Still not convinced? Let me give you an example from my own working life that might change your mind.

I'd been working in the prime minister's office for less than a year and I was unhappy. The hours were absolutely relentless; 14-hour days and 12-day fortnights were standard. I was struggling to finish my university degrees in the limited time I had outside work, which meant there was no room in my life for rest or relaxation. I was lonely. I barely saw my friends and family. While other university students were sinking beers and partying on a Friday night, I'd be sitting at my desk summarising what had happened on *Lateline*. I'd gained nine kilograms in nine months because I didn't have time to exercise and was eating my feelings. I hadn't told anyone close to me how I felt. *Having this job is an honour and a privilege*, I kept insisting to myself. *Quit whining and be grateful for the opportunity you've been given.*

Parliament had reached the end of its winter session. The staff and several of the politicians were gathered in one of the courtyards for a party. Kate Ellis, who I knew a little from my student politics days, approached me. She and her chief of staff, Shannon, made polite chitchat for a while, before Kate asked how I was going. She didn't ask in a perfunctory way either, she really wanted to know. I remember Kate put her hand on my shoulder, with an expression of genuine concern on her face. I probably looked just about as good as I felt that evening – which was miserable.

I'd just launched into my practised 'how great is life!' speech when – to my very great horror – I started to tear up. The warmth and kindness of a near stranger had broken my façade. Swallowing the tears, I let the whole sordid tale of my unhappiness at work escape. Kate and Shannon consoled me. Two weeks later, the prime minister reshuffled his frontbench and Kate was promoted. With her expanded ministerial responsibilities came a new position in her office. Shannon called me immediately. 'How about you come and work with us?' she asked warmly. I'll never forget the kindness of those two women and their willingness to give me a shot. By being vulnerable, I opened myself to new professional opportunities. By being receptive to that vulnerability, Kate and Shannon earned themselves immense loyalty and commitment from their newest staff member.

Emotional intelligence is the new black.

Hiding emotions at work isn't working for employees and it's not working for employers, either. An employee is actually more valuable if they are emotionally intelligent and aware. Emotional intelligence is a term that gets thrown around a lot without much understanding of what it actually means. One of my (bloke) mates recently described it as 'what chicks are good at – you know, feelings and stuff'. I stepped on his toes. In basic terms, having emotional intelligence means you're able to recognise and manage not only your own emotions but the emotions of others. It's characterised by three main skills:

1. **Emotional awareness**
   This means being self-aware, understanding what it is you are feeling and recognising emotional responses in others. For example, if you are feeling as though you want to cry, how good are you at recognising the cause of the tears? Is it anger, sadness, frustration or exhaustion?

2. **Harnessing emotion**
   This means applying emotion to improve performance in a task, like problem-solving. If you are stressed about an impending deadline, can you use that to motivate yourself? If your team is excited about an upcoming project, are you able to translate that to increased productivity?

3. **Managing emotion**
   This means managing both your own emotions and the emotions of others effectively. When a friend is upset, are you able to calm and comfort them? When you receive criticism from your boss, are you able to separate your emotional response from your functional response?

Academic consensus is that women tend to be better at emotional intelligence than men. At any one time, women are likely to have up to 30 per cent more neurons firing in the areas of the brain that control thinking and feeling. Remember, these neural pathways are mostly developed postnatally and so are shaped, at least in part, by how we are raised. This is what makes women go over and over the same emotional challenge in their heads – sometimes to a point of anxiety. If you've ever rolled over in bed at night and explained to a gentleman partner what's on your mind only to be met with a response of 'Huh? But that was *ages* ago,' you'll know this to be true.

Researchers have found that 'women are faster and more accurate at identifying emotions' as well as picking up non-verbal cues. Men are more likely to exhibit unifocal thinking, which means they focus on the end result, whereas women generally have more divergent thought processes. While the end goal remains in a woman's consciousness, there is greater consideration of what risk might have been missed, or what's not being seen clearly. What often gets called 'women's intuition' may actually be a type of unconscious reasoning that is based on recognising emotional patterns. This is what helps us to assess when it's appropriate to take risks and when greater self-care is required. Some scientists even believe it may be part of the reason women live longer than men. Men take more risks, which are less calculated. Women play it safe.

Some scientists think brain structure may even cause women to fixate more intensely on an event that has already happened. We consider carefully how things could have gone better, what we would have done differently and why a situation turned out the way it did. There is a small part of the brain called the cingulate gyrus, nicknamed the 'worry wart' by neurologists. It's the part of the brain that humans use to weigh up our options and evaluate errors. It's generally larger in women, which may make women better attuned to emotional responses because we have spent more time imagining possible variations. Put another way, women aren't better at feelings than men. We just spend more time thinking about and processing them. We've had more practice.

Building workplaces where feelings are a good thing

Research consistently suggests a balance of traditionally masculine and feminine approaches in workplaces yields the best results. One corporate finance study found that men traders produced better immediate results but lower portfolio results than women achieved over the long term. Men tended to suffer from *over*confidence, which meant they occasionally invested where they shouldn't. Similarly, inpatients treated by women doctors have a lower relative risk of death and of being readmitted to hospital within a month. Researchers think the reason for this discrepancy is the willingness of women doctors to invest time in preventative care and counselling. Companies with a higher proportion of women on their boards do better financially. While there is a place for competitive, aggressive and risk-taking approaches in workplaces, there is also a place for more collaborative, inclusive and creative behaviours. A mixture of the two seems to work best.

These kinds of studies explain the rising demand for employees with high emotional intelligence. Increasingly, it is considered vital to risk management and innovation. Emotional intelligence is also linked with the traits Brené Brown talks about – authenticity and vulnerability. Research by the universities of Wisconsin-Madison and Geneva has found that human beings are deeply aware of inauthenticity. In other words, we can smell bullshit immediately.

Most of us have experienced that hard-to-articulate feeling when we meet someone who is putting on a front. Sometimes it only takes a few words or even a glance, but it makes us uncomfortable. When someone is pretending to be something they're not, it's disconcerting and off-putting. The two of you are unlikely to feel a real connection. By contrast, that rush of happiness you experience when connecting with a work colleague intellectually and emotionally is invaluable. It creates an ongoing bond.

Emotionally intelligent managers are in demand because research is showing that 'servant leadership' is what yields the best results. This is defined as values-based leadership, in which feelings are seen as a positive not a negative. That's management mumbo jumbo for: your ability to feel is a positive for your career. Hiding emotions is exhausting and stressful. Being yourself is less difficult and is also what will allow you to feel the most confident. Being vulnerable with those around you can be both engaging and endearing. People who work for you remember that you are a human being, not just a boss. It encourages them to empathise with you, feel closer to you and therefore work more cooperatively with you. Employees with a sense of personal connection and investment in their workplace are more loyal and engaged than those who are in it for money alone.

The universal benefits of being yourself

This is it. You found it. The bit where I tell you that the secret to feeing more confident is being your genuine, authentic self. The bit where I say you are a magic unicorn, born quite unlike anyone who has ever come before you and that being your true self is the key to unlocking your special, mind-blowing potential.

Just kidding. There are no magic confidence beans. Or at least none available at your local grocer.

But you should be able to be yourself at work. Not because you're a mystical miracle of a human being, but because being yourself is *the easiest thing to be*. Suppressing your feelings at work *takes work*. And the more time you spend hiding emotions, the less time you spend doing your actual job. Pretending you're a robot automaton is an expenditure of emotional labour, and a waste of precious energy. Dr Sandi Mann, senior lecturer in occupational psychology at the University of Central Lancashire, says:

> The effort it takes to fake or hide emotions can be compared
> to physical labour and it causes huge mental stress – it can
> make you lose your sense of identity, as if your employer
> 'owns' your emotions.

We know that emotional intelligence is a valuable tool. We also know that women tend to possess rather a lot of it thanks to our conditioning. So why not embrace your feelings as something that will further rather than hinder your career?

To do this, you need to start by figuring out what you're *really* good at.

The Constitution of the United States of America lays down some universal truths. Now, it's questionable whether that country always respects and abides by those truths, but nonetheless they are considered to be self-evident. Figuring out what your universal truths are will help you feel more confident. What are the qualities you possess that are beyond argument? What are your core skills? What are your natural talents? What are you really, really good at? If you're currently facing a career crossroads and wailing, 'I'm good at nooooooooothing!' then get a handle on yourself, woman. Of course you are good at something. You glorious, gorgeous fool.

You're in exactly the same position that my friend and former colleague Lucy was in last year. Lucy had recently quit a job and was pretty burnt out by her previous role. She was ready to try something new, but wasn't sure what that something was. Months earlier, while handing in her resignation, Lucy had breezily informed me that her plan was not to have a plan! She would take some time to lie on her back in the middle of a park and gaze at the sky, to ride her bike and cook delicious hearty meals for her friends and family. Lucy was going to live free from the relentless ping of emails, and gain some longed-for perspective. She was going to see where the world took her . . .

Two weeks into her new life, the world had taken Lucy to my dining table and through the best part of a bottle of red wine. There's only so much time you can spend looking at clouds, she informed me. Lucy needed a new challenge. So we set about dissecting her future career prospects in an event I like to call a 'Whiteboard Night'. I've probably done this with various friends a dozen or so times over the years. You need a whiteboard or some giant sticky Post-It notes, tonnes of coloured markers and some people who know you well and from whom you can take both praise and criticism. Personally, I also suggest the presence of alcohol, but I'll leave that to your own excellent judgement.

Together, you need to drill down into the specifics of what you are really good at. This means the sort of skills you list on a resumé: tasks that you've perfected in previous roles. It also includes the stuff that is harder to define but is an inherent part of what makes you yourself. The natural talents and traits that make you an effective contributor to the workplace, like being calm in a crisis, or deeply methodical, or generously encouraging.

Whiteboard Night is not an easy process. It requires that your friends be honest with you about what you are and aren't good at.

It requires that you be honest with yourself, and make a distinction between what you love to do, what you'd like to do and what you're actually effective at doing. It also involves listening to effusive praise about yourself, something that can be even more difficult than hearing criticism. Once you have your complete list of talents, skills and abilities (and the wine bottle is empty), you can write them on a single piece of paper and label it your universal truths. They become self-evident, inarguable and incontestable facts. Your strengths and abilities are no longer negotiable. Next time you lack confidence at work, you can feel safer in the knowledge that you have these attributes supporting you and the language to express what they are. These are the positive qualities that would make any employer lucky to have you and that no amount of self-doubt can take away. They are what you can turn to in times of doubt and call on in stressful situations like interviews.

Fake confidence, never knowledge.

It can be easy to confuse faking confidence with faking knowledge or experience. However, the two could not be further apart. As we've discussed, faking confidence can help you feel more confident, appear more confident and even improve your chances of success. By contrast, faking knowledge or experience will cause you to feel *less* confident. Firstly, when you're 'faking it', you're worried about when you'll be discovered as a fraud. This means your attention is diverted from the task at hand. Secondly, when trying something for the first time, you want to be properly supported in case you do fail. There is learning and experience that can only come from having done something before. So while you should relish the opportunity to try something new, you should also be willing to caution against your own inexperience.

In the introduction to this book, I wrote about the great graduation speeches I found when attempting to write my own. One of the best I've read is from Jon Lovett, who delivered an entire address about fighting a culture of bullshit. He advised:

> Don't cover for your inexperience. You are smart, talented, educated, conscientious, untainted by the mistakes and conventional wisdom of the past. But you are also very annoying. Because there is a lot that you don't know that you don't know.

Lovett was speaking to university students who hadn't yet entered the workforce, but it's good advice for whenever you're faced with a new task. When you're at work, try to be honest about the skills you don't have while using the skills you *do have* to reassure others that you're up to the challenge. Frame it like this: 'I can't wait to get started. So you know, this is actually my first time chairing a meeting/writing a brief/cutting hair/taming a water buffalo, so I'd be so grateful for any extra advice you might have.' By setting a fair framework of expectation, your boss is more likely to be happy with your ultimate performance. Even more importantly, you'll feel more confident while carrying out the task, because you haven't lied about your experience.

TAMING YOUR FEAR OF FAILURE

Because we're not saving lives here, people.

When Cate Campbell emerged from the water after the 100-metre freestyle final in Rio, she already knew she'd lost. Swivelling her head, searching for the clock, the only question in her mind was by how much. Less than one second. Campbell's expression betrayed the scale of her disbelief. What is barely an instant for most of us is colossal in swimming terms. One second can be the difference between first and last. Campbell didn't just lose the race everyone had expected her to win – she'd been thumped. A month earlier she'd broken the world record for the same event. She'd anchored Australia's gold medal–winning swim in the relay over the same distance. She was cruising and in control during the Olympic heat and semifinal. That Campbell is a phenomenal talent is undeniable; she's one of the best swimmers of her generation. It appears to have been fear – not lack of ability – that got the better of her.

One of the great indignities of modern sport is that athletes are interviewed immediately after they lose. Distraught and obviously shocked, Cate Campbell stood beside her sister Bronte on the pool deck. She struggled to control her emotions as she answered the reporter's questions. When asked if she had a message for her fans back in Australia, Campbell's response was gut-wrenching.

'I love you,' she told her supporters. 'Please still love me back.'

What is often called fear of failure is actually a fear of *public* failure. It's not the actual failing that we're scared of. Failing quietly on our own terms, in our own time with nobody else to witness it, doesn't bother us. It's failure in the eyes of others that terrifies us. Human beings are social creatures. We fear both negative judgement and personal rejection. We don't want to feel alone. We want to do our best – not just for our own selfish reasons, but for the people we care about and who have cared for us. We want to be loved and we want to be special. Failure, we reason to ourselves, could cause us not to be.

It's a feeling that's rarely articulated out loud. In that raw moment immediately following her defeat in Rio, we caught a glimpse of it from Cate Campbell. Her vulnerability was on show for the world to see. I wanted to take her in my arms, give her an enormous bear hug and remind her how ridiculously great she is. Fear can be a powerful motivator, but this kind of socially constructed fear is rarely helpful. It holds us back in a myriad of ways. In later interviews, Campbell reflected that it was anxiety that got in the way of a victory she was indisputably capable of. For you, it might be not applying for a job you really want in case your application is rejected. Or it might mean not asking for a promotion in case the boss thinks you aren't up to it. It might mean avoiding taking on a project because your work could be viewed as less than perfect in the eyes of others. Fear of failure makes us conspirators in our own career sabotage.

Why would I put myself out there if I'm likely to fail?

Research shows that women tend to have a more pronounced fear of failure than men. This has been documented everywhere from the *New York Times* to the *Harvard Business Review* to *Elle* magazine. Most women can recall instances from their own lives that illustrate the truth of this. We're so afraid of what others will think if we fail that it cripples us professionally.

After falling out with a girlfriend who works in the same industry, I couldn't sleep properly for several weeks. Each night when I closed my eyes, I'd try to solve the dilemma of that lost relationship, playing out hypothetical scenarios in my head. If only I could think my way to a solution. My poor husband was baffled. Every night he'd counsel me that it was okay, that we'd be mates again one day, and that I was blowing the issue out of proportion. Finally, he forced me to drill down to the essence of what bothered me. 'I can't stand to think someone is out there in the world thinking badly of me,' I spluttered. 'But it's a big world,' Jeremy replied. 'There are always going to be people who don't like you. Probably lots of them.' I stared back at him, mouth agape, horrified by the proposition.

In my experience, women specifically fear being viewed as failures in the eyes of others. Certainly more than men. Women have been conditioned since childhood to strive to be perfect, even though we know perfection is impossible. Harvard professor Claudia Goldin noticed this in her economics classes. She was troubled that men outnumbered women enrolled in economics majors by 3:1. After analysing students' results she found that women who earned Bs (a high but not the top possible grade) in introductory classes were half as likely to stick with economics compared with men students. By contrast, there was no discernable difference between men who earned As and those who earned Bs in the introductory courses. Men who were outstanding and men who were quite good went on to complete economics majors in equal numbers. The women who were quite good dropped the class. Goldin hypothesised that one less-than-perfect result meant the women students changed majors.

Women tend to view failure as a permanent experience. We conceptualise fear differently to men, seeing it as a 'final destination' rather than a single point in time. For men, failing is a one-off occurrence – something that happened, and that they'll move on from. For women, failing once means you're a failure. Forever. We consider failure a perpetual judgement about who we are as individuals rather than a one-off bad result. I've watched my super-brilliant sister move from *I wasn't right for that job* to *I am right for* no *jobs because I'm a terrible person who is bad at everything* in a matter of seconds. She's an actress, and taking that mindset to the auditioning process can be soul destroying. My friends in other industries do the same thing. Viewing failure in such absolute terms makes it seem more significant, with the result being that women will go out of their way to avoid failing in the future. We'd rather play it safe or not play at all, rather than take the risk of playing and losing.

Former Obama adviser Valerie Jarrett suggests that the historical exclusion of women from professional life is part of the problem too. Many women, she argues, feel that they 'owe it' to those who went before them to be professional successes. For women of colour, who have historically been locked out of workplaces, that sense of duty to succeed can be even stronger. We look at how hard women and men of colour fought for us to lead the lives we do today. We think about how generations of our foremothers never had the working opportunities we enjoy, and we're desperate to deliver on their dream. That desperation further augments our desire to be perfect in a way that can be both debilitating and unobtainable.

There is mixed evidence that the differences between female and male brains has an impact here too. Some scientists have argued women have stronger responses to emotion-based memories because of their brain make-up. That is, our emotional memories may be more vividly recalled. Perhaps that explains why I can remember every romantic interaction my husband and I have ever had, and he forgets Valentine's Day. If your ability to recall painful emotional memories is strong, this is a powerful motivator to avoid making more of them. In other words, women may have greater fear of failure because they have clearer long-term memories of the *feelings* associated with past failures. We remember emotional distress more clearly and, so, we're more scared of it happening again.

When fear of failure becomes a problem.

It's important to remember that fear of failure is not always a bad thing. If you've ever watched the early audition stages of *Australian Idol* or *X Factor*, you'll agree. There is always at least one contestant who is a truly horrendous singer but who thinks they are dead-set brilliant. Fear of public humiliation is probably the only thing standing between me and being one of those people. In this way, fear of failure works in my favour. It only becomes problematic when the fear discombobulates otherwise rational decision-making. When fear of failure morphs from a feeling of unease into self-sabotage. Self-sabotage is psychologists' fancy way of describing 'screwing yourself over'. It manifests itself in three ways.

1. **Procrastination**

Guess how long I put off writing this paragraph for? Go on . . . Procrastination is the most common form of self-sabotage. It involves voluntarily delaying your planned course of action, despite being fully aware that you're going to be worse off after the delay. There's a misconception that procrastination stems from laziness. It doesn't. Procrastination is motivated by fear. You put something off again and again in order to avoid experiencing the anxiety that you might not do very well. Any chronic procrastinator can tell you that no pleasure is gained from this mindless avoidance. It's a form of mental paralysis. A lot of us joke about being bad procrastinators, but in its most extreme form procrastination can be quite serious. Researcher Piers Steel has found that procrastination is associated with lower salaries, poorer results, debilitating anxiety and other health problems.

Shit, eh? Better get on with it.

Steel also found that excessive procrastinators tend to struggle with visualising long-term success. The prospect of a project that will take a significant time commitment and sustained period of concentration is overwhelming to them. They have no confidence that they'll ever complete the project to a sufficient standard so they can't bring themselves to commence working towards it.

Procrastinators are not unintelligent. It takes serious mental fortitude to deliver when you have no choice but to complete a three-week project in a single evening, fuelled only by obligation, fear, energy drinks and Cottee's Ice Magic. Procrastinators simply require different incentives to other people. Research shows that the first 15 minutes of a task are crucial for procrastinators. Short periods of intense work with concrete goals in mind (i.e. I will write 400 words in the next twenty minutes, even if they're awful) tend to help them stay on task. As Elizabeth Gilbert, creative guru and author of *Big Magic,* advises, sometimes the only way to end that negotiation in your head about doing the important thing is to do it. If you tend to procrastinate, focus on setting short, measurable goals. Often it's the scale of the project that is reinforcing your avoidance. So break down big tasks into short, small, achievable ones. Aim for doing, not perfecting.

2. **Low self-esteem**

Low self-esteem is the result of internalising negative feedback you've received in your life. When your self-esteem is low, you begin to believe that you aren't worthy or capable of success. Excessive self-criticism and self-blame are the most common signs of low self-esteem. Researcher Timothy A. Judge has found that women tend to display lower self-esteem when they're at work, compared with in their social lives. Women feel more comfortable operating outside of traditional workplace structures. We prefer systems that fulfil our desire to be liked rather than punish us for it. Women with low self-esteem can find work particularly hard to navigate. That in turn can cause underperformance. Basically, you become so convinced that failure is inevitable that you make yourself incapable of success. You don't *try* in the first place.

People with low self-esteem can find it incredibly difficult to claim credit or acknowledge their strengths. They're good at recognising the talents and success of those around them, but can't seem to apply the same objective standards to themselves. They're also less likely to ask for or get raises, promotions or even apply for jobs in the first place, regardless of their abilities or qualifications. Low self-esteem becomes apparent in seemingly innocuous ways. For example, by asking permission for things at work that you already have the authority to do. Or by over-explaining yourself in a meeting and providing unnecessary justifications for legitimate decisions.

Remember that self-esteem and confidence are different. Confidence is how you feel about a specific ability in a specific situation. For example, you might not be confident chairing a meeting. Self-esteem is much more generalised and tends to affect multiple – sometimes all – realms of our lives. Chronic sufferers of low self-esteem are dealing with a mental health challenge that is about more than lack of confidence. Low self-esteem can be a symptom of depression, and can develop into a debilitating sense of powerlessness and learned helplessness. If that sounds like you, then consider seeking some help from a professional. A psychologist can give you the tools you need to cope with feelings of self-doubt.

3. **Perfectionism**

Perfectionism is the insistent need to be perfect or believing that people will only value you if you are perfect. Were you the kind of school student who handed in an assignment two weeks late because you couldn't bear for it to be marked until you were 100 per cent happy with it? That's perfectionism. Much like other self-sabotaging tactics, perfectionism affects women at a significantly higher rate than men. Perfectionism is often mischaracterised as positive when actually it can be devastating and even destructive.

Perfectionism can be a direct result of fearing failure. That is, perfectionist behaviour is motivated by a desire for social acceptance from others. You fear the negative judgement of people around you if you present yourself or your work as anything less than perfect. This can particularly be the case among women of Asian heritage who are subject to a prevailing stereotype within Western cultures of being high performing 'model minorities'. That is, Asian women are *expected* to be extremely hardworking and intelligent, which in turn creates greater internal urgency to attain perfection. The perfectionism obsession is closely connected with feelings of guilt, shame and inadequacy. In its most extreme form, perfectionism has been observed in the mindset of long-term eating-disorder patients.

Perfectionist behaviour gets mixed results in a work context. Sometimes it can earn praise because the standard of work delivered is so high, but more often than not it encumbers the perfectionist in the long-term. For example, perfectionism might cause you to avoid speaking up in a meeting unless you're entirely confident that what you say will be positively received. So you barely say a word. This all-or-nothing approach tends to make perfectionists less innovative because they're reluctant to give something new a go. Perfectionists can also be poor managers of people because they expect similarly extreme behaviour from others and become frustrated by those who don't have the same exacting standards. Their black-and-white view of the world means they become caught up in detail, unable to see the bigger picture. Of course, actual perfection isn't attainable by anyone. So this leaves perfectionists in a perpetual state of struggle. They never really achieve success according to their own standards. They're always dissatisfied.

Remember who you were at 22.

Exhaustion caused by excessive eye rolling is a real thing. I've fallen asleep at many corporate leadership conferences, so I know what I'm talking about. Normally I nod off after a particularly intense period of scepticism. It comes around the time the audience is asked, 'What would you do if you weren't afraid?'

What. A. Stupid. Question.

If I weren't afraid, I would do all sorts of things that would most probably get me killed or, at the very least, cause extreme embarrassment (see my earlier *Australian Idol* example). Fear can be a good thing. Fear keeps us safe. It tells us when we are in danger. The stress that fear creates can motivate human beings in positive ways – like telling us to *run very fast* in the opposite direction when there is a polar bear coming at us with its teeth bared. Fear is what tells us to stand up and leave the Tinder date immediately when a bloke says, 'Gay marriage just feels wrong and unnatural to me.' Too often society dismisses fear as a weakness, but it's one of our most valuable traits. Fear is why the human race is still alive.

The key to dealing with fear of failure is being able to recognise the difference between legitimate fear and socially constructed fear. Remember Cate Campbell's plea for her fans to still love her? That's a socially constructed fear, and one you've probably experienced. It's usually the by-product of low confidence. So having said that, I'd like to propose an alternative question: What would you do if you were 22 years old again?

At age 22, many of you would have been (or are!) studying or in the fledgling stages of your careers. At this time, the confidence engendered at school is generally intact. The workplace hasn't yet taught you that the system you had figured out is irrelevant now.

You haven't begun to doubt your abilities in the way you likely will by age 30 or even 25.

It's also an age where most people have entered the workforce but aren't yet expected to be any good. (If you were an early achiever who'd already fallen victim to the gendered trappings of low confidence by age 22, then simply reframe the question as if you were 17. There's nothing super special about 22 – I chose it simply because that's the last age I remember feeling pure, unabashed confidence.) Career success is generally something that 22-year-olds see as part of their *future* rather than something they demand of themselves in the present. This means they're more likely to take chances and be more accepting of potential failures.

Everyone who has ever been good at something did it for the first time without knowing how. That's important. Let me repeat it. *Everyone who has ever been good at something did it for the first time without knowing how.* My friend Ceri is a high-school teacher who stands up in front of 25 unforgiving teenagers each day and talks without notes. That would terrify me, but that's because I've never done it and I don't know how. My girl Bella is a doctor. People trust her to locate and identify cancer in their bodies and help make them better. That would terrify me too, but that's because I've never done it and I don't know how (and, sure, I'll probably never know how). My mate Em is a comedian and performer who wears sequined costumes and sings, dances and makes jokes for audiences in the thousands. That would terrify me most of all.

Each of my friends is good at what they do. In fact, they're great at it. They are confident in the knowledge that they've done it before and that they have a knack for it. But there would have been a time when, just like me, they had never done it before and didn't *know* if they'd actually be any good at it. When you're 22 years old and new to the workplace, that is true of pretty much everything. You've never done any of this stuff before, so you don't know if you'll be any good and, importantly, nobody expects you to be any good. With that knowledge comes a tremendous sense of possibility and freedom. You are allowed to fail. You're allowed to make mistakes. You're allowed to be less than perfect. You're *expected* to fail.

So next time fear of failure takes hold of you, try testing out the situation on your younger self. Would she behave differently? Would her list of reasons 'not' to do something be as long? Would she let someone get away with claiming credit for her work? Would she ask the question even if it might be a bit stupid? Would she quit because of one humiliating experience? Would she start her own business? Would she call a recruiter? Would she ask to be sent on a professional development course? Would she tell her boss she was bored and in search of a new challenge? Would she apply for that job despite her lack of experience? Would she ask for the promotion instead of waiting for it to come to her?

Would she? Would you?

Your younger self is going to help you separate legitimate fears from those that are the product of a gendered workforce. Twenty-two-year-old you may be living on cheap ramen noodles and drinking too many Vodka Cruisers on Saturday night, but she's one smart cookie. Twenty-two-year-old you might be scared, but she isn't going to let that stop her. She's going to give something a go because – who knows? Perhaps she'll be brilliant at it. As the late actress Carrie Fisher said, 'Stay afraid, but do it anyway. What's important is the action. You don't have to wait to be confident. Just do it and eventually the confidence will follow.'

Imposter syndrome: when fear of failure goes next-level

A former colleague contacted me on social media recently and asked for advice. Holly is a writer who was headhunted by a UK website to be an editor at just 24. Suffice to say, she's an impressive young woman. Having picked up her life and moved to the other side of the globe for a promotion, Holly was bubbling with excitement about her new job. However, once she started, she hit a serious roadblock:

> I'm in the role and I'm feeling really overwhelmed. I'm in charge of a team of seven women who are extremely respectful and welcoming. They are mostly my age or older, and all fantastic writers. Better writers than me, really . . . Every day I worry I'm going to go in and someone is going to jump out of a cupboard and tell me it was all a big prank, that I need to clean up my desk and go home.

Holly is suffering from imposter syndrome. Imposter syndrome is when you experience persistent feelings of inadequacy even in the face of overwhelming evidence to the contrary. Someone with imposter syndrome lives in a near-constant state of fear at work. They are scared of being 'found out' and discovered for the imposter that they think they are, and sufferers struggle to understand why others have faith in their talents and abilities. In their own minds they are frauds. Like Holly, they're waiting for the day when their bosses and colleagues realise the truth.

This kind of thinking forms a vicious cycle. The imposter is given a task by their boss and they're terrified. They're anxious that they won't be able to perform and are plagued by self-doubt. In order to manage those feelings, they neurotically overprepare or work harder than is necessary to complete it. They work them-selves up into a lather any soap company would envy, and throw all their energy into doing or worrying about the task. Once the task is complete, the imposter doesn't experience the natural buzz of accomplishment. Instead, they just feel relieved that they 'got lucky' once again and that they weren't exposed as being not good enough for their own job. This reinforces their feeling of inade-quacy. They view the mammoth effort they put into the task as confirmation that – unlike others – they must put in an inordinate amount of hard work to succeed. *Normal people would just do a few hours and get away with it,* they reason. *But I have to work around the clock for weeks to get by.* The sheer scale of their effort reaffirms the imposter status in their head.

Imposter syndrome is common among high-achieving people. By constantly needing to validate their success, imposters will push themselves to achieve more and more. Every promotion or oppor-tunity or new job needs to be justified, which means they work twice as hard to 'keep up the façade' of success. Imposter syndrome is so much more prevalent in women that researchers previously believed it only affected one gender. While the syndrome has now been observed among men, it generally isn't with the same intensity or frequency. Imposter syndrome is even more common among women of colour, women from minority communities and women working in industries dominated by men.

People are susceptible to imposter syndrome when they feel undeserving of their place in the workforce. When they feel like they don't belong. As we already know, white, male corporate struc-tures tend to reinforce the idea that women and people of colour don't belong. So if these people do make it to the top, their percep-tion is that it's by accident rather than on merit. Women and other minorities may feel pressured to keep proving to others that they are deserving of positions they already hold.

Note to self: feeling like an imposter doesn't mean you are one.

Overcoming imposter syndrome starts with recognising you have it. The first step, friends, is always recognising you have a problem. And recognising that you have imposter syndrome means recognising that you are *not* in fact an imposter. Here are three facts, which might help you along the way to this realisation:

1. **Real imposters don't know they're imposters.**
    Sociologist Jessica L. Collett describes this both beautifully and bluntly. 'People who are dumb are too dumb to know they're dumb. They don't feel at all like frauds – they feel they know exactly what they're doing and how could other people not know what they're doing . . . turns out, they don't know enough about how little they know.' Simply put, people who suffer from imposter syndrome probably need to worry about being a fraud the least.

2. **Talk to girlfriends you admire who feel the same way.**
    My friend Rosie has struggled with imposter syndrome for much of her career, and says it's actively stopped her pursuing opportunities. Hearing Rosie (who is so talented it's ridiculous) talk about her experience of self-doubt actually helps me deal with my own. I would never question that Rosie is deserving of every success that comes her way. She is undeniably excellent. So listening to her describe the same feelings of inadequacy that I have is reassuring. Sometimes we can't see the truth of our own talents,

but we can almost always identify the abilities of people we care about.

The celebrity world is full of kick-ass imposters.

If you don't personally know any women who suffer from imposter syndrome, then look to your good friends in Hollywood. Meryl Streep, Tina Fey and Oprah Winfrey have all experienced imposter syndrome despite being the best in the world in their respective fields. Closer to home, Australian journalist Leigh Sales has spoken about her feelings of imposter syndrome. When she was first awarded the prestigious gig hosting the ABC's flagship current affairs program *7.30*, Sales was terrified. She told the *Daily Telegraph*:

> The worst bit of my day is the five minutes before we go to air . . . my five minutes of hell. It's just me in the studio with the camera and the cameraman hidden behind it, waiting to start. There's literally nothing else to do but sit there and wait, and all I have to think about is not messing it all up.

If your heroes feel like this and they aren't frauds . . . then maybe, just maybe, you're not either.

COPING
WITH
SETBACKS

Because sometimes stuff will inevitably go a bit shit.

Choosing the right anecdote to kick off this chapter was problematic. Not because I haven't failed in my life. My career has provided ample failure fodder. Choosing the right anecdote was difficult because failure is so contextual. Failure looks very different to you, to me, to your mum, to your cat, to Aung San Suu Kyi. Whether an event was a failure, a setback, a criticism or entirely insignificant is all a matter of perspective and context. Viewed in a particular light, failure can even look pretty good.

The narrative of human history sentimentalises failure. We revere artists whose brilliance wasn't acknowledged in their lifetime. University graduates speak fondly of their wayward youthful years spent skipping lectures, scraping pass marks and living on heavily discounted minced meat. Career failures can seem rather romantic when viewed as a single point on a pathway that ultimately leads to success. You've probably heard these dreamy idealistic stories of 'failure' before: a dozen editors rejected the original Harry Potter book before J. K. Rowling eventually found a publisher. Oprah Winfrey was fired from her first television job for getting too emotional on air. Vera Wang was a figure skater and narrowly missed out on the Olympic team before turning to fashion. Julia Child didn't release her first cookbook until age 39. Viewed against the backdrop of these women's hugely successful careers, their failures are reduced to charming anecdotes. The devastating becomes inconsequential because of what they went on to achieve.

When I look critically at my own (far less glittering) career, I observe the same thing. The pain of recent failures still cuts deep. Some hard moments are genuinely difficult to recall. A lump forms in my throat. The red blotchiness of humiliation climbs up my neck. By contrast, the pain of failures that took place years ago is less. Failures that felt monumental and world-shaking at the time don't really matter much any more because I went on to pursue other things. These moments of failure, which I presumed I'd carry with me for life, have become speed bumps in the rear-view mirror. Current Me wishes I could go back and reassure Past Me that each of those disasters wasn't actually that big of a deal. She probably wouldn't listen.

My very best failures and fuck-ups: a cheerful trip down memory lane

I got braver and better at attending those scary chiefs-of-staff meetings that I told you about. So much so that the minister wanted to give me the job permanently. For this to happen, she needed approval from higher up. There is a committee that oversees and approves senior staff appointments in the government. I wonder now if my boss foresaw the outcome because she put my name forward to the committee without telling me first. My promotion was soundly rejected. The cartoon-like image that accompanies my memory of the rebuff involves an oversized, old-fashioned stamp with bright red ink. REJECTED. It stamps the paper again and again, darker and stronger each time, so that I definitely get the point. REJECTED. REJECTED. REJECTED. Youth and inexperience made me unfit to fill the role, the committee said. They were probably right.

One year later, I applied to do a masters degree at the London School of Economics. I'd completed a summer course there several months before and wanted to return for a longer stint. My friend Marielle was applying too. We had the whole thing planned. Our glamorous, exciting life in London would be cosmopolitan and academically rigorous at the same time. Our student budgets would be no barrier to acquiring European designer wardrobes and renting a light-filled classical apartment in Notting Hill. My undergraduate grades were lower than required for acceptance to the school. I didn't have the necessary honours degree, either. Entry was going to be difficult. Still, I convinced myself that my extracurricular activities and persuasive cover letter would get me over the line. They didn't. Marielle set off for London alone and I was left behind.

One year after that I failed again – this time with a much larger audience. I should have anticipated that criticising breakfast TV host David 'Kochie' Koch would create a stir. I'd written an article in a hurry and pressed publish without double- and triple-checking my facts. That's the ultimate sin for an opinion writer. There is no excuse for it. My error became something bigger when an intern failed to publish a comment left in response to my article. The comment had been posted by Koch himself. He deserved a right of reply and was denied that chance. The next morning Koch lambasted me for several minutes on live television. I choked back tears as I watched it. My social media accounts erupted with vitriol and hate. When the story ran on pretty much every news website in the country, I received death threats. Two years later, when David Koch came by the office for an interview, I hid in a gazebo like the very mature adult person I am. He probably didn't remember my name.

I don't recount all these screw-ups to seek reassurance, but to reveal how we make and re-make our own narratives. We tell stories based on paths taken rather than those left untravelled. The passage of time has changed how I feel about all those failures. Instead of dwelling on the rejection, I can see that my inexperience meant I wasn't right for that government job. Instead of seeing the degree I missed out on, I value the career that took its place: a move to the media that would never have happened if I'd pursued politics. Instead of berating myself over and over for the same careless error, I've become rigorous in checking facts and made sure I won't ever repeat the mistake. Context and time have turned those failures into setbacks. The pain I felt in the moment they happened is mostly gone. I can look at them with grace rather than throwing myself a pity party. The same will be true for you.

Men and women fail the same. But we respond differently.

Retrospection is powerful. It creates perspective most of us lack in the moment. It's the reason why so many inspirational quotes tell us we should view failure as a positive, as an opportunity to learn. Failure, we're told, is simply an obstacle on the path to success. We should embrace it as a glorious chance to better ourselves for the future. Pick yourself up, dust yourself off and try, try, try again . . . Which is easy to say when the failure is behind you and when the happy future has become the present. It's harder to be positive about failure when success seems like a barely visible dot on the horizon.

Perspective is basically impossible to come by in the *actual moment* that failure occurs. Or even in the days and weeks that follow it. Changing the way we look at failure will not make up for the immediate humiliation and hurt it causes. Even the most starry-eyed, splendour-filled viewpoint can't change the fact that failing feels awful. In the face of setback, disappointment or criticism there is a normal and natural human desire to curl up in bed, ensconced in your doona with a loaf of sourdough and re-read *Pride and Prejudice* for the 32nd time. In the moment, failure really, really, really sucks.

Women and men tend to respond to failure differently. For women, failing often feels enormous, immovable and permanent. This makes recovering from it harder. Where men tend to move on quickly, women dwell on where they've gone wrong. Women are also more likely to blame failure on themselves. Men, on the other hand, will blame the workplace or their equipment or lack of resources when they don't succeed. As part of a famous Indiana University experiment, students were introduced to a stranger and told to 'persuade them' of something. Afterwards, they were asked to evaluate their own success. Overall, women and men performed equally well, but their self-evaluations were significantly different. The women who performed badly were devastated. They berated themselves for being poor communicators and apologised for not having concentrated harder on the task. The men evaluated themselves positively regardless of how they'd performed. When the men who performed badly were shown their poor results, they blamed the task itself for being 'too hard' or 'stupid'.

Taking the time to assess your failures and establish where you might have gone wrong is a good thing. Going through this process reduces the likelihood of future errors. You can't learn from your mistakes unless you properly reflect on them. However, women sometimes do more than that. They respond to failure in a way that awards it greater significance than it deserves. Too often, women allow their failures to become a permanent part of how they view themselves. We take each failure and store it away for the future, so we can use it to berate ourselves at a later date. We incorporate failure into our idea of self-worth. At the extreme end of the spectrum, we see patterns of failure that simply aren't there. We are harder on ourselves than we would be on anyone else.

A sensible person's guide to failure

The period when failure is at its most recent and raw is full of feelings. You might be angry, sad, resentful, scared, bitter, confused, humiliated, crushed, helpless, ashamed, or even a bizarre and agonising combination of all of them. In my experience, those feelings tend to prompt less-than-sensible behaviour. Inconveniently, this period is also the *most important* for getting your response to failure right. The exact time you really need to act sensibly is when stupid feelings get in the way. Dealing with failure effectively requires that you put down Jane Austen, come out from under the doona, put away the sourdough and behave sensibly. And because behaving sensibly is very hard in a moment of failure, I'm going to guide you through it with this helpful list of eight Very Sensible Things To Do (and Not To Do) After You've Failed.

1. **DON'T shave your head to show an ex that you're over them.**
    Some people – particularly the hypersensitive among
    us – respond to a setback or failure with extreme behaviour.
    In the romantic world this might translate to getting a tattoo,
    a dramatic new haircut or collecting your former lover's stuff in
    a giant pile in the local park, setting fire to it and then dancing
    around the flames nude singing Adele's 'Someone Like You'.

While it might be okay to do these things when you're in a more stable mindset, they probably shouldn't be undertaken in the immediate aftermath of a break-up. When you're wounded, the irrational can seem rational. So you need to wait for the wound to heal a little before taking drastic action.

The same logic applies to your professional life. Within a fortnight of returning to work after maternity leave, I wanted to quit. Each night I would arrive home in tears, my husband would listen patiently, console me and convince me to wait one more week before quitting. Again and again we went through this routine: me sobbing, Jeremy listening, me raging, Jeremy cautioning me to wait one more week. It was so exasperating that I considered squirting him in the eye with my breast milk. After several turbulent months I did eventually quit. It was an enormous relief. A big part of that relief lay in knowing I had made a considered, sensible decision. If I'd resigned in the heat of my frustration, it would have been far more likely that I'd come to regret my choice.

When we experience failure or criticism, most of us want to respond immediately. You might be in a performance review and are told you're not up to scratch. Or you might have applied for a promotion and your boss has said you're not ready. Every fibre of your being wants to respond, to defend yourself or to try to fix the situation. The single most sensible thing you can do or say in that moment, though, is nothing. Take some time away (even a few hours) to sit with your feelings. Time will make your response more rational and decrease the chances of you spending a fortune at the career equivalent of a tattoo-removal parlour.

2. **DO be the best wallower you can be (and set a time limit).**
Everyone's brave face looks different. Some are angry and
loud. Some are silent and defiant. Some are silly and self-
deprecating. Many brave faces don't look particularly brave
at all. What they have in common is their purpose. A brave
face is about putting on a front for the sake of those around
us and not giving in to our feelings. In the period directly
following failure, a brave face can actually prevent you from
processing pain. You might recall my earlier astute insight that
failure really, really sucks. It does. There is nothing wrong with
feeling crap about it for a while. Get used to the pain. Accept
it. Wallow in it, if you need to. Be kind to yourself while your
brain processes the disappointment and shock.

　　Career coach Hillary Rettig advises that you should permit
yourself to 'cope lavishly'. Lavish coping is a thoroughly
attractive proposition and one I heartily endorse. Rettig says:

> We're often in shock, after a traumatic rejection, and so may
> not be conscious of the full extent of the hurt. And the tendency
> toward denial is strong. I find, in fact, that many rejections are
> like icebergs: small on the surface, but much larger underneath.
> I would therefore err on the side of caution and assume I'm
> hurting worse – and need more healing – than I may realize. If
> you need a crying jag or a sulk, take it: you're not hurting anyone.

The less fun part of coping lavishly is that at some point you
have to stop. Once you've wallowed for a bit, the wallowing
must come to an end. Set a time limit for your wallowing. That
time limit might be a day, or even a week, depending on how
spectacular your failure was. When the time limit comes, you

aren't expected to be magically recovered and over it. That's
unrealistic. The purpose of the time limit is to put an end to
self-indulgent sulking. The time limit is a forced stop. A signal
that it's time to get back on the field, or the horse, or whichever
of the sporting analogies you prefer. It's a hard line in the sand
that means the feeling-sorry-for-yourself bit is over now.
Brave face goes back on.

3. **DON'T drink poison and hope someone else will die.**
    Feeling angry after you've been criticised is normal, but anger
    is a temporary state. It will pass. Eventually. And if it doesn't,
    there are cafes where you can pay for the right to smash up
    all the crockery, which sounds like a deliciously exhilarating
    option. What you need to be really cautious of is letting anger
    transform into resentment. Resentment is far more detrimental
    than anger. Resentment can quickly become a way of life.
    If you resent your boss or your colleagues or an organisation
    that didn't give you a job, it can be utterly fixating. Resentment
    actually *alters* the way we view the world. Psychotherapist
    Mark Sichel says:

> Resentments embody a basic choice to refuse to forgive, an
> unwillingness to let bygones be bygones and bury the hatchet.
> We review and rehash our painful past, even as we profess to
> want to let go of it. We do so because we believe the illusion
> that by belaboring our resentment, we will somehow achieve
> the justice we believe we are due. We cling to a futile need to
> be 'right,' which overrides the capacity to heal and be at peace
> with ourselves. We hang on to perceived offences because we
> don't know any other way of coming to grips with painful
> feelings of hurt, rejection, and abandonment.

The desire to be 'right' – and for someone else to know they were 'wrong' – is intense. Resentment has even been compared by psychologists to addiction because it is literally drug-like: it's something you grow dependent on day-by-day. You begin to crave that 'hit' of resentment. You indulge in imagining scenarios where the person who wronged you realises, or pays for what they've done. You focus on the potential for retaliation, revenge becomes singular, and that means you can miss new opportunities.

Most of us have *that* friend who can't stop talking about that time they were incorrectly blamed, badly treated or unfairly chastised. The repetitiveness of their angst quickly becomes annoying. It certainly isn't helpful to them or their work. You want to tell your mate to make like Elsa in *Frozen* and just let it go (while also suspecting they may no longer be capable of doing that). The best option is to avoid indulging resentful feelings in the first place. Harbouring resentment is like swallowing poison and then hoping some other guy will die. It will kill you (or, at least, your chances of career success) well before it kills them.

4. **DO believe in climate change.**

Have you ever watched a climate-change sceptic on a televised political panel? Ranting and raving that 99 per cent of scientists have it wrong, they'll pull out a graph that at first glance appears to show the planet *is* getting cooler. It's not. Look closer at the graph and you'll discover it shows data collected over a very short, specific period of time. It's usually a brief period during which climate data didn't follow long-term trends. The graph shows a *temporary* occurrence. A blip. An outlier. So while technically correct, the graph is deliberately misleading.

When we experience career setbacks, we tend to behave like climate-change deniers. Instead of objectively assessing the curve of our career graph in its entirety, we focus in on the specific occurrence of failure. We become fixated on what's *just happened* to the exclusion of the bigger picture. This is problematic because climate change is real, you guys. Also, nobody's career is entirely linear. Nobody experiences absolute success *all the time*. Nobody has God-like clarity about which opportunities they should pursue and which they should allow to pass them by. A career only ever looks like a career in retrospect. At the end of our working lives we can consider all the points on the graph and draw a smooth, even line of upward trajectory. But at the beginning and even in the middle of our careers, the bigger picture isn't there for us to see yet.

5. **DON'T compare your behind-the-scenes with everyone else's highlight reel.**

The misleading graph problem is exacerbated when you inevitably start comparing your career to others. Most people suffer in silence rather than out in the open. Women in particular don't tend to advertise our imperfections. This means that when you have a setback, you take a look around you, and everyone else's life seems flawless. Everyone else's graph is sloping upward. Or, at least, that's how it seems. Women's silence about our errors has perpetuated a falsehood that we're all doing fine. That life is easy and manageable and careers are calm, smooth and successful. At a *Huffington Post* live event in 2013, American television host Mika Brzezinski said:

> Women, one of the things we do . . . is make everything look so easy. We're supposed to be perfect. We're supposed to be

beautiful. We're supposed to be thin. And it's all supposed to come easy . . . And it isn't. On every level.

So be careful when you look to the experiences of others and use them as a yardstick to measure your own success. In all likelihood these people have spun a pretty poem about their career that erases the less beautiful parts. Instead of comparing yourself with people you hardly know, speak to friends or colleagues who will be honest. Everyone experiences criticism or failure at some point. You are not the only one who has messed up or missed out. Don't let strangers' Instagram stories convince you otherwise.

6. **DON'T kid yourself. Nobody but you is thinking about you all the time.**

One summer, my brothers and sisters-in-law decided they'd learn how to surf. It took several days of inexorable peer pressure for me to join them. I made all sorts of protests about why I couldn't do it. I was scared of sharks. I didn't want to hurt myself on holiday. I had to look after the baby. I had an old tennis injury that meant I couldn't. It was only in the privacy of my own head that I admitted the actual reason for my hesitation: I was scared of looking like an idiot. But once I'd had a few hilariously awful attempts, my fear fell away and I started to enjoy myself. Why? Because what I'd been afraid of wasn't actually failure. I was afraid of what the others might think of me when failure happened.

There are five basic fears all human beings share. Of those five, four of them are related to fear of physical harm. They are (for the record) death, disfigurement, being trapped and being abandoned. Scary. The fifth fear is what researchers

and philosophers delightfully call 'ego death'. Ego death
is basically fear of being humiliated, shamed or made
to question your worth. It's a fear everyone experiences,
although in varying degrees. Women, you won't be surprised
to learn, tend to have a greater fear of ego-death than men.
So when you're upset about having failed, it's worth reflecting
on what exactly is upsetting you. If your boss ticks you off,
are you genuinely worried about losing your job? Or are you
simply hurt that your boss doesn't have as high an opinion of
you as you'd previously thought? If you mess up a presentation,
are there actual consequences that deserve to consume your
thoughts? Or are you just embarrassed about losing face in
front of your colleagues?

If the real source of your distress is fear of ego death,
then I have good news. As painful and gut-wrenching as
embarrassment can be, it will not kill you. It is *always* a bigger
deal to you than it is to others. It's easy to get trapped in your
own head and lose perspective of the fact that people rarely
measure us as harshly as we measure ourselves. Think back
to the last time you saw someone speaking in public who
was obviously nervous. Did you think that person was stupid,
or unqualified or pathetic or worthless? Of course you didn't.
You probably empathised with them while they were speaking
and had forgotten about it by the time you left the room.
Your brain would have moved on to bigger issues, like which
Subway sandwich bread you'd order for lunch. By contrast,
the person who made the nervous speech probably worried
about it for the rest of the week. Moral of the story: everyone
has their own stuff going on. You and your stuff aren't that
big a deal to anyone but you.

7. **DO accept that your brain is wired to protect you from lions, not criticism.**

    If you want to develop a thicker skin, consider writing opinion columns for a living. Last year I was writing for Australia's number one news website. I write about politics, multiculturalism and feminism, three topics that never fail to piss lots of people off. Every week my column goes live and my Twitter feed erupts like a volcano. I've been called stupid, vain, silly, insolent, rude, a whinger, a 'femonazi', pathetic, a bitch, a slut, irrelevant, unqualified, crazy, demented, a dill and, yes, even a terrorist. (Unfortunately that's the go-to insult for someone with a Muslim name). Every awful comment lodges itself inside my head.

    Negativity bias means we give more psychological weight to our negative experiences than our positive ones. We remember the bad and gloss over the good. Our brains react so strongly to negative emotions that you need at least five positive encounters to counterbalance a single negative one. There may also be biological reasons why humans have developed like this. The human brain has systems to ensure we notice danger, register it, remember it and take it seriously. This is very helpful if you're a cave lady and the neighbouring tribe want to cook you and eat you for dinner. It's less helpful when you're being reprimanded for missing a key deadline. When you've received a ticking off from your boss, remember that this is a single piece of criticism. It doesn't erase or discount the many times you've received praise from that same boss or from others. Remind yourself that your bias will cause you to focus on the bad over the good. Don't let a single negative incident dictate the overall picture of your work performance.

8. **DON'T forget, it's the receiver who makes
   the criticism constructive.**

I've never been good at responding to criticism. I become defensive. I go silent and unintentionally start glowering at my chastiser. As I grind my back teeth and push my tongue to the roof of my mouth, my temples throb threateningly. To complete the effect, I open my eyes wide and avoid blinking. These aren't conscious actions – they're reflexive. Friends and family tell me that the combination is terrifying. My mum – who was on the receiving end of my defensive routine a lot during my teenage years – calls it 'the Rizvi look'. A former boss called it 'the blinking', and my vividly descriptive husband named it the Silent Fury. 'All the heat drains from your body to fuel the fire in your eyes,' Jeremy says dramatically. Told you it was scary.

Mine certainly isn't a smart way to deal with criticism, and I like to think I am slowly getting a handle on it. But being defensive isn't the only unconstructive response to critique. I've worked with team members who would nod along with criticism but never take in the substance of what was being said. These employees tended to become trapped in their own cocoon of silence. Unable to learn from criticism, they would make the same errors over and over again. Other people I've worked with have gone immediately to water when faced with criticism. By apologising profusely and repeatedly, they'd incorrectly assume they were giving me what I wanted. When, really, the over-the-top response showed that they hadn't registered the critique properly or appropriately.

The best thing you can possibly do when receiving criticism is listen. Try to understand what you're being told.

Do the old 'put yourself in the other person's shoes' and consider: how is your behaviour affecting or how has it affected everyone else? Ask questions of the manager who is reprimanding you. Make sure you understand the criticism fully. After the criticism is over, request the opportunity to go away and think about it before you respond. Take the time to sit with it, to mull it over, to look at it from all angles. Perhaps ask someone you trust to weigh in. Criticism becomes constructive not by how it is delivered but by how it is received. It's up to *you* to take the criticism and use it as an opportunity to be better.

MANAGING UP LIKE A BOSS

Because it's what every boss you've ever had wishes you knew.

Every day working for the prime minister, my alarm would sound at 3.15 a.m. It was set to that piercing tone of the standard 2009-model Nokia BlackBerry. It was also set for the latest possible moment of wakefulness. I had exactly 30 minutes to get out of bed, shower and dress, scrape the frost from my car windscreen and drive to the newsagency. I would park illegally out in the alley-way, not bothering with the hazards. Standing under the still-black sky, I'd hug myself for warmth, jiggling from one foot to the other and waiting for the first light to flick on inside the shop. My only company was a serious-looking young man who worked for the opposition leader. Every morning he and I were charged with iden-tical pre-dawn tasks: we would collect the daily newspapers for every capital city and painstakingly summarise their contents.

As the most junior member of the team my job wasn't intellec-tually difficult. While the pace was relentless, the bulk of my tasks were mundane. It should have been exhilarating just to be in that lofty environment, but six months into the job I was bored. I was desperate to do something more challenging, more interesting.

In politics, opportunities come to those who shine, but not ahead of those who 'do their time'. I was still an ingénue. I didn't have the requisite notches on my belt. The problem was that I couldn't find an avenue to demonstrate my capability for doing more. There was no opportunity to prove myself worthy.

Lots of women experience feeling overlooked at work. You're ambitious and hungry, but nobody seems to notice. You want to prove that you're ready for more, but don't know how to do that without first being given more to do. You're stuck. There is a scene in the movie *Strictly Ballroom* where a couple become 'boxed in' or 'blocked' on the dance floor. You probably know the moment: handsome Scott (be still my beating heart) is dancing the samba with the beautiful but deadest nutty Liz (she of the yellow feathers and platinum-blonde hair). Their performance becomes confined to a tight corner of the floor. They're out of the judges' eyeline. It doesn't matter how well they dance because they're hidden from view. They can't win.

That is exactly how I felt in my job. There was so much frenetic activity and important work to do that the career trajectory of one junior staff member meant nothing. The people working there had bigger priorities than me, and fair enough. But I was a kid in my first full-time job and desperate to shine. Again and again I was overlooked, so I started to think that maybe I wasn't good enough. The feeling of being undervalued took far more of a toll than the early hours or heavy workload. By the time I left, my confidence was shot.

Stop waiting for your boss to give you a tiara.

Being overlooked does not feel good, and unfortunately it happens a lot. As many as one in two millennial women feel like they've been passed over for career advancement. They probably have.

Among early-career employees, men outnumber women in leadership positions. Postgraduates, women in middle management and even those in executive positions also report struggling to be recognised for their contribution at work.

Women consistently say that despite their skills, abilities and willingness to work harder and longer, they feel unseen. More often than not the promotion goes to a man who is good at self-promoting over the woman who has worked diligently and effectively. The advantage is bestowed not on the hardest worker but the superior publicist – and the superior publicist tends to have a penis. Being overlooked causes women to lose confidence. When you're working harder than ever but still not being rewarded, motivation wanes. You look inward and wonder if maybe you're not good enough. Maybe everyone else is better than you . . .

Carol Frohlinger and Deborah M. Kolb, the founders of Negotiating Women Inc., call it 'tiara syndrome'. Here's how it works: a woman enters the workforce determined to succeed. She throws herself into work with everything she's got. She prepares fastidiously for meetings. She reads the fine print. She practises and perfects her trade. She enrols in educational courses to further her knowledge. She takes every bit of feedback to heart. This, she reassures herself, will eventually be recognised. She will be promoted. She will get a raise. She will be awarded an opportunity she really wants. She expects that her effort and good results will speak for themselves. She is operating under the misguided belief that her boss will one day come along and place a shiny, sparkly tiara on her head. When that doesn't happen, she tells herself that she must work harder. She redoubles her efforts and waits again for the tiara to come . . . It probably won't.

Because tiaras don't come to those who wait, tiaras come to those who hustle.

A nice girl's guide to self-promotion

Ilhan Omar was the first Somali American elected to the US House of Representatives. She says that 'women and minorities often wait for permission to be invited to something; we need to stop doing that.' Women need to find the courage to be honest about both our potential and our achievements. That means pushing back when the opportunities go to people who claim the credit without really doing the work. It means realising that you weren't overlooked because you weren't good enough, but because women are systematically overlooked and undervalued at work. It means stop waiting for permission and start *asking* for the tiara. It means persistence and knowing what you are worth and being unafraid to say it out loud.

Self-promotion is an uncomfortable thing to do. It feels distasteful. Most of us are put off by people who talk up their own achievements all the time. Australians, in particular, don't like people who have tickets on themselves. Tall poppy syndrome is our national sport. We love a winner, but not a bragger. We prefer to back the underdog. 'You think you're so good!' was one of the meanest things you could say to another girl when I was at high school. And because women engage in bragging behaviour less often than men, it means we're especially harsh on women when they do. A woman who is confident to the point of cocky is social poison. After all, nice girls aren't show-offs.

But self-promotion shouldn't have to be distasteful. There is a time and a place for talking frankly about your skills and abilities. Making sure that your employer appreciates your hard work is not a shameful activity – it's a necessary one. In an ideal world, your employer would notice your hard work and good performance without having to be told. Promotions and rewards would be based on merit, and merit alone. Sadly, that isn't the world we live in. If it were, then there would be a whole lot more women CEOs, board directors and members of parliament. Merit alone is *not enough* in a gendered workplace. Some degree of self-promotion is required if you want to succeed in spite of an ingrained bias that says leaders are white men in suits. You have to position your lovely noggin in the direct eyeline of your boss, so that next time they're scanning the room with a spare tiara in hand, your head is impossible to ignore.

If you're cringing inwardly at this, there is a simple solution for those who prefer a more subtle form of self-promotion. It's called managing up. Managing up is about developing the best possible working relationship with your superiors. It means being the employee who can anticipate their manager's needs and solve problems without prompting. Just like a good boss helps their employee be the best that they can be, a good employee helps their boss to be better too. Managing up reduces the power imbalance between an employee and their manager. It helps the manager adjust their view so that the employee is seen as an equal – a worthy contemporary rather than a subordinate. Managing up is not about manipulating your boss. It involves more *actively* demonstrating your value to them, in a way that benefits you both. This means you can gently but firmly push back against structural barriers that could otherwise see you overlooked.

Managing your boss is the most important part of the job.

There are seven steps to managing up effectively.

1. **Reframe your boss as your client, not your employer.**
   Managing up requires you to reframe how you approach your boss. Stop thinking about your boss as someone whose primary

purpose is to guide, support and direct you. Instead, pretend you are a business and that your boss is a client. Servicing your client's needs effectively involves understanding their motivation and goals. Doing the right thing by your client means that sometimes you have to give them advice they don't want to hear. You also have to know their shortcomings. Your client may be a bit slack or they might be indecisive or a poor communicator. This is annoying, but it's something you have to deal with if you want to get paid. You have to support them to get the best possible outcome. Ultimately, your client needs to feel like success *without* you is impossible. They have to rely on you and think you're indispensible to their success. That's how you ensure their repeat business.

2. **Your boss isn't perfect, and that's a good thing.**
   Remember when you were in primary school and saw your classroom teacher at the supermarket? It was always the most shocking experience. Your kid mind had never contemplated the fact that teachers might do stuff outside of school. They didn't have families of their own, or interests beyond their students! They didn't get sick, or use the bathroom, or run out of dishwashing tablets the way your parents did! They were all-powerful, perfect authoritative beings that existed only within the confines of the school walls and the hours of nine to three. As adults, many of us inadvertently take this same approach with our bosses, particularly in steeply hierarchical workplaces. We assume a boss's judgement and time management and general skill level is infinitely better than our own. It's not. We expect them to have an innate knowledge of how to be a good boss. They don't. So when a boss inevitably reveals their imperfections, we're left shocked, frustrated and angry.

Your boss is human just like you. There will be areas they excel in and areas where they struggle. There will also be pressures on them that you are unaware of, like there are pressures on you that they're unaware of. When you're managing up, part of your job is to plug the gaps in your boss's abilities; to be their complement, the yin to their yang. Make a study of your boss the same way you would a new area of work. Learn about them. Understand their strengths and their weaknesses and look for patterns. Then consider how those weaknesses might be an opportunity for you to help them and, through them, the whole team. Perhaps time management isn't their strength, and you could propose a better scheme for guiding the team towards a deadline. Perhaps they've got a big-picture vision for your organisation but keep forgetting the small and niggly parts. That weakness might be a chance to demonstrate your stringent attention to detail.

A word of caution: It's important here that you differentiate between your boss's *weaknesses* and decisions they've made that you happen to disagree with. Managing up is primarily about making your manager's job easier. It's not about trying to do the boss's job for them, and it is certainly not about you actively undermining things that are their call.

3. **Boundless enthusiasm masks all manner of deficiencies.**
Sometimes your boss will give you tasks that are thrilling and rewarding. Enthusiasm will flow naturally, like water gushing from a luxurious fancy-hotel showerhead. That is excellent but it is also unsurprising. It's easy to be passionate and to reveal your best self when you're doing something you enjoy. The challenge comes in attacking *everything* you do with that same enthusiasm. Your boss knows some work is mind-numbing,

and assigning that boring task to one of their team is probably
something they dread. If you can respond with enthusiasm to
a less-than-pleasant task, you do your boss a great service.
It means they'll remember you positively, regardless of how
good you were at your actual job. Children's author and
gentleman of untold wisdom, Roald Dahl, expressed it far
more eloquently than I ever could:

I began to realize how important it was to be an enthusiast in
life . . . If you are interested in something, no matter what it is,
go at it at full speed ahead. Embrace it with both arms, hug it,
love it and above all become passionate about it. Lukewarm is no
good. Hot is no good either. White hot and passionate is the only
thing to be.

I once worked with an executive assistant called Dimity. This
was Dimity's first full-time job and it took her a while to get
a handle on the competing demands and ever-lengthening
to-do list. Dimity's tasks often involved things she'd never done
before and there were more than a few fumbles along the way.

But Dimity attacked every task with such boundless
enthusiasm that it was impossible not to fall in love with her.
She was an essential part of our office's culture. She would
part-rally, part-bully everyone into group activities, she never
forgot a birthday and she was genuinely passionate about every
aspect of her job – no matter how tedious. If I asked her to
get coffees for guests I was meeting with, she'd respond like a
kid with a free pass to Wet'n'Wild. After nine months as my
assistant, Dimity moved into a more senior role in the business
where she proceeded to shine brightly, like the diamond she is.

Dimity has since decided to go back to university and pursue a different career. She works as a nanny to my toddler in between her studies. Why? Because my memories of Dimity aren't of her inexperience or mistakes, they're of her being an utter delight to work with and to be around.

4. **Fold up the washing (but don't think you have to clean the whole house).**

I'm not a particularly domestic person, but the one chore I am deeply committed to is folding washing. That's because it's the household task my husband dislikes most. He finds folding clothes boring and repetitive (unlike all those other *super-fun* chores like vacuuming or watering the garden). He hates folding clothes with the burning fire of a thousand suns. Jeremy and I are a team, which means dividing tasks in line with our respective strengths but also in line with our preferences. Folding up washing isn't a task I relish, but I don't find it particularly distasteful. It's an easy burden for me to take on and an enormously welcome gesture for him. I call this marital leverage.

Discovering what elements of the job your boss loves and loathes is part of being a good team member. In every partnership – either personal or professional – we look for someone who can balance our shortcomings and preferences without causing us to feel insecure about them. Try to do this for your boss. If there's a job they find particularly boring or draining, perhaps you can share some of that burden. Be willing to go above and beyond your job description. If the additional tasks you're taking on are ones that your boss hates, they're even more likely to notice your contribution. They're also more likely to see your contribution as one they can't live without.

A note of caution: don't think you are expected to take on every rubbish task in the office. That's not fair or reasonable. Managing up doesn't require dutifully completing every task your boss hates. This isn't about doing someone else's job for them. Fold up the washing but don't clean the entire house just to get noticed.

5. **Motivation is everything, and you need to know theirs.**

In job interviews, the prospective employer always asks why the candidate applied for the role. *Why do you want to work here? What is it that drew you to this position?* When I was 14 I applied for a casual position at my local Bakers Delight. I earnestly informed the head baker that I'd always dreamed of a job in the bread industry. It was clearly bullshit, but he laughed and hired me anyway. I've interviewed prospective employees for lots of jobs, and candidates rarely answer this question well. Intent on delivering a suitably worthy reason for wanting the role, people tend to cobble together meaningless sentences full of words like 'inspired' and 'passionate'. Just once, I'd love to hear someone be honest and say, 'Because you guys pay better' or 'I was caught photocopying pictures of my bum and think I should resign before I get fired . . .' Even better would be a candidate turning the tables and asking their prospective manager the same question: *Why did* you *want to work here? What is it that drew* you *to your position? What about the work makes* you *happy to stay?*

Most of us know what our own motivation is for getting out of bed in the morning and heading to work. We might not be able to name it precisely, but there's a feeling, a rationale, a purpose for doing what we do. There is something driving us. When you're managing up, you need to flip this. You need to know what your *boss's* motivation is. What is driving them at work? What are their goals? What is their big picture? What is their plan? What is their unspoken purpose? What are they afraid of? What are the pressures from above? What is it that they're trying to accomplish above and beyond the day-to-day grind of work? If you can answer those questions then you can make the motivations of your boss your own. This is an invaluable act of upward management. It creates a stronger, more trusting dynamic between the two of you.

6. **Know what they need before they know themselves.**
   You need to understand the communication style of your boss and adapt your approach to match theirs. If they prefer having time to think and reflect before responding, then you do yourself no favours by coming to their office unannounced, expecting a serious talk. If your manager is a parent of young children then contacting them around bath or bedtime might be a no-go. There may be some subjects your boss finds difficult to discuss, or times when you need to anticipate what they need without a specific request. Good communication means taking a step away from the content of your work interactions and examining their style. Helping your boss in an emergency is one thing, but learning the ordinary rhythms of their day-to-day needs and wants means you can stop emergencies happening in the first place.

   I witnessed the ultimate act of upward management when Kate Ellis, my colleague Marielle and I were travelling in regional Western Australia, visiting childcare centres. A visit from a federal minister was a big event in these small country towns, each with populations of less than 1000 people. One centre even built and planted a new flowerbed in anticipation of the minister's arrival. At each visit, there was a morning tea for which the local mums and educators had prepared the most magnificent spread. We ravenously devoured the deliciousness at the first centre, then the second, and then the third. By the time we reached the fourth centre we were stuffed. There is a stomach-space limit for even the most delectable of Country Women's Association homemade scones.

Kate had it the worst. As minister, everyone wanted her to sample their baked goods. She was starting to look a little ill, but well-intentioned strangers kept forcing food into her hands and then checking in to see she'd definitely eaten it. Kate was in an impossible social position. That's when Marielle decided to intervene. At this point it will become clear that Marielle is a little bit brilliant (she's the same clever friend who went off to study in London without me). Marielle is one of those once-in-a-generation policy minds – but on this occasion it was her body, not her brain, that she put to work in service of our boss. For the remainder of the day, Marielle got between the minister and every proffered delicacy. She was an eating machine. Insatiable. Unstoppable. When we arrived in Perth late that afternoon, the usually tall and slim Marielle could no longer hold her burgeoning tummy in. Her waist-high belt popped out of its clasps and fell onto the pavement. She'd literally eaten herself into the next dress size, such was her commitment.

7. **Get specifics, determine priorities and provide options.**
'Could you take care of this?' is one of the most galling phrases bosses say. It's a question for which they want only one answer: 'Yes.' It's also a question that obliges at least half-a-dozen more questions, including:

- When do you want me to take care of it by?
- What resources can I use to take care of it?
- What does taking care of it look like, exactly?
- Is there anyone else who is taking care of this with me?
- How should I take care of it?
- Should I stop taking care of other things to take care of this?

Managing up is made simpler when you are purposeful about three things. First, you need to get specifics. If your boss asks you to complete a task for them, you have to fully understand their expectations to execute it effectively. Sometimes this is hard to achieve in the moment, but can usually be followed up by email or in person later in the day. To get specifics you need to *be* specific. Don't make vague requests for more information. Ask direct questions that will get you the answers you need. Insist on deadlines. Be clear about when you can make calls for yourself, and when your boss would prefer you returned to them for guidance. Often it can help to repeat things back to the boss in your own words. This will ensure you have a shared vision of what success looks like. And if your boss has a tendency to change their mind or shift goal posts? Then repeat things back to them in writing so you have a record of their agreement.

Second, you need to determine your priorities. Being able to prioritise effectively is a critical workplace skill. Employees who can balance competing day-to-day tasks with longer-term projects and the inevitable interruptions of a workplace are the most valuable people in an organisation. To prioritise well you need to understand that priorities are constantly changing, and so the order of your to-do list should be too. Your list of tasks should shuffle around like an Olympic medal tally. Prioritise and reprioritise. When you're confused, ask for help. Ask your boss short, easy-to-answer questions that won't take them long to respond to. For example, 'I'm pressed for time today – would you prefer I rushed to finish projects A and B, or can project B wait, so that I can deliver a higher standard on project A?'

Third, offer options. Managing up requires you to be a problem-solver. Your boss needs to see that they can trust you to make decisions. Always go to your boss with a solution and not just a problem. Even better, go to the boss with several solutions. Give them options. The boss will generally be more aware of the bigger organisational context of your work than you. So when you offer a single solution there may be a range of reasons it might not work that you're unaware of. Furthermore, there is rarely a single perfect solution to a workplace problem. By presenting your boss with a number of choices, along with your primary recommendation, you demonstrate how carefully you've thought about the issue. You also make your boss's job easier by simultaneously setting out the relevant considerations and offering multiple paths forward.

Two pitfalls of managing up (or how to avoid tripping over your own feet)

We've gone through the 'do's'. There are also 'do nots' of managing up:

1. **Managing up does NOT mean sucking up.**
    The Mamamia website was at its best on the days Mia Freedman and I fought. Morning editorial meetings that dragged on for longer than usual because we were at loggerheads could be exhausting and playfully antagonistic.

But they were always worth it. If there was a point of tension between my boss and me, then that same point of tension was likely to exist among our readership. It meant we needed to argue our way to common ground or run multiple opinion pieces putting forward divergent points. We did a better job for the people who read the website on the days we challenged one another. The same rule went for the entire team of senior editors. Our many differences of opinion were what made us good at our jobs.

Don't be afraid of disagreeing with your boss. Do it respectfully and appropriately. Remember that, as the boss, their decision is ultimately the one that counts (and make sure they know that you know that). But don't be fooled into thinking that managing up requires you to fall in line with their opinion each and every time. Managing up does not mean being a suck-up, a sycophant or agreeing with everything your manager says. While managers tend to have big egos, they want to be successful more than they want to be flattered. Hearing other perspectives and having your view challenged makes you a better contributor. Workplaces are stronger when everyone in the team can make a contribution. The old cliché of two heads being better than one is *true*, so don't fall victim to becoming a weak wax figure of your boss's head.

2. **Beware the competency trap.**

The competency trap is when you're so good at what you do that nobody wants to promote you because that means you won't be doing it any more. This happened to my friend Kellie, who was an office manager at a graphic design studio. She desperately wanted to move into a creative role but couldn't find a path to get there. Her colleagues and bosses kept emphasising how damn *good* she was at the administrative roles she'd always filled. They were telling the truth. She was good. Kellie was such an effective operator that her bosses couldn't imagine her doing anything else or how they'd get along without her administrative support. Her career became limited by how successful she was at her current job.

The competency trap emerges when, in the desire to be recognised and appreciated, employees restrict themselves to only doing tasks they know they do well. They expect advancement when they've unintentionally convinced others their skill set is specific to the role they're currently in. To avoid this, the skills you demonstrate to your manager need to be transferable. Versatility is key. Expertise and knowledge in a particular area are valuable, but so are generalist skills like being innovative, accountable, reliable, creative and efficient. These are skills that would be helpful in any role, in any workplace. Managing up effectively means showing your boss that you can thrive in multiple environments and in multiple roles. If you focus on being good at only your specific job – to a point that your boss can't imagine anyone else replacing you – then you are never going to be offered advancement. Look for opportunities to learn and to develop *and display* new skills. Play to your strengths, but make sure you're broadening your skill set, not just perfecting it.

HOW TO ASK FOR MORE

Because asserting your worth isn't 'greedy'.

Historically, women have been paid less than men. It was way back in February 1869 that a letter to the editor first appeared in the *New York Times* questioning why the government's men employees were paid more than the women. Your grandmother can probably recall positions being advertised in the classifieds, with two different rates of pay – one for women and another for men. Anti-discrimination laws in most developed countries now make it illegal for employers to expressly pay a woman less than a man for the same job. But that doesn't stop it happening in more covert ways. The proof lies in the gender pay gap. This gap has remained between 15 and 19 per cent in Australia for more than a generation. It widens to 23.1 per cent once bonuses, benefits and other perks are factored in. It is an irrefutable fact that Australian women are still paid less than men, and the same is true all over the world.

Even Hollywood actresses earn less than their men co-stars and admit to finding it hard to ask for more. Amy Adams, Charlize Theron, Robin Wright, Jennifer Lawrence and Carey Mulligan have spoken openly about it, which begs the question: if some of the world's most privileged, powerful women find negotiating pay difficult, what does that mean for the rest of us? What does it mean for a migrant who has to start from the bottom in her new country because foreign qualifications aren't recognised? What does it mean for a single mum whose pay barely covers her childcare costs, let alone her rent? What does it mean for the woman with an observable disability for whom mere entry into the workforce is a battle against discrimination? Negotiating fair pay for women's work remains one of the world's great challenges. When women ask for more money, we are up against a tidal wave of history that says our work simply isn't worth as much as a man's.

Women also face ingrained cultural bias about what is and isn't ladylike, and talking about money isn't polite. They won't like me if I ask for a higher salary, we tell ourselves. It's nicer to wait and be awarded the promotion rather than chase after it, our inner voice counsels. Women's conditioning is that asking for more money isn't appropriate. Almost every woman I know has given up money that should have been hers because she didn't want to have a conversation about it. Several of my girlfriends have accepted new jobs without asking what the salary was first. One friend put off requesting a pay rise that she knew she deserved for over three years. Another acted in the position above her own for 11 months before being formally offered the promotion. She never asked to be back-paid for the work she'd already done and the company didn't offer. Dozens of my colleagues have worked overtime without ever expecting compensation, despite being legally entitled to it.

Women regularly forgo their own prosperity to avoid a few short minutes of social discomfort. Far too often we assume that negotiating won't work, or that we won't be any good at it or that it's not allowed. It isn't our fault we feel that way. It's a reaction to the ingrained workplace bias that says women are inherently less valuable than men. But, nonetheless, it costs us. Dearly.

Your hunch was right. You're probably not very good at asking for more.

Women understand how important negotiating is, but we still go out of our way to avoid it. One in five Australian women say that they won't negotiate over money at all. Ever. Not for a salary. Not for a promotion. Not for flexible hours. Not for a car. Not even in a game of Boggle. Researcher Linda C. Babcock conducted a study where she actually asked university students to do just that. After several games of Boggle, she told them, the students would be given between $3 and $10 to compensate them for their time. After playing the game four times, students were each given $3 and told, 'Here's $3. Is $3 okay?' Babcock found that the women students were nine times less likely to ask for more money than the men. Nine times less likely to ask for more! The women performed equally as well as the men in the game and complained just as angrily about the stingy compensation once they were outside the room. But they weren't willing to actually ask for more.

Women are 2.5 times more likely than men to admit they have a 'great deal of apprehension' about negotiating. This means they either let someone else do the negotiating for them, or refrain from it entirely. This reluctance to negotiate extends to areas where negotiation is not just expected but actually factored into pricing structures, like buying a car. Men tend to be much more comfortable negotiating and confident in their ability to attain a satisfactory outcome. One study comparing students with masters degrees from the same university found that the men's starting salaries exceeded the women's by an average of $4000 a year. When questioned about why this might be, 57 per cent of the men said they'd simply asked for more money than what they were originally offered. Only 7 per cent of women had done the same.

My husband is a lawyer. He gets excited in anticipation of a day spent in court, or a high-stakes mediation. He gees himself up like he's competing in the AFL grand final or running a marathon. I honestly wouldn't be surprised if he carb-loads before a big case. It's all a game to him. A serious one, but a game nonetheless. His approach is pretty standard for his gender. Men tend to enjoy negotiating, whereas women actively dislike it. When asked, American men compare negotiating to 'winning a ballgame', whereas women consider the experience akin to 'visiting the dentist'. Unsurprisingly, men's relative enjoyment of negotiating makes them more likely to engage in it. It's why men initiate salary negotiations at *four times* the rate of women.

Over time, all of this negotiation avoidance adds up. Studies estimate that by not negotiating harder on starting salaries, women miss out on as much as $500 000 during the course of their careers. That's half a million dollars! The equivalent of the prize money for winning *Survivor* – but without the indignity of 55 days on a remote beach having your every move filmed, living on nothing but rice and beans and searching for hidden immunity idols in the sand. It's a jackpot, and women are just letting it pass us by. Why? We find talking about money uncomfortable.

What makes women so reluctant to ask for more?

Actively pursuing career progression isn't typically 'feminine' behaviour. Asking for more – even when more is objectively our due – goes against women's conditioning. Children's stories illustrate the point. The fairytales on which we were raised have a common moral: little girls who ask for more get what's coming to them. Consider selfish Goldilocks, who took more and more from those three bears before being firmly put in her place and having to go bush to avoid being eaten. By contrast well-behaved Cinderella didn't request her shoe back off that thieving prince – she waited patiently for it to be presented to her. *Sleeping Beauty*'s Aurora spent almost a hundred years napping in a castle before being rescued. Heaven forbid she'd had the gumption to ask someone to get her the hell out of there earlier. It would have been a less gripping story, but a far sweeter life for her.

Women tend to assume that good things come to those who behave nicely and wait patiently. This messaging is so powerful that many of us don't even realise we're exhibiting this behaviour. So when it does come time to negotiate, to hustle or to ask for more, something about it feels inherently wrong. We can't quite put our finger on *why* we hate negotiating so much. We just know that we hate it. If you're a woman who faces multiple barriers to workforce participation, then the process may be even more difficult. For example, women with disabilities have been historically locked out of the paid workforce, which means asking for more becomes a radical act of self-assertion. Requesting more money or a promotion or better conditions is itself a form of protest against the assumption that women with disabilities aren't entitled to a place in the workforce at all. Disability advocate Carly Findlay says there is a widely held expectation from employers that people with disabilities should be 'grateful' to have a job at all.

Part of women's anxiety about asking for more is linked to a fear of making others socially uncomfortable. For me – and most of the women I've worked with – it's important to be liked by colleagues and employers. This makes discussions of money, with their high potential for disagreement, all the more undesirable. Researchers Bowles and Babcock explain that 'women get a nervous feeling about negotiating for higher pay because they are intuiting – correctly – that self-advocating for higher pay would present a socially difficult situation for them – more so than for men.' Negotiations about money aren't the stuff of friendships, and, increasingly, that's how we view our workplace relationships. Work is about more than a pay packet for most people. Employees put a high value on a positive culture and a happy, warm, welcoming environment. Employers know that and use it to their advantage. More and more, workplaces are putting resources towards marketing themselves as a great place to work. It's why you hear clichés at work like: *We're all in this together, catch me as I fall during this trust exercise, here's a certificate for team member of the month, rah-rah-rah!* Of course, building a workplace that is a positive, inclusive environment – somewhere you want to be – is a good thing. But there are also some potentially negative consequences. The closer you personally feel to your employer, the harder it makes any discussion of pay or conditions. Asking for a salary increase begins to feel like a social transaction instead of a commercial one, like asking a really big favour from a friend. It's a shifting relationship that effectively advantages the employer in a negotiation.

Additionally, the growing number of women in the workforce has coincided with a blurring of the lines between home and work. Technology means our personal and professional spheres are increasingly interconnected. There used to be work and home – two neatly divided spheres. Now they feel like they're basically the same. They overlap with one another, and this makes salary conversations more complicated. The social complexities of navigating what used to be straightforward 'more money or I leave' negotiations are enormous.

Any time I have resigned from a job to pursue the next opportunity I've felt desperately guilty. I prepared for the resignation discussion in the same way I once prepared to break up with a boyfriend. I practise my 'lines' in my head. I make sure to explain that it was 'not you, but me' and do everything I can to maintain the relationship with my soon-to-be former boss. Perhaps you're the same. These feelings reflect that modern working relationships are about more than simply earning a living. Our sense of self, our sense of belonging and our sense of loyalty are tightly intertwined with our jobs.

I've experienced the same thing as a manager when team members have requested a pay rise or a promotion. More often than not, women employees have apologised in salary negotiations. They were sorry for taking up my time, sorry for being dissatisfied, sorry for having the *audacity* to want more money. While managers assume that from time to time employees will ask for more, women feel it's discourteous to do so. They don't want to appear arrogant or entitled or selfish or above their station. They don't want to 'put anyone out'. In my experience, new women employees rarely try to negotiate on starting salary. Some don't even ask what the salary is before accepting the role. Young women, in particular, are so appreciative to be given a job in the first place that they don't consider asking for better than they're being offered.

The 'tiara syndrome' we spoke about in the previous chapter impacts pay negotiations as well. Women instigate pay negotiations less often than men because we would rather wait for the offer to come from above. That is, we think of a salary bump or a promotion as a tiara, something that will be presented to us in recognition of our hard work and good performance. It rarely happens that way. Studies show that women are more likely to delay asking for more money because they want to build a positive long-term working relationship with their boss. They justify the decision *not* to ask by reassuring themselves that in the long-term they'll be rewarded for not rocking the boat. Women also tend to be more focused on fairness, and are less likely to relish being paid more than others at the same level. Men – having been raised to aggressively push for advancement – are more individually motivated.

The double disadvantage of being a woman who asks

Women are disadvantaged in negotiations because they fear the social backlash of being 'pushy'. That is, women have been conditioned not to ask for more and others have been conditioned to *expect* that women won't ask for more. When women behave contrary to societal expectations, they're punished for it. Sara Laschever, co-author of *Women Don't Ask: Negotiation and the Gender Divide*, explains it like this:

> We teach little girls that we don't like them to be greedy,
> pushy or overly aggressive . . . Once adulthood is reached,
> studies are conclusive that neither men nor other women like
> women who are too aggressive.

For many women, the chief concern when negotiating salary or asking for a promotion is being labelled. Women report being scared of appearing entitled, of asking for too much before they've proved themselves worthy, of being labelled as 'aggressive' or 'pushy'. Note the very particular wording I've used here. Women aren't afraid that they'll *be* aggressive or pushy. They're only afraid that they'll be *seen* that way. This is also why women may need to be encouraged by a superior to apply for a promotion or request better pay. It feels less pushy that way. The request is being made because someone else suggested it, not of one's own volition. This gives the woman permission to ask. It allows her to rationalise that she is not asking for *herself* but for somebody else.

It's perfectly rational that women fear social penalties if they ask for more money. The very fact that managers are less used to women negotiating means they tend to react more defensively when it happens. Indeed, women managers are often the harshest critics of women employees who ask for more. There is an underlying assumption by women and men bosses that women employees won't ask for more money. Bosses expect women to conduct themselves differently. They expect that women will be team players, supportive and unselfish, and not mess with the status quo. Asking for more money or demanding better conditions – while a totally reasonable thing to do – goes against that expectation.

The truth is that women tend to be excellent negotiators. Research shows that when negotiating on behalf of *someone else*, women are at least as good as – if not superior to – men. Some of the fiercest negotiators I've ever seen in action were women. They took no prisoners and consistently delivered the goods when tasked with negotiating a better deal with a supplier, or a fairer outcome for their team. But those same women could fall down when it came to negotiating for their own personal benefit. They would defer asking for a raise in the first place and when they did, they would ask for far less than a man in the same position would.

Women are more likely to succeed when the purpose of the negotiation doesn't require them to make an assessment about or to actively assert their own self-worth. Research shows that women's salary expectations fall anywhere between 3 and 32 per cent *lower* than those of men for the same job. And the gap between the expectations of women and men grows over the course of a career. In other words, the more time women spend at work, the more their salary expectations fall below what they're really worth. In addition, as their careers progress, women are more likely to base their salary expectations on comparisons with women colleagues only, which necessarily lowers how much they ask for.

Organise and unionise – because we're better together.

Negotiating can be incredibly daunting so it's crucial to remember that you're not alone. Most of us are employed in organisations where there are other people in the same position as us. This means that your interests are likely to overlap. Just as Captain Planet was born out of the collective powers of his Planeteers, you and your colleagues' negotiating strength is greater together than it is individually. That's where unions come into the equation. A union is an organisation that represents the interests of employees within a particular industry and bargains on their behalf. The union movement has been at the forefront of fighting and winning positive outcomes for working people throughout Australia's history, and women have been a central part of that.

One of my favourite stories of women working collectively to advance their interests comes from way back in 1912. After a group of tram drivers were told they couldn't wear their union badges on the job, thousands of workers in Brisbane decided to protest. They were fighting for the right of these specific workers to wear their union badges but also for workers all around Australia to be members of a union. Emma Miller, a seamstress, suffragist and pioneer trade unionist, led a group of 600 women and girls to participate in a march to Parliament House. In those days, for women to take such an active and visible role in protesting was unusual. Miller herself was a teeny-tiny woman in her 70s; she is estimated to have weighed less than 40kg. Nonetheless, when policemen entered the crowd of protestors and began attacking the workers with batons, Miller held her ground. Legend goes that she pulled out her hatpin – the only weapon at her disposal – and stabbed a policeman in the leg to stop him from hurting the women and girls around her.

Now, the world has changed a lot since 1912, and I certainly wouldn't recommend you engage in hatpin-related violence (or any violence for that matter). However, the enormous negotiating power of employees who band together is absolutely relevant today. Unions have played a leading role in arguing for equal pay, paid parental leave, anti-discrimination laws, affordable and quality childcare and flexible work arrangements. Ged Kearney, president of the Australian Council of Trade Unions, tells me:

> It is about power. Men have held positions of power in the workplace for much longer than women, and mostly still do. Men will not give up that power easily, so consciously or subconsciously they defend it by discriminating against women or by making it harder for women to get ahead, forcing us to triple efforts and go far beyond [what] any man would have to. For some women who have made it through to positions of power, they also often guard it rather than using their positions to help other women succeed. Women need to work with other women, stand together, give them a hand and support each other to move onwards.

We can't assume better conditions for working women will flow naturally as a consequence of having one or two more women at the very top. It's exciting and worthy of celebration when one woman becomes the CEO and is paid accordingly. However, until the fair pay and progression of women through *every level* of the workplace is the norm – rather than a novelty – real change for women won't be achieved. This is why it's a far more effective negotiating tactic to ask for more as a group, rather than as individuals. It is fundamental to shifting the power imbalance between a single woman employee and a group of (usually men) decision makers. As women, we will ultimately rise together, or not at all.

The power imbalance between an employer and an employee is part of what makes negotiating so intimidating. Even when you're friendly with your boss, the unspoken status differential between you is ever-present. They get to make decisions about your salary or wages, but not you about theirs. If you believe you're entitled to higher pay or improved working conditions, then chances are the person sitting next to you feels the same way. A union can take advantage of those mutual interests to help win a better deal for you both. Unions are also critical in maintaining the pay and conditions you already have, which may come under threat from time to time. If you're at risk of unfair dismissal, or benefits that were previously in your contract have disappeared, then a union should be your first port of call.

Going it alone: the dos and don'ts of asking for more

If the pay increase or promotion you're seeking is for you as an *individual*, then you're ultimately going into the negotiating room solo. While unions and employee associations might be able to help you up-skill for that meeting, it is still going to involve a discussion between you, your boss, a chair and a table. Gulp. I understand that this is mildly terrifying. I've seen employees literally get the shakes when asking for a pay rise. I have also been the employee with the shakes while asking for a pay rise. Working out how to go to your boss and ask for more is daunting. I suspect the gender influences I've outlined earlier in this chapter haven't done much to fill you with confidence, either.

But, in a funny way, they should.

Good negotiating requires that you know as much as possible about the person you're negotiating with. So being aware of gender biases and how they might affect your employer is actually going to make you a better negotiator. Understanding that the doubts you have about your negotiating ability are caused by social conditioning, not a reflection of reality? That's got to help, too.

Now I suspect that you're sitting there and thinking, *But what if I am the exception to the rule and I really am a terrible negotiator?* Well, I say otherwise. I say that you can actually be very, very good at negotiating. Especially if you follow this simple seven-step process.

1. **Stand back and objectively assess your situation.**
   There's a famous saying that goes something like this: *First comes conditioning. Next comes me.* It means the first thought that comes into your head is rarely your own. That first thought is a product of your conditioning. Or put another way, it's what the world has taught you to think. The second thought is the one that reveals the truth of who you are. It's the harder one to think your way towards, but is also more likely to be accurate. The second thought is the more objective one – it's the rational assessment of your skills and abilities. This thought is often pushed away by the first because conditioning is so

persuasive. Indulging the second thought requires separating yourself from stereotypes, expectations and your own personal biases. But the second thought is the correct one.

Before asking for more, you need to follow the second thought through to its natural conclusion by objectively assessing the situation. I find it helpful to pretend that I'm supporting one of my girlfriends to make a decision, rather than making it for myself. This improves my ability to be objective and assists in eliminating personal insecurities from the equation. Ask yourself: *Would you advise someone else in your situation to apply for a promotion or ask for a raise?*

That question will prompt a bunch of other questions, which will help you determine if asking for more is a reasonable request at this time. These might include: What's changed between now and when I was last given a pay rise? Has the company become more profitable? Have I been offered jobs elsewhere? Have I become faster or better at my job in some other way? Have I acquired new skills or experience that makes me more valuable? Has my role expanded to include responsibilities that weren't there before? Have other people who do the same job as me been rewarded with more money or other benefits? Has the market changed? Have other similar businesses started paying their staff more? Is there greater demand for my skill set than there was before?

2. **Time your request with precision.**
   Timing is crucial when it comes to asking for a pay rise. Remember that your place, position and pay occupy your thoughts most days, but the same isn't true for your boss. Your boss has other demands on their time and budget that have nothing to do with you. Think about what those

might be. What months is cash flow best for the business? When are promotions easier to come by? Is there a standard review period? When are budgets set? When is your boss most stressed? When might they be open to an unexpected conversation? Have you just come off a stellar few months of performance or have you been operating at less than your best recently? How long have you worked with the organisation?

I once had an employee provide a compelling case for why she should be promoted. I was a little puzzled, though. She'd only been employed about four months, was my memory. She was a solid performer, but she didn't have a good enough handle on the nature of the business yet to warrant a promotion. I asked her to remind me how long she'd been working with us. 'Oh, about eight weeks now,' was her reply. Safe to say, her timing was out of whack.

3. **Prepare, prepare, prepare.**
Asking for a promotion or a pay rise isn't something to do on a whim. Nor should it be a last-minute decision. You want to avoid your request being a shock for your manager. The groundwork for a negotiation should be laid in advance of the actual conversation. Find ways to articulate your professional ambitions to your superiors. Remember that your boss isn't a mind reader and won't necessarily know you're interested in a higher position or moving to another area of the business. They may well believe you're 100 per cent comfortable and happy doing what you're doing now. We don't necessarily appear as ambitious as we feel. If you want more, make sure people know it.

Being prepared also means doing your homework before asking for more. This involves researching your market value. Knowing what sort of salary your skill set attracts in the marketplace gives you leverage at the negotiating table. Market value is rarely a specific number. Usually it's a range of values made up of the average salaries for your role, what kind of company you are working for, and your individual value to the company, both currently and in the future. There are websites that collate salary data and can give you an overview of what others with your job title and description are earning. You also need to account for factors like location, industry and company size, which all shape the capacity your employer has to pay you more. Arm yourself with information. Be prepared.

4. **Focus on outcomes, not effort.**

There's nothing more frustrating than when you're mid-argument with your partner and you can't remember all the things they've done wrong. You know they exist. Your rage reminds you that your partner has messed up so many times, but you can't quite find the words or the examples to prove it. I've been involved in more than a few salary negotiations that mirror this sort of lovers' quarrel. The employee asks for a raise, but fails to provide any real reasons for why they deserve it. They should be offering examples of what they've achieved, how they've contributed and where they've excelled, but instead? Nothing. Employees tend to fall back on describing how hard they work. They talk about effort instead of results. Hard work is great, but hard work isn't enough to warrant more money. The organisational value of hard work lies in the results it produces.

When asking for more, you need to bring your employer examples of *outcomes*. Just like in fights with your partner, these outcomes can be really hard to remember the night before your big meeting. We tend to forget this stuff once we've moved onto the next work project. You can avoid this panicked, brain-racking moment by keeping track of your achievements over time. It doesn't have to be a formal record. Keep a Post-It note in your top drawer or a folder in your email where you file away reminders of what you've accomplished, or praise you've received. It's like a private gold-star chart. This record will make your arguments more compelling when you're asking for more. It serves as objective evidence that your request is a fair and reasonable one.

5. **Emphasise your worth, not your need.**
   Another trap employees fall into is justifying their request for a pay rise based on their personal circumstances. I had an employee ask for a pay rise because she was saving for her wedding, and another because she'd moved house and the rent was really expensive. Those are both good reasons for those employees *wanting* a pay rise. Neither are good reasons for the *employer* to give the employee a pay rise. As career strategist Jenny Foss explains:

> Your future employers do not care how much your rent, your car payment, or your kid's braces are costing you. They care about what you're going to walk in their doors and deliver. So if you've got that offer in front of you and are ready to negotiate, you absolutely must pull together a pitch that demonstrates that you're worth the extra cash.

We fall back on these needs because we don't want to appear greedy. By arguing that you need more money to live your life, you avoid having to make the case for why your skills are *worth* more money. Women find it hard to state their self-worth in monetary terms, but being able to do this is essential to salary negotiation. Remember your employer isn't paying you because they're a generous soul who wants you to have nice things. They're paying you to do a job, and if that job is highly skilled, you do it brilliantly and it contributes hugely to the success of the organisation? Well, you're worth more money, damn it.

6. **This doesn't have to be a contest. It's a cooperation.**
Linda Babcock and Sara Laschever, authors of *Women Don't Ask*, advise reframing the way you view salary negotiations to be a cooperation rather than a contest. Consider it like this: an organisation would like you to work for them (or continue working for them) and you would like to do that. That's cooperation! To make this mutually agreeable future a reality, however, the two of you need to find some common ground. More cooperation! This is what a salary negotiation is. Aggressive negotiation can absolutely be effective, but it's usually not the most effective approach. Some studies suggest that cooperative negotiation tactics are more than twice as likely to succeed than aggressive negotiation. So there's no need to prepare like you're going into gladiatorial battle. This is not *Game of Thrones*. Nobody owns a dragon. Instead, think of a negotiation as two people coming to the table with different aims, who will probably meet somewhere in the middle. You just have to figure out where.

Aggressive negotiation also includes threatening behaviour. Threatening to quit or using phrases like 'that's my bottom line' will end a negotiation quickly but not always positively. Any hostage negotiator or parent of a toddler will tell you never to make threats that you don't intend to follow through

with. Negotiation is called negotiation for a reason – it's not
a demand and deliver scenario. You're not necessarily going
to get everything you want. Threats to quit or walk away put
the employer in a binary position where they must either meet
your demand or not. If they decide not to, then you either
have to walk away or look really, really, really silly by trying
to backtrack on your threat. Don't make threats unless you're
genuinely committed to acting upon them. Your final offer
actually has to be the final offer.

7. **There is more to life than money.**
My dear, there is more to life than money. I don't mean this
in the Pollyanna, airy-fairy, 'let's quit our jobs, move to the
country and live a life without stuff' kind of way. I mean
that there are benefits you can negotiate that aren't purely
monetary. Perhaps your employer isn't in the position to give
you the 10 per cent salary increase you've requested. What
else would you like? What other conditions or flexible work
arrangements would benefit you? A title change, even without
an accompanying salary bump, might better reflect the kind of
work you do and be critical in helping you land the next job.
The chance to learn new skills or work directly with someone
you admire might be better for your career in the long run than
an immediate promotion. Culturally, you might value having
greater input into some aspect of the organisation you work
for. Perhaps a nine-day fortnight, or the option to leave early
on a Friday, or an additional week of annual leave could be
agreed upon? Negotiating requires an open mind. Don't enter
into it with a single fixed picture of what 'success' looks like.
Be prepared to find compromises that will meet the needs
of both you and your employer.

HOW
TO BE A
MANAGER
OF PEOPLE

Because you're a boss lady now.

I was curled up in a hotel room bed in Kuala Lumpur when I received an urgent series of text messages. They were from my housemate and fellow political tragic, Anika. They read as follows:

> GILLARD.
>
> DID YOU JUST SEE THAT?
>
> HOLY SHITBALLS. THAT WAS ACE.
>
> IF YOU AREN'T ALREADY, GET IN FRONT OF A TV IMMEDIATELY.

The messages were followed by a series of emojis conveying a level of excitement that can't be expressed in words. There are some rare moments in life that are so incredibly special they require the use of the dancing lady in the red dress. That day Anika sent several dancing ladies in red dresses. This was a big deal.

I opened my laptop and started streaming footage from the Australian parliament. 'I will not be lectured on sexism and misogyny by this man; I will not,' Julia Gillard blazed from the dispatch box. Her steely gaze fixed on Opposition Leader Tony Abbott, a man renowned for his 1950s-esque views on the role of women.

The speech was an epic smackdown. Unprepared, and raw with the emotion of having recently lost her father, Gillard spoke largely without notes, just a few scribblings on a piece of paper. She was angry but reasoned throughout – a master debater.

As prime minister, Julia Gillard suffered horrendously sexist treatment at the hands of the media, the opposition and even some within her own party. On top of the usual irrelevancies that women in positions of power endure, Gillard also faced a barrage of conservative disapproval over her childlessness, her atheism and her marital status. Her 'misogyny speech', delivered in October 2012, is now the stuff of political legend. The video footage from that day reveals a woman at the pinnacle of her career, brimming with frustration. Gillard wanted only to be allowed to get on with the job. When Gillard announced her resignation from the Australian parliament, she spoke about the role gender had played in her prime ministership. Standing soberly with two Australian flags behind her, Gillard said of gender, 'It doesn't explain everything. It doesn't explain nothing. It explains some things.'

The same will be true for you once you become a Boss Lady.

Who would you rather work for: Heidi or Howard?

When a woman lands a leadership position, the job description matches that of the man who (usually) had it before. However, her experience is likely to be quite different. The varied treatment of women and men at work becomes more acute at the management level. Being aware of this from the outset means you will be better prepared to cope with its consequences.

Women leaders can be disliked for displaying the very attributes that are *required* for effective management. Being women, they are expected to behave in the same stereotypically 'feminine' way that other women employees are. They must be kind, caring and supportive employees. They must be likeable and contribute to a pleasant working environment for their colleagues. Being bosses, however, they also have to exert authority, a traditionally masculine activity. When a boss makes decisions it isn't always possible to please all parties. This means that when women are in leadership positions, they face a complex trade-off. They can live up to people's expectations of their gender, or people's expectations of their position. Successfully doing both is a fallacy.

This exact conundrum was captured in the now famous Heidi versus Howard experiment. If you're not familiar with it, here's how it goes: one group of people were given the resumé of a highly successful entrepreneur named Heidi Roizen. A second group were presented with *exactly the same* resume but the name Howard was substituted for Heidi's. Both groups assessed Heidi and Howard as equally competent candidates for a job. But while Howard was described in glowing social terms, Heidi was assumed to be 'selfish'. The people participating in the experiment – both women and men – described Heidi as 'not the type of person you would want to hire or work for'. Success and likeability are correlated for men, but not for women. That is, successful and ambitious men are popular with their colleagues. People assume they'd make good bosses and are nice to be around. Successful and ambitious women are presumed to be competent bosses but not very pleasant to be around.

Why are we harsher on women leaders?

There are several reasons women leaders are judged more harshly than men. The first is something called role congruity. While women bosses are growing in number, they remain unusual. When children are asked to draw pictures of a 'boss', the artwork they return inevitably shows a white man in a suit. We expect bosses to be men, and when we see something that runs counter to that expectation, our brains struggle to process it. Therese Huston, author of *How Women Decide,* explains it like this:

> This idea that when we think of a leader and we think of a man, those two concepts have a lot of overlapping qualities. We think of men as ambitious and action-oriented and we think of a leader as ambitious and action-oriented. Whereas when we think of the qualities of a woman and a leader there doesn't tend to be much overlap.

The fact that there are fewer women leaders means our expectations of those who do reach leadership positions are higher. Women in high-profile positions are still achieving 'firsts': a country's first woman prime minister, a company's first woman CEO, a charity's first woman managing director. So when women reach these positions of power, they attract a brighter spotlight than if they were men. It means that when they falter, more of us are watching. A colleague once remarked to me that a rubbish man politician is one of many, but a rubbish woman politician is the reason women shouldn't be in parliament. That double standard runs deep. It extends to women who hold less lofty, middle-management leadership positions as well.

The spotlight on women leaders can play out in the positive. Women in high-profile positions become role models for others, heroes for women like you and me. We are more invested in their success than we otherwise might be, simply because they're women. There aren't many other role models of women with power and influence for us to choose from – so we expect a lot of those we've got. The weight of that positive expectation can be dangerous. When a woman leader inevitably fails to live up to the varied hopes and desires of everyone who admires her, we're *extra* disappointed. Far more so than we would be had she been a man or one of many women leaders. Her failure is more likely to be viewed as a failure on *behalf of all women*.

When a woman is the first or only woman to hold a particular position, she attracts extra scrutiny. It is as if her colleagues are waiting, watching with bated breath and more than a tinge of doubt, to see whether a woman can really 'do it'. If the only woman director in a company makes a major error, people who work for the company are more likely to think another woman would make the same sort of errors. When a man makes a major error, his failure is a personal one. When a woman leader makes a major error, women are collectively failures. Gender researcher Associate Professor Farida Jalalzai describes it like this: 'We have to acknowledge that men are not faced with the suspicion that they can't be good leaders simply because they are men'.

That double standard is also the cause of 'the glass cliff' phenomenon. This refers to the fact women have a much better chance of being made leaders of organisations that are already in a precarious position. For example, Marissa Mayer was chosen as CEO of tech company Yahoo! when it was flailing and then blamed when she couldn't turn its prospects around. Women who are chosen to lead only when an organisation is already in crisis are vulnerable to greater criticism. The glass cliff phenomenon is regularly observed in politics, where women leaders are awarded the top job only when a government is seriously on the nose and likely to lose the next election anyway (think of Theresa May in the United Kingdom, or former NSW premier Kristina Keneally). It's as if decision-makers are thinking, *Well, nothing else is working – maybe we try a woman and see how that goes?* These women are set up to fail because they're being used as a last-ditch effort.

The harsh standards we judge women leaders by take their toll, and so do the impossible expectations we place on them. Psychologist Michelle Ryan says you can see evidence of this in women's changing levels of ambition. She told *The Guardian*:

> If you do surveys about the proportion of men and women aiming for the top, you can see differences in their levels of ambition . . . They don't start off that way. We've done the surveys for numerous professions, and whether it's police officers, surgical trainees, or women in science, men and women have absolutely equal levels of ambition and want to make it to top in equal numbers . . . While men's ambition increases over time, women's decreases. My research suggests that this drop is not associated with wanting to have kids, or to stay home and look after them. It's related to not having support, mentors or role models to make it to the top, and the subtle biases against women that lead to their choices.

In other words? The unfair expectations we place on women leaders makes other women less ambitious to become leaders at all.

Is there a women's 'style' of leadership, and is it any good?

The concept of 'women's leadership' started to gain traction in the 1950s. As women began entering workplaces in greater numbers, people were interested in whether they would behave differently to men. Specifically, we wanted to know if there was a universal 'feminine' leadership style and whether it was any good. Research over the next 65 years has shown that, overwhelmingly, women and men lead in similar ways. However, there are a few gender-related differences that have been observed.

Research suggests that women may be slightly more cooperative, collaborative and less hierarchical in how they approach leadership. This difference is more pronounced in industries where there is a 50/50 gender split, or where women dominate – presumably because women feel less pressure to conform to masculine stereotypes when there are fewer blokes around. Some researchers have found that women are better at creating supportive working environments, the kind of workplaces where informal mentorship flourishes and colleagues are invested in one another's success. There is also evidence that women leaders tend to produce more benevolent outcomes. That is, women are focused on the ethical and social impact of the companies they lead, not just on making a profit.

There are also anecdotal reports from senior executives that women leaders behave differently to men. General Motors CEO Daniel Akerson wants to see more women in his executive team because he believes women 'have a higher emotional quotient, and they deal with change, radical change [well]'. Mamatha Chamarthi, now VP and CIO at TRW Automotive Holdings Corporation, described women as having 'inherent strength, a collaborative capacity that may not come as naturally to men'. This positive, feminised view of women's leadership has won popular support and agreement. It's assumed that women leaders will make for a kinder, more participatory and fair environment. I've sat on boards that are dominated by men who say they want women among their number to make the place gentler, or more collaborative. One gentleman even told me he liked the 'feminine touch' I brought to board meetings. Seriously.

It is great that workplaces are starting to recognise and value women leaders. Really, it is. But if we only value women leaders for having a uniquely 'feminine' set of attributes, then it will ultimately be detrimental. A narrow casting of what women can contribute to leadership limits their capacity to be successful in other ways. Indeed, women leaders often find that they're only praised for their traditionally feminine attributes. Stereotypes of women's leadership also make life more difficult for women who don't live up to them. When women leaders display masculine traits (like insisting on pursuing their own course of action rather than deferring to the majority), they're socially penalised. You've probably seen this happen in your own workplace. A woman manager is more assertive than usual. She insists that her decision is the right one, despite considerable opposition and – snap! – she is being talked about behind her back. 'That was a little bit *aggressive*, don't you think?' says Eliza from accounts. 'She was being a pushy bitch, if you ask me,' responds Mike in marketing. (You really should never listen to Mike in marketing.) It's a series of quite small steps from 'women are effective leaders because they have these traits' to 'for women to be leaders they *must* possess these traits'.

Neelie Kroes, the former European Union commissioner for competition, claimed that women-led banks did better during the global financial crisis because 'women have a better ear to listen, and they are less likely to pretend to know everything themselves. They are team players with less ego.' The view that women leaders are good for business is also gaining traction and does have an evidentiary basis: companies with more women on their boards, for example, are more financially stable. Again, while this sounds positive, we should be wary of a message that says 'hire and promote more women because it's good for business.' This reduces the benefits of equality to only an economic argument. Supporting women in leadership positions is beneficial because it creates a more equitable society, not just a profitable company. When Abraham Lincoln abolished slavery, he didn't do so because it made good financial sense. It was because slavery was a racist abomination. It was cruel, unjust and a fundamental breach of human rights. Gender equality is a worthy aim in and of itself, and shouldn't be justified solely by reference to economic arguments. There is also little ground to cover between 'we need more women to make the company profitable' and 'profits haven't gone up since we promoted a woman, so why bother promoting any more?' Women leaders need to be valued for their many varied and individual traits – not just for being women. The arguments for women's leadership must be bigger and broader than economics and so-called 'feminine' qualities.

Doctor Jennifer Wheelan says that lumping all women leaders together like this does women a disservice. Stereotypes about women – positive or negative – will always hurt them, Wheelan explains:

> Once we focus on gender differences we don't just trigger the positive aspects of gender stereotypes, we trigger the negative ones too. Worse still, whether complimentary or critical, stereotypes impose narrow expectations on both men and women that constrain their choices and perpetuate misconceptions about their capabilities.

Indulging the positive stereotypes makes it harder to dispel the negative ones; for example, that women are too sensitive to make tough decisions. You can't pick and choose which stereotypes people draw on to make judgements about one another. Encouraging one stereotype about women leaders encourages them all.

The implications of stereotyping for women leaders who belong to multiple minority groups can be even more severe. These women may face dual, intersecting stereotypes. Research from the Human Rights Commission has identified a 'bamboo ceiling' in Australian workplace culture. Australians from African, Middle Eastern and Asian backgrounds are rarely promoted into leadership roles because 'the ethnic and cultural default of leadership in Australia remains predominantly Anglo-Celtic'. Ming Long, an experienced finance executive says that as an Asian–Australian woman she had to doubly adapt her leadership style: first to be more masculine, second to be more 'white'. 'I think there is an assumption that if you're an Asian woman within this country you're meant to be quiet, meek and mild, and sit in the background and not say much,' Ms Long told the ABC.

No matter who you are, being a boss is bloody hard work.

While it can be helpful to talk about 'feminine' and 'masculine' leadership styles, most leaders exhibit some combination of the two. Women tend to mix nurturing and participatory leadership with more direct and goal-oriented action when required. This may be because they've witnessed backlash against women leaders who are deemed too 'masculine' in their approach, so they attempt to avoid being labelled in the same way. Or it may be that women have simply found this androgynous approach is a more effective way to manage.

Regardless of gender, being a boss is hard work. It's a task made more difficult because there is rarely explicit training in how to do it well. The transition from employee to manager can be a brutal one. Management is a skill like any other – it takes practice. When you're really good at your job, then the promotion to a management role seems like the logical next step. But it can rattle your confidence when you find that the skills needed to do a job and the skills needed to support others to do that job are quite different. This shift can throw you off track. A few mistakes early on can dent your confidence long-term. You might begin to think management isn't for you when really you're just learning.

When you're new to management, you need some basic foundations for how to do the job well. I've been a good manager and a bad manager. I've been managed well and managed badly too. There is endless writing and advice on this topic in which leaders are categorised into neat little boxes. I'm not going to try to do that here. Instead, I am going to share 10 pieces of information that should remain in the back of your head as a manager. They'll help you to navigate the murky waters of management a little more clearly.

1. **Everybody is the star of their own story.**
   Human beings are inwardly focused beasts, and remembering this is essential to being a good boss. In an average conversation people spend 60 per cent of their time talking about themselves. That figure jumps to 80 per cent when the conversation isn't face-to-face. We think about ourselves and talk about ourselves because it feels good. It floods the parts of our brain associated with motivation and reward with neural activity. The people who work for you will take every instruction, interpret every decision and respond to every piece of praise or criticism you deliver as if it were *all about them.* When you're the boss, you're paid to think about the bigger picture. Your team isn't necessarily doing the same.

They're focused on their own job and what they've got going on personally. Keeping this front of mind will help you engage with them in a more effective way.

During my first week in a new management job, I make it a rule to sit down with each member of the team individually and ask how the organisation could be improved and to inquire about any concerns they might have. I focus on the employees as individuals instead of on the business as a whole. I ask them to spill, to run off at the mouth, to tell me everything – from the trivial to the extreme – about what is working for them and what isn't. I never promise to fix everything, and I certainly don't promise a pot of gold at the end of the rainbow. What's important is giving them an opportunity to air their grievances. It's preferable to having those grievances aired repeatedly in private, behind management's back. It also lets team members know that you're on their side, there to help them and, through them, the organisation as a whole. This is critical to building a strong team.

2. **Your team needs to know that you know they're important.**
Part of helping the people who work for you feel valued is showing appreciation. A Templeton Foundation study found that people are less likely to show gratitude in the workplace than anywhere else. Isn't that sad? We spend a third of every weekday at work and we rarely bother to be grateful to the people around us. It's also unproductive because there are huge benefits for employees and leadership when staff members feel properly appreciated. Increased loyalty, productivity, personal satisfaction, lower absenteeism, less stress and better teamwork and retention rates have all been linked to staff who

feel appreciated. It's something that should matter to managers because it makes the business better. That staff members are happy should *also* matter to managers, because not being an arsehole is a smart move. Being an inclusive and supportive manager who cares about her colleagues makes good economic sense, sure, but it also makes good human sense.

The most effective way to help employees understand the importance of their role in the organisation is to show them. Your team members need to understand how *they* contribute to the bigger picture, why their particular contribution is important and valuable. They need to know and believe that without them the company, the department – and you personally – would be worse off. Most importantly, they need to know that *you* know this. The good opinion of the boss is something team members desire. It helps them feel safer and secure in their employment and motivated to do their best. The prospect of being replaceable does not inspire positive behaviour. When your team members understand why their job matters and that you value their individual contribution, they'll likely achieve better results for themselves and the group.

3. **Sometimes your team needs reminding why their jobs matter.** I'm a great believer in the show-don't-tell strategy when it comes to conveying ideas. Show-don't-tell refers to the fact that people are more likely to believe something if they see it in action, rather than if they're just told it is so. It's commonly used in marketing and advertising. When you have lots of people working for you, making sure they feel valued becomes all the more difficult and important. This was the case when I was working as an editor-in-chief. It presented a big challenge,

so I blatantly ripped off reality-television show *Undercover Boss* and recreated it in the office.

The job of site coordinator is one of the most junior positions in an online newsroom. It's also one of the most important. It involves a lot of low-level, repetitive tasks, but when done badly the flow-on effects hurt everyone in the business. The complex juggling act that is a site coordinator role means it is hard to master quickly. It takes a while to get the hang of it. Every four months, I would pretend we had nobody to fill this role for a day and announce to the team that I'd be doing it myself. I didn't have to try very hard to stuff up. My failure was inevitable. The other team members would all have a good laugh before jumping in to save my skin. I'd be the butt of the office's jokes for a solid week afterwards, but the effect was magical. The junior staff members would walk around with this wry smile on their faces. The importance and high degree of difficulty involved in their job had been acknowledged very publicly thanks to my mistakes. Telling the junior staff they were indispensable would have been far less persuasive than them seeing it in action. All the adjectives in the world couldn't convey the message that my own ineptitude did.

4. **How your team likes to be managed might not be the same as how you like to be managed.**
Here's a lesson I learned the hard way. When you're the boss you have to manage people the way they like to be managed, not the way you like to be managed. That sounds rather like an *Alice in Wonderland* riddle, so let me explain. One of the better working relationships of my life began with constant clashes. Remember Lucy, who quit her job to lie in the park and look

at the sky? We met for the first time as colleagues. Lucy and I
liked one another personally, but we couldn't seem to master
our office interactions. As her boss, I tried to show my faith in
her through increased responsibilities and lots of autonomy.
But Lucy would react with panic, not pride. I couldn't for
the life of me work her out – until we both took a workplace
personality test. The test assessed how employees like to be
managed and plotted it on a graph. My line was red and Lucy's
was blue.

If you can imagine a big X – that's how our lines
intersected. Lucy and I were polar opposites when it came
to how we liked to be managed. I work best when I'm given
a goal, a deadline and then left alone to get on with it. Lucy
preferred more detailed directions and the opportunity to
check in regularly to ensure she was on the right track. I wasn't
managing Lucy how she liked to be managed. I was managing
her how I liked to be managed. No wonder we clashed. As the
boss, part of your role is to figure out what your employees'
approach is and how you can use that to help them achieve the
best possible results. You can train a team member to be better
at a task, but their overall approach to work is a fixed part
of their personality. While no personality test alone can (or
should) determine the career trajectory of an employee, they
can be useful tools to decipher why an employee behaves the
way they do.

5. **Your way is not always the best way.**
The best leaders are confident in their abilities but modest
about their potential. They're intellectually humble, which
means they understand the limits of their own knowledge.
Just because you are the boss does not mean you're instantly

expected to be the fount of all knowledge. In fact, you don't want to be. If you were, there would be little left for your team to do. Being humble about what you do and don't know, and being willing to ask for help, are qualities all good bosses possess. Humility doesn't require you to be a pushover. It's more about eliminating intellectual pretentiousness by accepting that you're going to get it wrong sometimes.

Perhaps you've come across someone in the workplace who keeps hiring less-than-impressive people. The 'logic' here might be that they don't want any of their team members to outshine them. The logic is hugely flawed. Surrounding yourself with smart, capable people and being humble enough to listen to them will make you better at your job. A wise lady once told me, 'Hire people who are smarter than you and you'll always shine.' I've always approached recruitment with that principle in mind. Effective leaders are open to the advice of others, and go searching for it when they don't have all the information.

6. **An unpredictable workplace is like doing trapeze without a harness.**

When you're asked to manage people for the first time, you generally have big plans. You think back on all the bad bosses you've had and imagine how much better you'll be. You think of all the great leaders in history and envisage how closely you'll emulate their style. You set out boldly, intending to be remembered as strong, kind, inclusive, brave, innovative, forward-thinking, nurturing, successful, or all of the above. But the single most important thing you can be as a boss is the adjective least likely to cross your mind: predictable. PREDICTABLE! Can I get a 'hells yeah!' for all the predictable bosses out there? Woohoo!

A really great boss is someone who builds structure and provides consistency for the team. This creates a working environment – a *predictable* environment – where people feel safe. In 2015, Google conducted a study of its employees to determine what makes a cohesive and productive team. They discovered that employees work best when they trust their co-workers and managers. That trust is what allows them to take risks, rely on one another and work towards their shared goals. Google's company rules for successful teamwork all emphasise the need for a safe, predictable and structured work environment. Predictability is what provides Google's employees with the security to be able to dream big, try new things and innovate. Predictability is also important so that team members feel safe during tough times, such as during a company restructure or sale.

Predictability and consistency are interlinked. When a boss is consistent in their decision-making, the people who work for them actually have more freedom. The employees know what they can and can't do because there are clear parameters – but within those parameters? They can experiment. If you are consistent in the way you approach decision-making and deal with your team, then they are able to predict your behaviour. Predictability is closely intertwined with fairness and trust. Employees like to know that the boss will respond the same way if the same situation were repeated. When this happens, the workplace is perceived as a fair place, and employees are more likely to trust their boss. A good leader sets clear roles, plans and goals for their team, giving employees a straightforward understanding of what their purpose in the organisation is and what expectations are.

7. **Share the credit but not the blame.**

   When you're the boss, you tend to get more praise from above when things go right. Those higher up the totem pole will credit you with the success of your team. That praise might even come with further opportunities for you. Opportunities like promotion and even public accolades or awards. All of that is very nice. You deserve it and you should enjoy it. After all, you were in charge. But for your employees to be genuinely happy for your success during the good times, they need to know that you will also take the heat for them in the bad times. My advice is to do everything you can to share the credit of a win, and everything you (reasonably) can to take the blame for losses. Building a culture where team members feel safe means they have to know you would take a hypothetical office bullet for them. That you would stand up for them and make sure they weren't reprimanded unless it was genuinely deserved. This is critical for bosses who want to build teams that don't indulge in blame-shifting and in-fighting.

8. **Your team is more than just employees. They're people.**

   Work can be a creative outlet, provide intellectual stimulation and, of course, it's socially important. Most people spend upwards of 90 000 hours at work over the course of their lifetime. Having friends at work boosts morale and employee satisfaction by a whopping 50 per cent. So as a manager, you can never forget that the work environment isn't just about productivity – it has to be fun. As a leader, you have a critical role to play in setting the tone for your team. Some of the happiest days of my life have been spent at work in the company of wonderful colleagues. Much of that was thanks to bosses who encouraged us to play hard as well as work hard.

Looking after the wellbeing of your team extends to what is happening to them outside of work. Being a manager means recognising that your team has pressures external to the workplace and that these can affect their performance on the job. It's important that you build an environment in which these ups and downs are acknowledged, and allowances are made. As the boss, you need to recognise that there will be times when the personal and the professional collide and your employees need a little extra slack, or a little extra support. I once worked in a team that developed a brilliant tradition of going to play laser tag whenever someone had their heart broken. We were a small, close-knit bunch, and it was our way of showing whoever was struggling personally that their colleagues cared. There is nothing quite like shooting your workmates in the dark with lasers to help you forget romantic tribulations.

An aside: this fun stuff is not something you can opt out of as the boss. The fun isn't fun for the sake of it. It's critical team-building activity and that means you *have* to be a part of it. As leaders, our time is the most valuable thing we can give our employees because we can never get it back. It's better than money. Better than awards. Better than a promotion or a car space. You can't skimp on camaraderie.

9. **Don't take on more than your fair share of emotional labour.** It can be easy to fall into the trap of always being the one to deal with employees' emotional stuff simply because you're a woman. Emotional labour has previously been considered as confined to the private domain. It is the work of remembering birthdays, worrying about how a child is fitting in at school, taking the time to drop in on an elderly neighbour or generally

managing the emotions of others. But emotional labour is actually just as relevant in the workplace. And like they do at home, research shows that women tend to shoulder a disproportionate amount of emotional labour at work. Women are more likely to be lending a sympathetic ear to unhappy employees, to be organising social events, or tolerating an egotistical, erratic boss.

Women managers are assumed to be more emotionally available, as though their time and dedication to helping others process their feelings is unlimited. The consensus is that 'women are just better at that stuff', and perhaps some are. But being emotionally aware and understanding is a skill required of all managers. You should absolutely do your bit; however, it shouldn't feel like you have to pick up the slack for other, less emotionally supportive managers. Emotional labour can be exhausting. If you're carrying more than your fair share it can detract from your other responsibilities.

My experience as a boss and a woman is that employees have greater expectations of your emotional availability. They want and anticipate more support from you than they would a man in the same position. The reverse is also true. Women bosses often struggle to balance their desire to support employees personally with their responsibility as a manager. When you're the boss, you need to remember that having a relationship of trust with each of your team members is more important than having a friendship. Focus on building trust, not finding a buddy, among the people who work for you. Don't risk emotional burnout. It's not practical or appropriate that you help the same employee sort through the same emotional baggage time and time again. No matter how much

you want to be their shoulder to cry on, you need to know
when you're giving them that shoulder a little too often.
That's what an employee's friends and family are for.
You're the boss. It's up to you to set the boundaries.

10. **Use your power to advocate for those without it.**
Being a manager of any kind comes with a greater degree of
power and influence. It also comes with a responsibility to
advocate for those who don't share that same power or who
face systemic barriers to ever gaining it. Acknowledge that your
experience of the workplace won't be the same as everyone
else's. As a woman you will probably have faced gender bias
at work, but may have been immune from other kinds of
discrimination. For example, you might have benefited
from the privilege that comes with being white, or straight,
or cisgender, or financially independent, or able-bodied or
highly educated in ways that others haven't. Recognise that
your colleagues will likely have had negative interactions with
the workplace that you may not be familiar with. Be open-
minded and take the time to understand experiences that
are not your own. Make sure that your team members know
you're an ally, that you're someone who has their welfare and
best interests at heart. Then use your power and influence to
advocate for a fairer, more equitable and inclusive workplace
for everyone – not just the people who are exactly like you.
This is what sets a leader apart from a manager, and a person
of integrity apart in an unjust world.

EXHAUSTION AND BURNOUT

Because using your time well can make more of it.

I can't remember the last time I was woken by something other than the sound of my son crying. But this time it's clearly an alarm. The brightness on my iPhone is set a little too high for comfort, so I keep one eye closed and adjust the other to the narrowest of squints. A low, whispered moan escapes my throat as I take in the hour: it's 4.35 a.m. I've got 40 minutes to get ready. Standing in the shower, I fiddle with the knobs, trying to find the elusive perfect temperature that will gently guide me to wakefulness. It's my first day back at work after maternity leave, and every minute of my morning is scheduled and accounted for as though it were a military operation. *The GHD has landed. Milk encroachment may commence. Taxi en route, GO GO GO.*

Little do I know that in four minutes everything will go to shit. Literally.

My 15-week-old son starts howling. He's managed one of those mysterious, defy-the-laws-of-physics poos that explodes out of the nappy and reaches all the way up his back. He's uncomfortable. He's smelly. He wants to be fed. I'm standing in the door of his room, naked, with water dripping from the ends of my wet hair and milk spraying out at a weird right angle from my left nipple. It dawns on me that travelling interstate for work on my first day back may have been a bad idea. I should have pushed past my guilt and insisted on another week's leave. It's too late now. By some miracle, 20 minutes later we are hurtling down the stairs to get in the taxi. I rush past the pram in the foyer of our apartment building and see a note taped to the hood. Why, oh why, oh why do I pick up that note? What good can come from picking up that note?

This is a communal area and should be kept clear.
Please find an alternative parking space for your pram.

I shove the piece of paper in my pocket and, swallowing down my hurt, clamber into the cab. Forty minutes after that we're still on the highway, traffic is bumper to bumper, and there is no way I am going to make this plane. I'm trying not to panic. I'm planning the kind of emotional manipulation I'll need to employ to convince the airline staff to let me on the flight. By the time we pull up at the terminal, my breathing has slowed and I'm embracing a 'What will be, will be' mantra in my head. *What will be will be. What will be will be.* 'That's $59.40, love,' says the driver. *What will be will be. What will* — I forgot my wallet. I can see it in my mind's eye on the top right corner of the kitchen table. Bright-pink, gold embossing, unmissable and yet somehow . . . 'Fuck,' I mutter.

Some rapid-fire phone calls save the day and a colleague who is departing from Melbourne on a different flight rushes to the curb less than 10 minutes later. She pays for my cab before sprinting back to her gate. My sobbing-first-time-mother routine works and soon I am sitting down with two boarding passes and a cup of tea that will never be drunk. There is a grizzly baby in my arms, spit-up on my clothes and breathing deeply is doing nothing to calm my rapid pulse rate.

Welcome to the jungle, I think to myself.

What happens when you work all the time . . .

That shocking morning aside, work-life balance wasn't something I fought to maintain when I became a parent. It was something I *discovered* when I became a parent. For the first time in my adult life, work was no longer my single overarching priority. Prior to that, working at one inch away from breaking point had been my status symbol. It gave me a perverted sense of pride that I could sustain working that way and others couldn't. I'd hurry through the city at lunchtime, firing off emails on my phone, annoyed by the interruption of having to buy my mum a birthday present. If I bumped into an old friend, they'd ask, 'How are you?' I would reply, 'Busy, always busy,' or sometimes, 'Crazy busy!' It was my coded way of saying, 'I don't really have time to talk to you' and also 'I am very important'. Busy was my badge of honour, and it was only when I stopped working 24/7 that I realised it wasn't doing me any good.

I was lonely. Despite being constantly surrounded by people I rarely made space in my life for those I didn't work with. My family, my husband and my friends outside of work had been neglected for a long, long time. It had an impact on them, but it also had an impact on me. I didn't have the time or space to be a particularly good friend. Remember when you were little and your parents would tell you that it's far nicer to give a gift than receive it? Well, I'd spent my working life receiving gifts. I was the one everyone helped out and was generous towards because I was always *just so busy.*

While I was grateful for the support, I missed out on the opportunity to help in return. I didn't give myself space to *be* the good friend. I just reaped the benefits of having good friends. I was never the one who took the bins out for an elderly neighbour, or offered to babysit a cousin's children. I was the worse off for it.

I was boring. By working all the time, I resigned myself to being a not particularly interesting person. My life was dictated by my work and I failed to prioritise other things I liked to do. I remember travelling to a regional centre when I was working in politics. A local resident asked what my hobbies were. She was friendly and kind and trying to strike up conversation with a tired-looking 20-something in a crumpled blue suit. I looked around awkwardly before responding that I didn't have any. Eating, sleeping and politics was all I ever did.

I was less effective. My unrelenting commitment to work meant that eventually I became less effective, not more. In the year before I went on maternity leave my work life was relentless and reactive. It was ruled by the vibration of my phone, the ping of our internal messaging system and incessant text-message exchanges with my boss. What was urgent came first, and because there was always something urgent I rarely got to what came second. I had no time to *really* think, to reflect, to innovate and to be creative. The best ideas come when you have space to develop them, and I'd eliminated every inch of empty brain space by filling it with my busyness.

I was unappreciated. When you only ever work at 110 per cent, your efforts and energy become unremarkable. They're not appreciated in the way that they once were. Going above and beyond in my job had stopped being worthy of note or thanks. It was assumed. Expected. Human resources expert Liz Ryan describes it like this:

You Turn Into Wallpaper. When you are always at work or always reachable outside of work, your incredible effort stops being exceptional. Your personal time devoted to work is taken for granted at that point. Everybody you work with is used to seeing you killing yourself for the job, and they don't think about it anymore.

Once I was able to find some semblance of balance between freelance work, writing, my family and my friends, I became a happier person. I also found that my creativity returned, with newfound freedom giving me space to imagine and problem-solve in original ways. While I'm someone who finds incredible fulfilment through paid work, work alone isn't enough. I wish I had realised that before starting a family.

There is a myth that says only parents need help finding time for life outside of work. It's because when we talk about work-life balance, we really mean work-parenting balance. That's a shame, because every working person needs time for the personal as well as the professional. Every human being requires more than one activity to occupy them, more than one source of fulfilment and happiness. Whether you have children or not, work shouldn't be the only thing that matters to you. Focusing on work to the exclusion of your romantic life, your family, your friendships, altruism, sport, music, literature, travel, art, faith – whatever it is that makes you happy – is a mistake. Yet with the way our world is evolving, finding time for the personally pleasurable is harder than ever before.

So what do we do about it?

Well, as employees we must genuinely believe that leading varied, free and full lives actually makes us better at work. Then we have to enact that in our own lives. And as employers we need to put that same belief into practice, valuing the personal lives of all people who work for us. Not just the parents.

The most important career decision you'll ever make

The take-out message of Sheryl Sandberg's career manifesto was that women should 'lean in' to their careers. But, for me, there was a far more valuable piece of advice in her book. One that often gets overlooked. It's a recommendation around how the personal and the professional merge. Sandberg says:

> I truly believe that the single most important career decision that a woman makes is whether she will have a life partner and who that partner is. I do not know of one woman in a leadership position whose life partner is not fully – and I mean fully – supportive of her career.

Sandberg was spot on. Reading this passage made the news of her husband Dave Goldberg's death in 2015 all the more heartbreaking. Sandberg's chosen partner was more than the father of her children and the love of her life. He was her greatest cheerleader and supporter. The immense success Sandberg has achieved would not have been possible without her choice of partner. Too often we pretend that love and work are entirely separate spheres of our lives. Yet they're as dependent on one another as Jenga blocks in a tower.

There are a whole lot of good things about falling in love. For more detail, see Shakespeare's sonnets or Michael Bublé's greatest hits – I'm going to leave the pretty platitudes to them. What I want to say about love is directly related to your career, and it is this:

the best thing about choosing to share your life with someone is becoming a team. This is closely followed by having someone to turn the light off when you've been in bed reading, it's very cold and you don't want to make the mad semi-nude dash across the room. Being a team means you're no longer alone in the big bad world, fighting solo battles and wielding a single sword. In the career context, you've got someone who is on your side, and who desires your success and achievement for no other reason than they love you and want you to be happy.

Of course, love is a two-way career partnership. It means no longer making decisions that benefit only you. Relationships require compromise, including about competing work priorities. It may be that one party is offered a promotion with unusual working hours that will limit time spent together. Or one of you might be given an opportunity that requires moving interstate or abroad. Throw children into the mix, and a whole host of new challenges arise. Who will stay home with the baby during the early months when their needs are unrelenting and constant? Who will skip work and stay home if a child is sick and can't go to childcare? Who will do the school pick-up or deposit various children at extracurricular activities, condemning themselves to an afternoon of free taxi services? When you're a couple, you think about what is best for the team rather than what is best for the individual. And, inevitably, this will at some point lead to clashes.

For heterosexual couples, making the decision that is best for the team usually favours the career of the man. Why? Women earn less money than men. The gender pay gap means the bloke's salary is usually a more important part of the family budget. I've explained earlier that this causes families tend to 'weigh up' the cost of childcare against the potential salary of the mother.

Her earnings are seen as less valuable because they come at a 'cost' of her not being home with children. But really we should be weighing up the cost of childcare against *both* parents returning to work. While 60 per cent of Australian fathers have a stay-at-home wife, less than four per cent of women have a partner who is the primary carer of their children. Even when a mother is working, the responsibility for childcare arrangements is far more likely to fall to her. In *The Wife Drought*, Annabel Crabb notes one example where 57 per cent of senior women business leaders identified themselves as being the decision-maker on childcare arrangements, compared with only one per cent of senior men.

I'm doing that thing where I depress you again, aren't I? Let's talk solutions instead of problems. Throughout your career the support of a partner will often be the difference between your moving forward or standing still. While that might come down to choices you make together at the time, there is one thing you can do *now* to increase your chances of optimising your career.

Choose. The. Right. Partner.

Choosing to spend your life with someone shouldn't just involve a conversation about where you will honeymoon. It should involve conversations about your working lives and how you plan to make decisions when your interests are in conflict. Having a partner who supports you means someone who recognises the benefits of you having a challenging and fulfilling career that can't be expressed in dollars. Your partner should be someone who appreciates your commitment to work and how it benefits you as a human being, not only as an earner. Your partner should be someone who treats your time with respect and supports you as an equal. And you owe them the same in return.

How to make more time (when there is none)

We've established how important it is to regulate your professional life in order for the personal stuff to thrive. Equally, we've established how your personal life is essential to success at work. This neat equation doesn't function unless you've got the time and space to dedicate to both. For many of us, the pressures of our professional lives are so great that there is no room for anything else. It's the reason that an entire self-help book genre is dedicated to helping people squash more stuff into the same amount of time. My experience is that those theories and magic formulas don't achieve an awful lot. Time management and efficiency are buzzwords that every boss likes to throw around, while most employees have no idea how to actually make them happen.

I used to work with a woman called Monique whose work ethic was something to behold. A former Australian basketballer, she used to make us do squats during morning meetings. She was wacky in the best possible sense of the word, and obsessed with discovering the 'secret' to efficiency. Each day Monique arrived at the office with a new time-management hack that she was convinced would revolutionise her life. One week she only wore black skivvies and jeans like Steve Jobs to eliminate energy-consuming clothing choices from her mornings. For a while she worked with white noise playing in her headphones to improve concentration. On one occasion, she demanded I show her, step-by-step, how I dealt with my emails, while she took compulsive notes.

As a manager I regularly fielded questions about how to be more efficient. Lots of people, especially high-achievers like Monique, want to improve their time management. They want to know how much time and focus each task should receive, and then jump back and forth from one to the next, struggling to prioritise. Rarely does anyone spend much time thinking about the inverse. Rarely do we think about *which hours and minutes* should be awarded to which tasks. Instead of focusing on time management, it can actually be more helpful to focus on energy management. Understanding how your personal energy levels fluctuate through the day can make you more productive.

Let me use myself as an example. My standard freelance work pattern originally looked something like this: wake up, help get my son ready for childcare, and then spend an hour or two having a slow breakfast and several coffees while working my way through emails. All the administrative stuff would be out of the way by 10.30 a.m., when I'd normally schedule meetings. At 3 p.m. I would do my most important work, writing this book or filing an article for publication, or working on a strategy document. I'd break at 5.30 p.m. to collect my son, get him fed, bathed and to bed. Then my husband would arrive home, we'd eat together, watch an hour or so of television and then I'd pop open my laptop and do another hour of work on whatever I'd been writing.

The problem with this schedule is that my most intellectually demanding tasks weren't aligned with my most productive hours. I am the definition of a morning person. Not in the 'I get up at 5.30 to salute the sun, run a half-marathon and drink a green smoothie' kind of way. My brain is simply at its best earlier in the day. It starts to slow around 4 p.m. and stops working completely around 10 p.m. The arrangement of my freelance days meant I was doing the tasks that required the most mental energy when I was least equipped for them. So I started organising my day differently. I now begin work earlier, leaving the morning childcare duties in the capable hands of my husband. I begin with the biggest, most daunting piece of work, and schedule meetings for the afternoons, when the stimulation of fresh company and conversation ensures I avoid a 3 p.m. slump. The necessary but dull administrative work waits until the evening, when my brain can simultaneously juggle emails and the hilarity of *The Wrong Girl*.

I. Get. So. Much. More. Done.

Conserving mental energy for use when it's most needed is a strategy that can be helpful beyond the 24-hour cycle. You might be someone who experiences a Wednesday hump, or you may have an emotionally draining dinner with your in-laws scheduled on Mondays that makes Tuesdays a bit slow. Thinking about your productivity over the course of a week allows you to be more realistic. We all have off days occasionally. If you think about your to-do list in terms of a 168-hour week, rather than a 24-hour day, it will feel a lot more manageable. Your energy may also change depending on the nature of your work in a particular week. Scheduling a set period of time in advance, say three hours on Thursday morning, to attack an intellectually daunting task can work well. It allows you to gear up and build energy and anticipation as you move towards your 'start' time, the same way an athlete does before a big race.

This method is popular at tech giant and famously awesome-place-to-work Google, where employees are encouraged to set 'Make Time'. This refers to a scheduled half-day of work when a specific important task will be completed, rather than simply planning to 'do it this week'. This approach results in a 91 per cent completion rate, compared with a 29 per cent completion rate for tasks that are not given a specific predetermined time. It makes sense. We make plans for how we eat, when we exercise and to ensure we get enough sleep, all of which are about maximising energy. Yet when it comes to the *expenditure* of that energy, we don't necessarily make sensible choices. By having a plan for energy expenditure we automatically make more time for ourselves.

Stop panicking. Start prioritising.

If there were a single trait I could gift every employee it would be the ability to prioritise. Making good decisions about what deserves your attention and what doesn't is crucial. Less experienced employees tend to find prioritising really hard. That's because at school or TAFE, during an apprenticeship or at university, someone else has been doing the prioritising on their behalf. Assignments, exams, class schedules and the rest provide a comforting, predictable structure for students. The workplace tends to be less rigid. There is more autonomy and flexibility, deadlines are more fluid, and priorities more likely to compete and conflict. It causes many employees to fall down. So next time you feel overwhelmed by your entirely urgent, ever-growing to-do list, try this four-step approach:

1. **Make like Nelly Furtado and take a bird's-eye view.**
   The day-to-day grind of work makes us lose sight of the bigger picture. Often we get so bogged down in the task immediately in front of us that faster, more efficient methods of moving forward aren't visible. The same goes for your overall career path and goals. You get so focused on what you're doing this hour, this day, this week, that you can get to the end of the year and be confused about why you did it all in the first place. If that sounds familiar, then you need to make 'like a bird'. (It is mandatory that you sing the previous phrase. Please go back and comply if you failed me the first time.) Rise above what's going on right this minute and consider the whole picture. When you're lost in the middle of a foreign city,

every building and street starts to look the same, and finding your way becomes impossible. A map – or a birds'-eye view – means alternative paths to the same destination become apparent. Think about what your eventual goal is and re-order your priorities towards that specific outcome.

2. **Write down your priorities and read them like a menu.**
When you have a whole bunch of important tasks at once, it can create stress and weaken your confidence. Particularly if your manager is breathing down your neck and expecting you to deliver multiple projects simultaneously. But having multiple priorities is actually a good thing – really. It forces you to make choices. You have to consider the merits of pursuing each priority in that particular moment and make a decision about what deserves to come first.

Comparing priorities, weighing up and making choices (often several times over) is a little like reading a menu at a restaurant. Over time, you may end up eating lots of dishes you like, but on each occasion you've only got so much stomach space. You have to pick a combination of dishes that will satisfy you on that particular day. That same decision-making process applies when you're comparing and ranking your priorities. While it can be uncomfortable, it will also be the making of you. The higher you climb in your career, the greater the consequences of each prioritisation you make at work. You may as well get good at it now. And start eating.

3. **Make a plan (because there is nothing I love more than a plan).**
I read a lot of *Famous Five* as a kid, and if there's one thing I learned from those 21 children's adventure novels it's this: you feel better once you have a plan, even if it isn't a very good one. Whenever the Five would get into a pickle (that's Enid

Blyton's awfully British way of saying clusterfuck) they'd sit down together and come up with a plan. Inevitably someone would say, 'Well, it's the best plan we've got,' admitting its possible faults, but the kids always seemed comforted to have it nonetheless. Having a plan is like a hug from your mum. It doesn't necessarily fix the problem, but you feel *so much better*. The problem-solving process is less daunting and everything seems more achievable once you've gone through the mental process of planning.

So after you've looked at your priorities like a bird, written them down and read them like a menu, make a plan to move forward. It will be an imperfect plan. When you have conflicting priorities, there is rarely a single silver bullet. Yet making a plan, based on the information you have at the time and the assessment you've already done, will always lead to a better outcome than no plan. Make your plan. Pursue it. Be ready to come back and reassess it, if required. If something changes, make a new one.

4. **Remember the cost of doing anything is *not* doing something else.**

Having too many priorities can be the result of taking too much on. This is a mistake many women make when they're starting out, and I include myself in that group. Career coach Jenn DeWall warns that women in the early stages of their careers are prone to saying yes to every project that comes their way. She cautions against the allure of this. It makes you less likely to stand out in one particular area. You end up doing a decent job many times over instead of being brilliant at just one or two things. By contrast, DeWall says men typically choose fewer but more highly visible projects. This means their efforts are more focused and their wins more noticeable.

When optional opportunities come your way at work, take the time to really consider them. Ask whether or not they'll help you meet your eventual goal, or if they're a side project you don't need to take on right now. Be careful not to say yes only because you want to please other people, or because you think it's expected of you. Say yes to a new project because it will further your career, challenge your mind or bring you happiness. Remember that you only have 168 hours in each week of your life. Every hour you devote to one thing is an hour you *could* have devoted to something else.

When working for a workaholic becomes unworkable

Sometimes having an achievement-focused boss can be really motivating. And sometimes bosses have entirely unrealistic and impossible expectations. I've had managers who fell into both categories, and also managers who moved *between* those categories. There is no question that a workaholic boss can make your life really hard. They might expect 24/7 responsiveness and constant face time, or will load you up with a ridiculous amount of work. Workaholic bosses rarely provide the support needed to help you achieve your own work-life balance. This reduces your productivity and leaves you at risk of burning out. If you have a boss who consistently fails to respect your time outside of the workplace, then 'pushing through' is rarely the best strategy. You need to take action to preserve the working relationship, the job and your own sanity.

Begin by considering your boss's perspective. They may be completely oblivious to how unrealistic and intrusive their demands are. If this is the case, then talk to them about it. Before you do this, make sure you're really clear on exactly what is frustrating you and what needs to change. You need to be able to articulate what the problem is in a precise way. There is no use going into your boss's office and complaining that they're generally making your life miserable. Saying 'I've just got too much work' is similarly unhelpful. You need to identify the specific problem(s) and provide specific solutions to those problems. Ask yourself: What *in particular* is making me crazy? What *practical changes* could actually improve the situation?

Offering an alternative way of doing things really helps. Linda A. Hill, professor at Harvard Business School, suggests that in order to make a potentially uncomfortable conversation with your boss easier, you need to focus on how they can help *you* to be better at your job. She advises setting clear boundaries. These boundaries should be framed as conditions for success, and not as rules to stop the boss being *awful*. Talk to your boss about how you work best and when you're at your most productive. Frame the conversation in terms of how much you want to succeed, how much you want to deliver for them. Explain why the status quo is making it impossible for you to do a good job.

I once had an issue with a manager who was hugely demanding outside of regular business hours. The situation was becoming unworkable. I felt resentful and unappreciated, and my manager was frustrated that I wasn't as responsive as she expected me to be. The trigger point for our disagreements came daily at around 8.30 p.m. This was when I used to spend time with my then boyfriend and wanted space from my work. For my manager – who was a busy working mum – this was the most convenient time because she'd been offline with her kids for the previous six hours and they were finally in bed. Once we actually talked about our different daily patterns, we were able to find common ground and restructure the way we communicated.

Burn. Out.

It's day 17 of the 2010 federal election campaign. That means I haven't slept in my own bed for over three weeks and probably won't for another three. I'm homesick and cranky. Weekends have been relegated to the stuff of dreams. Most evenings I receive an update from campaign headquarters, confirming the minister's itinerary for the next 48 hours. It almost always involves getting on a plane. There was one day when my feet touched the ground in four separate states over a 24-hour period. That night I fell asleep with my head on a hotel-room desk in Townsville and woke up with ink marks down the right side of my face. I have the permanent sensation of a lump in my throat, like I've swallowed a slightly-too-big potato chip. I'm worried it's cancer. Google says it's probably cancer. I'll learn once the campaign is finished that it's a symptom of anxiety. And while the election campaign period had a clear end date, my anxiety didn't. It's still with me today.

Large employers often have entire departments devoted to 'human resources'. This terminology that makes me uncomfortable because what do we do with resources? We use them up. We use them until they're completely depleted. It's an approach that far too many employers take towards their staff, and increasingly employees have it about themselves as well. There is an assumption that you work until you break and that work never ends. Anecdotally, I've noticed a tendency among women friends to keep loading more and more and more onto their plate. They manage to fit 26 hours' worth of work into every 24 by sacrificing their sleep and their self-care. In their efforts to please others and not let anyone down – including their families who rely on them financially – they lose sight of what is physically, mentally and emotionally sustainable. None of us can work at a frenetic pace forever. At some point something has got to give.

Sometimes we develop work patterns that are unsustainable and sometimes we have them thrust upon us by our employers. More than 50 per cent of Australian employees report that their current workplace isn't mentally 'healthy'. One in five people have taken at least one day off in the past 12 months because they were mentally unwell. The minutiae of what work pressures are fair and reasonable and what aren't are beyond the scope of this book. However, if you're looking for more information, the Fair Work Ombudsman, Heads Up, the Mentally Healthy Workplace Alliance or your union are good places to start. Those organisations will help you determine if what's being expected of you at work is actually appropriate. If it's not, there are avenues to enforce your rights to a fair workload and reasonable hours. If your workplace's arrangements are appropriate but you're still struggling to cope, then please don't push through in fear and silence. There are people who want to and can help you.

Work can affect our mental health in a myriad of ways, and at its most extreme can cause us to fizzle and even burn out. Psychologist David W. Ballard describes burnout as 'an extended period of time where someone experiences exhaustion and a lack of interest in things, resulting in a decline in their job performance' – and often their personal life. Burnout has been observed at higher rates among young women, and if you're working multiple jobs to make ends meet you're also at risk. You may have a friend or colleague who has experienced it. Burnout is caused when the body and mind have been under chronic stress, and when you've neglected both your physical and mental health by working constantly. The demands on your physical and mental resources become so great that you are no longer able to process them. You can also become apathetic about that job you started off wanting to work so hard at. When left unchecked, burnout can have a significant effect on your health, mental wellbeing, relationships and career.

There are several warning signs that may indicate you are headed for a burnout. The most prominent is chronic exhaustion – mental, physical or emotional. You feel as though you are 'completely spent' and have no capacity to exert energy for things you once enjoyed. With a lack of energy comes lack of motivation. It becomes more and more difficult to drag yourself out of bed, and your work ethic begins to disappear. You may feel as though nothing you do is making any difference. Frustration, cynicism and negativity are all common signs of impending burnout. Burnout can also have a real impact on your cognitive abilities. You may become unable to focus on things or be in a near constant 'fight or flight' state due to chronic stress. Your memory can also be affected. You might start to isolate yourself and become detached from others or your environment.

If this sounds like you, then you should seek medical help. The same advice applies if you're feeling consistently anxious, panicked or depressed about work. Your GP can provide you with a mental health plan and may refer you to a psychologist. It's all too easy for us to treat physical illness as a big deal and dismiss the mental stuff. Please don't fall victim to this myth. Don't assume that your symptoms are insignificant simply because they're in your head. After getting some assistance, you may be surprised by how quickly the true cause of your symptoms becomes clear. Perhaps you're in the wrong job and need to plan an exit strategy. Perhaps there are pressures in other parts of your life that are affecting you at work. Perhaps medication, or a change in diet or lifestyle, might help ease your anxiety or depression. Perhaps your employer is actually behaving inappropriately and unfairly. Perhaps you just need to talk and to have someone who gets it listen.

A psychologist will support you to work through all of that. If necessary they can also make a plan for speaking to your employer about what they can do to help as well. When I was managing a large team, we had several contingencies and adapted work arrangements in place for employees with mental health challenges. It's an entirely normal and reasonable thing for you to request. Mental health matters. It deserves attention from you, understanding from your employer and expertise from your medical professional.

SEXISM AND SEXUAL HARASSMENT

Because this stuff deserves to be taken seriously.

I'm at a hotel bar in Perth with a dozen or so colleagues. Everyone is drunk. It's after 11 at night. We have an early start in the morning, but that doesn't seem to bother anyone awfully much. The more senior men in our group occupy the armchairs; dark wood and faded velvet upholstery that once would have passed for red. Their bodies reflect their status – stretched out, feet crossed lazily at the ankles and hands clasped behind the head when not cupped around a whisky glass. The more junior guys are on stools hastily grabbed from the bar, pushed into the circle so as not to miss the action. There are only two other women, neither of whom I know very well. We're seated together on a long couch, sitting primly with our knees together. Not that there is any real alternative when wearing a skirt suit. The conversation hums along, punctuated by the occasional burst of laughter, happy as a Hyundai Excel in third gear.

The man who has been sitting on my left stands to make his goodbyes. He's a married father with teenage kids. We've been chatting for much of the night. The way he talks about economics reminds me of my dad holding court at the breakfast table back when I was at school, when arguing was a method of preparing me for an exam. His questions are confrontational, but his tone is warm and encouraging. Oozing with charm, my new friend makes a point of singling out everyone in the group for individual mention as he departs. They all feel special. He's an important guy. Being recognised by him makes them feel important, too.

As he walks off I realise he's left his hotel room key on the table in front of me. I jump up and call out his name, waving the plastic card in the air. 'Forgetting something?' I ask. He walks slowly and deliberately back towards us. He comes right up close beside me to collect the card. His fingers clasp unnecessarily around mine as he leans in, face inches from my own. 'You're mouth-wateringly naïve,' he says. 'That was *meant* for you.' He speaks in an exaggerated faux whisper. The whole group can hear him and that's exactly what he wants.

Everyone is looking at us. Everyone laughs. I am mortified.

A brief (and yucky) history of sexism in Australia

Documented sexism in Australia dates back to colonisation, and quite possibly before. Between 1788 and 1830, approximately 55 000 men convicts were sent to serve their sentences in the new British colony. Eight thousand five hundred women prisoners accompanied them, with dual roles of serving life sentences and populating the new colony. By the middle of the nineteenth century, white men still vastly outnumbered white women in Australia. Author and political commentator George Megalogenis suggests this gender imbalance – which continued for decades – was an initial contributor to Australia's blokey culture. At that time few women were employed outside of the home. Only a small minority had access to further education. Women who did work were treated appallingly and were mainly employed in so-called 'female factories', which were a combination of workhouses, prisons and maternity wards.

Demand for women's equality grew over time, as sisters decided that having 11 babies, then dying in childbirth wasn't the most fulfilling path for everyone. The first women workers' riot occurred at the Parramatta Female Factory in 1827. Women protested against the working conditions and the fact they'd been deprived of sufficient food. A 'working woman' was about as low as you could fall in society at the time. After all, you only worked if you were husbandless and therefore worthless. This was seen as reason enough to treat working women appallingly.

The Australian Suffrage Society was formed in 1884. If you need a mental picture of the brilliant women who campaigned for your right to vote, think Mrs Banks in *Mary Poppins* but recast as a bushranger's wife with an Aussie twang. White women were given the vote in 1902. Indigenous women weren't extended those same rights until 1962. With each hurdle jumped, however, women were exposed to more instances of sexism. The more they worked, the higher they climbed, the broader their reach – the more opportunities for sexist behaviour and treatment arose. Early women politicians all ran as independents rather than as representatives of political parties. Why? Neither side of politics would endorse or support a woman's candidacy.

The world wars increased autonomy and working rights for women, but it wasn't until the 1960s that more meaningful cultural shifts began to occur. The contraceptive pill arrived in Australia in 1961, a Herculean step forward for working women as it gave them control over the size and timing of their family.

Women who worked outside the home slowly began to gain social acceptance. The determination of the Equal Pay case of 1969 meant that – at least in theory – women were entitled to receive the same pay as men for the same work. And in 1983, Australia signed the United Nations Convention on the Elimination of All Forms of Discrimination Against Women. This treaty is enshrined in Australian law too in the form of the Sex Discrimination Act 1984. It is illegal to 'discriminate against someone on the basis of gender, sexuality, marital status, family responsibilities or because they are pregnant'.

We've come an awfully long way. Legally, women's position in Australian society is drawing ever closer to genuine equality. However, the law alone can't prevent the sort of sexist behaviour that happens in Australian workplaces day-to-day. This is the stuff that sneaks in under the radar, the stuff that isn't reported, the stuff that women know is wrong but don't feel they should 'make a fuss' over. Sometimes it is wrongdoing that's so subtle you don't even realise it's sexist in the moment it's happening.

Would you recognise sexism if it danced around in front of you wearing a funny hat?

I settle into my seat for the first night of the Melbourne Writers Festival. One of my favourite Australian authors, Maxine Beneba Clarke, is giving the opening address. I'm pretty excited for what's to come, fidgeting with anticipation like a toddler before a Wiggles concert. I smile when a colleague from the media industry claims the spot behind me. We exchange pleasantries, remark on the cold weather and discuss the political issues of the day. He's an older gentleman and jokes about having finally mastered the art of Twitter so he can follow both Maxine and myself. He likes reading my observations on family life as well as politics, he tells me. 'Where's little Rafi tonight?' my companion inquires and I reply that my son is with his father. 'Lucky man, your husband!' he winks at me.

I smile back. He's trying to be kind, I tell myself.

As the welcome to country gets underway, the gentleman impolitely starts speaking again. I give him a 'time to shut up now' glare, but he can't help it. He has to share the tremendously *funny* joke he's thought up. With laughter bubbling in his throat, he picks up where he left off: 'He won't want to leave you – not even for all those virgins in heaven!'

We both turn out attention back to the stage, me with a meme-worthy confused face. I'm thrown by the bizarre comment. Slowly, I put the pieces together. The gentleman was talking about my husband. He must have assumed that my Muslim name meant my husband was Muslim and so trotted out a clichéd stereotype about what he presumed our beliefs were. This bloke who I barely know, who I'd only ever spoken to before as an industry associate, was commenting quite specifically on my private life – and, by implication, my sex life. Gross.

There were two 'isms' at play on the night we listened to Maxine painting pictures of pain and strength with her words. She told stories of childhood racism and not quite realising the truth of what was going on because she wanted to believe the best of people. She spoke powerfully about standing up to prejudice and having the courage to name it for what it is, to call it out. I hung my head with shame because I was not as brave as her.

Modern sexism can sometimes be hard to identify. It wreaks havoc while going unrecognised, including by those who are victims of it. During your working life, sexism will show up in countless different costumes. Sometimes it's mixed up with other biases and concealed all the more. Sometimes it's in the form of blatant and illegal sexual harassment. Sometimes it's unspoken expectations about how women should and shouldn't behave. Sometimes it masquerades as a joke or a double entendre. Sometimes it's a blatant and insulting stereotype. Sometimes it's a double standard. And, like the cast of a Shakespearean comedy, we all fall victim to sexism's trickery. We fail to notice that it's the same shit every time, just dressed up as something else.

Journalist Karen Middleton wrote a column detailing many instances of sexual harassment she'd experienced while working in the media. She was overwhelmed by the enormous response. Men colleagues and friends approached her, shocked and unsettled by the stories she'd told. What they didn't realise is that Middleton's stories were only remarkable in their ordinariness. Women live these stories daily. Men tend not to notice sexism unless it is literally standing in front of them screaming at the top of its lungs. In fact, research shows most men believe the obstacles that once made it difficult for women to get ahead at work have been eliminated. Men make comparisons between today and 50 years ago, and think things look pretty good for women. If they don't *personally* experience anything to counter this view, they assume it to be correct.

What's more surprising is that women can fail to identify sexism too. This is the case even for overt forms of workplace sexism, like illegal sexual harassment. Michelle Ruiz and Lauren Ahn conducted an extensive survey for *Cosmopolitan* magazine in 2015 where they asked women if they'd been sexually harassed at work. Sixteen per cent responded that they had. When the questionnaire probed more deeply, it turned out that the *actual* percentage was at least five times that. Eighty-one per cent had experienced some sort of verbal harassment, including inappropriate comments or sexually suggestive jokes. Forty-four per cent had been victims of unwanted physical contact or sexual advances. Twenty-five per cent had received unprompted lewd texts or emails from colleagues. Of all the women who had experienced some form of harassment, a whopping 71 per cent never reported what happened to them. The Sex Discrimination Act 1984 defines it as 'an unwelcome sexual advance, or an unwelcome request for sexual favours, to the person harassed, or engages in other unwelcome conduct of a sexual nature in relation to the person harassed'. These include 'making a statement of a sexual nature to a person, or in the presence of a person, whether the statement is made orally or in writing'. That means every single instance described in the *Cosmopolitan* survey could potentially meet the legal definition of sexual harassment. Yet barely a handful of women recognised the behaviour for what it was: against the law.

Women (who want to get ahead) don't tell.

Many women acknowledge the difficult, embarrassing or unfair situations we experience personally, but don't draw a link with gender. When something awful happens at work – like what's described in *Cosmopolitan*'s survey – we focus on our own behaviour instead of the perpetrators'. We look inwards and blame ourselves. We worry that we acted in an overly flirtatious way. We wonder if we're being naïve. We question whether we somehow invited it. Recognition that the inappropriate behaviour was motivated by sexism often doesn't come until later. It's only once time and the immediacy of our emotional response passes that we can stand back and say, 'Ah yes, THAT was sexist. THAT was sexual harassment. THAT was not okay.' By then the moment is long gone. People have moved on, workplaces have restructured and there doesn't seem to be any real reason to talk about it.

But we should talk about it.

So far in this book we've looked at how being a woman influences the way you experience work. For the most part, I have tried to focus on the positive and the practical, to empower and excite you about the possibilities of your own brilliant career. In this chapter I want to do something different: I want to make you angry. Why? Because you should be angry. There is so much to be angry about. Blatant sexism and sexual harassment should not be the price women pay for being part of the workforce. It's not fair that men go about their business unaware of how bad the situation is for women. Nor is it fair that women are made to feel responsible and isolated for behaviour that wasn't their own.

So instead of sharing more statistics in this chapter, I want to share stories. Stories from women who have been treated appallingly in the workplace. Stories from women who were at work in the 2010s, not the 1950s. Stories from women who are dental assistants, plumbers, policy advisers, waitresses, midwives, architects, aged-care workers, PR managers, university students, graphic designers, and doctors. Stories of women whose names must be changed because their careers could be damaged if they were identified. Stories of events that really happened and will keep happening if our community doesn't stand up and say: Enough.

Six stories in 60 seconds

Alice was 24 when she started working for a man who, over time and quite deliberately, transforms a team of young women staff into a sycophantic posse. Those who don't conform are ostracised, socially humiliated and in constant fear of firing. The boss begins inviting Alice to after-work drinks, rewarding her with titbits of workplace gossip and information that makes her feel special and included. In a matter of weeks, what was a slightly over-friendly working relationship descends into incessant, menacing and sexualised messaging outside of office hours. When Alice and a colleague who experienced similar treatment find the courage to fight back, they are shunned in the office and accused of being 'obsessed' with their boss.

Marta is a doctor and was one of the top students in her graduating class. She's applied and been selected for training to become a surgeon. If you've watched as much *Grey's Anatomy* as I have, you'll know that means she's the best of the best. While technically brilliant, Marta finds the emotional side of her job taxing. Watching people die is part of the gig. When called in for a meeting with her superiors to discuss her 'lack of resilience', Marta can't help but tear up. She is sitting across the table from fully qualified surgeons when she drops her face downward and begins crying. Once she has composed herself, she looks up to see one surgeon filming her on his iPhone. He's smirking. Within a week, the whole hospital has seen the 'hilarious' video of Marta 'being a sook'.

Anna is a marketing executive whose job includes servicing existing clients, but also, importantly, winning new business for her firm. After leading a team that successfully pitches and wins a major piece of business, Anna is feeling rather chuffed. The new client is so impressed with Anna's work that they request she personally head up their account. They don't want to work with anyone else, they inform Anna's boss's boss, the CEO. The CEO later asks Anna – who has delivered an enormous financial windfall for his company – how she won the new client over. 'Did you show him your tits or something?' he queries.

Yasmin is an adviser to government. She's walking rapidly down a corridor one day when she trips and drops paperwork all over the floor. She bends over to start pulling the mess of folders and paper-clips and pages back together. As she stands up, she notices a close colleague is facing her and can't stop laughing. He's guffawing, covering his mouth. She smiles at him, perplexed and hurt that he found her fall so spectacularly hilarious. Then she realises another colleague is standing behind her, thrusting vigorously with his pelvis as if he is screwing her. Yasmin fixes her gaze straight ahead and keeps walking down the corridor. The blokes never mention what happened.

Beth is an engineer, far more comfortable on a construction site than she is in a boardroom. Every few weeks, however, she has to be in her company's head office for meetings. She hates it, says her feet get itchy. 'I build stuff, I don't talk about it,' she tells me. The worst part is the men she meets with. These are men who aren't engineers, men who have no technical experience with what Beth does. They treat the boardroom like their kingdom. Those meetings are unbearable. Beth is interrupted far more often than anyone else. When she makes a reasonable point, she's belittled and dismissed. When she makes a particularly salient point the conversation moves on until one of the men makes that same point and everyone congratulates him on his cleverness. When the tea and biscuits arrive, everyone looks to Beth to do the serving.

Qian-Qian is an event manager who has worked with some of the biggest companies in Australia. Her organisational skills are legendary and she boasts some of the best contacts in the industry. Once she turned forty, however, Qian-Qian decided she wanted a change. She was sick of the corporate world and thought she'd take her considerable expertise and head to the not-for-profit sector. She wanted to do some good. Her first call was to a charitable organisation, which put her in a room with one of the senior managers within a week of her phone call. They didn't have a job for her, but they'd create one. Her boss-to-be noted that charities cannot afford to pay the way big business does. Did Qian-Qian have a high-earning husband? That would make the pay cut easier to manage, presumably.

Six women. Six jobs. The same sexist story.

It's the same story as Jo, an electrician, who was asked when another woman was employed at her company how she felt about 'no longer being the only hot girl in the room'. Or Tahlia, a pint-sized radio host, who was told she needed to lose weight before the new billboards were produced. Her co-host was morbidly obese but nobody had a 'talk' with him. Or Sari, a senior lawyer who had a paralegal tell her that she was his 'favourite' masturbation fantasy. Or Salina, who complained about having to be reimbursed for company expenses, rather than being given a credit card, and was told, 'You spend all your money on clothes and shoes anyway.'

The same story, over and over and over again.

Why we all need to start being 'that girl'

There are stories of unquestionably illegal behaviour that the victim worries are too 'trivial' to be worthy of complaint, but ultimately each of these has a common thread. They are stories of women who have been made to feel small, unimportant and worthless. They are stories of men taking advantage, taking liberties, and taking women's dignity and self-respect. Stories that most of us are too scared to report or protest about or push back against because we fear being labelled as 'that girl' . . .

That Girl is the one who calls out a mate at the footy over a sexist remark about a player's wife. She objects to being affectionately called 'sweetie' or 'darling' by her boss. She follows the sexual harassment procedures when a colleague sticks his hand up her skirt at Friday night drinks. That Girl isn't a girl at all – she's a woman. A woman who wants to be treated fairly as a colleague, a boss, an employee . . . as a human being.

You never want to be That Girl. That Girl can't take a joke. She's no fun. She's – insert eye roll – politically correct. She's boring. She should just learn to be cool. Learn to be a team player. You know? Why does she have to suck the humour out of everything? She should stop playing the victim. How come she doesn't get that the boys were only kidding around? The boys were just *being* boys.

I've been That Girl, but you know who I've been far more times? I've been Not Her.

I've let things go. I've smiled politely, prettily, and avoided having an argument. I've even laughed along with the joke when I know it's wrong, and it makes my skin crawl to pretend I wasn't bothered. Often it was because I felt exhausted by always being the one to say something. Or I let it go because it didn't seem like a big enough deal to call out and make a 'thing' over. There have been times when I simply didn't know how to handle a situation and felt out of my depth. There are occasions when I've watched someone else be treated badly, humiliated or unfairly criticised, and known she would have been cut more slack if she was a man. Sometimes I've still stayed silent. Sometimes I've been scared. Because being That Girl is really, really hard.

But there comes a point when you have to do what is right even when it is hard. There comes a point when you have to say it out loud. If not for yourself, say it out loud for the benefit of other women. Say it so that other women don't feel alone. Say it so other women know it wasn't their fault. So the young women who answered that *Cosmopolitan* survey know what happened to them is not okay and they don't have to put up with it. So that good men know the truth of what others do in their name and that standing silently watching it go on makes them complicit.

Say it so it stops being normal. And report so it doesn't go unchecked.

Be That Girl.

Because That Girl is a hero.

WORKING
WITH
MEAN
GIRLS

Because sometimes men aren't the problem.

'CATFIGHT' screamed the newspaper headline. It was a good yarn, as we say in the business. A former prime minister's daughter caught in a bitchy back and forth with a woman who used to work for her dad. That woman would be yours truly. The online reporters were in click-bait heaven on what was otherwise a perilously slow news day. Jessica Rudd is a novelist, entrepreneur, mother, and also happens to be the eldest child of Kevin Rudd. At the time she wrote a column for women's magazine *Cleo* and her foray into commentary was getting a lot of attention. In her latest piece she'd compared working in Parliament House to the cult American high-school movie *Mean Girls*. I'd responded in an online opinion piece, defending political staffers and putting forward a different view.

Two women who disagree with one another publicly? In the media world that's a catfight. The far less headline-worthy and actual version of events went something like this: I disagreed with parts of Jess's column. I called to give her the heads up that I planned to write a response. We had a good catch up and chat because Jess is an all-around ace chick. Then we included links to each other's articles at the bottom of our own, so readers could understand the nuances of our discussion and read both points of view. What Jess had to say was eloquent, clever and gracious, as she always is. I simply had a different perspective. When the stupid catfight headline was published, she sent me a message that said, *Well that was just about the loveliest catfight I've ever been a part of. Next time let's do it over a cup of tea and biscuits, shall we?*

The mean-girl stereotype isn't new.

The myth that all women secretly hate one another is a favourite of the media. Think about the much-publicised celebrity feuds between Taylor Swift and Katy Perry, Miley Cyrus and Sinead O'Connor, Chelsea Handler and Angelina Jolie, Kim Kardashian and Paris Hilton, Beyoncé and Rihanna, Madonna and Gwyneth Paltrow. A Hollywood spat between two men doesn't spring to mind in quite the same way, does it? That's because when those disagreements happen, they don't make the *Daily Mail* homepage. While two men can have a heated debate, shake hands at the end of it and move on, two women are rarely assumed capable of the same. Readers are encouraged to focus on the personalities of the women, instead of the substance of what they have to say. The media – and, through it, our community – think that when women argue it's *always* personal. A disagreement between women is framed through a lens of primal jealousy, the women reduced to competitors for the attention of men. Blokes who argue are professional people exchanging opinions, and women are hysterical balls of hot mess. Audiences fall for it every time.

Researcher Alana Piper says the mean-girl stereotype flows from history's ongoing struggle to understand women's friendship. The legitimacy of women's friendships has been consistently

questioned, she explains. The idea that women are incapable of
true friendship can be traced back to the Victorian era.

> Victorians celebrated romantic friendships between women,
> but also depicted them as superficial passions that simply
> prepared women for marriage. Rather than enjoying the long-
> lasting friendships found among men, bonds between women
> were depicted as short-lived, unable to withstand women's
> quarrelsome natures.

It was once believed that girl-on-girl crime was biological.
Women – as natural rivals for the male gaze – could never be genuine comrades. Friendships between women were regarded with
suspicion as recently as the Romantic Era. Groups of women who
were physically or socially close have variously been snubbed as out-
casts, accused of harbouring criminality and even burned as witches.
The word 'gossip' originally referred to a woman friend who would
spend time with a woman in the late stages of her pregnancy and in
the months following the birth. A word that once described intimate and loving conversation between two women has become
pejorative. 'Gossip' is a term steeped in disapproval. Confidential
discussion between women is something to be wary of.

The unfair reduction of women to mere competitors for men's
affection has been directly translated into the workplace. Writer
Rebecca Traister argues that history's inaccurate and unfair dim-
inution of women's friendships has actually become *worse* since
women began pursuing careers. In the Western world, women's
mass entry into the workforce in the 1950s and '60s coincided
with changes in how society viewed marriage. Marriage became a
union based on love, rather than solely an avenue for reproduction

and the transfer of wealth. Traister says this created new spheres of 'competition' between women: love and marriage, and work. This affected our social understanding of how women relate to one another. It reinforced our community's belief that two women's interests are never in alignment unless they are mother and daughter. The media's casting of women as 'hair-pullers, back-stabbers and bitches, always after each other's jobs, wardrobes and men' was just the next in a logical series of steps.

Women aren't worse. They're exactly as bad as men.

'Can I tell you something awful?' my colleague Erin says in a half-whisper. 'The worst stuff that's happened to me at work was because of women.' Her tone was secretive and embarrassed. The admission felt like a betrayal of the sisterhood. Erin is a feminist who doesn't want to feed the stereotype that women are out to get one another. The problem is that sometimes the stereotype matches reality. I grimace in response to Erin's confession. The same is true for me.

I once had a woman manager who regularly undermined me in front of my own team. One small instance – which still sticks in my head years later – happened after I sent a group email. My manager objected to parts of what I'd written, but instead of speaking to me about it one-on-one, she hit 'reply all'. 'Please disregard the contents of Jamila's email,' she informed a dozen of my colleagues, including people who directly reported to me. It was like I'd been slapped in the face. My skin burned with shame and indignation. For the rest of the day it felt like everyone was looking at me with pity, talking about me behind my back. They were. When I got home I picked a fight with my husband over nothing at all, which was absolutely a mature and sensible way to deal it.

But there are no innocent victims here.

I'm ashamed to say that I have also been the perpetrator of crappy treatment towards women at work. There was Jenny, a brilliant writer I'd hired to do a job she just wasn't the right fit for. Instead of taking the time to sit beside her, check she had the best possible support, value her inarguable strengths and find a role that *was* a good fit for her, I gave up. I pushed the problem away and let someone else handle it. Almost two years later I contacted Jenny and took her to lunch. I apologised. I half-expected her to tell me sweetly not to be silly, that I'd done nothing wrong and to sweep the conflict nicely and politely under the carpet. But Jenny looked me straight in the eyes and said evenly, 'I appreciate your apology.' The experience had hurt her. It wasn't her job to clear my conscience. I had an opportunity to embrace and support another woman who didn't share the positional power I did. I failed to do that and Jenny suffered as a result. She owed me nothing.

A 2011 study found that 95 per cent of women report having had their careers undermined by another woman. That's basically everyone. If you're anything like Erin and me, when you reflect on your career you can see more instances of women treating women badly than men treating women badly. It makes you uncomfortable. There's a niggling voice inside your head that quietly wonders if maybe the sisterhood isn't all it's cracked up to be.

It's okay to be hearing that voice. Every day the media bombards us with portrayals of women as malicious and undermining. Our conversations with one another and the stories we share with friends and family reinforce this view. None of us is immune. The niggling voice is a product of what we have all been conditioned to notice. It's not that women treat one another any worse than men treat one another. It's just that we *notice* women treating one another badly, while skimming over it when men do the same. This is called confirmation bias. The very fact that we *expect* women to treat one another badly means that we notice it more.

Let me explain in more detail. Conflict involving women violates social norms: the ones that say women should always be kind and nurturing, supportive and sweet. At work it's inevitable that behaviour inconsistent with this expectation takes place. Workplaces are competitive environments where people are bound to disagree or rub one another up the wrong way from time to time. When blokes compete or debate or engage aggressively with one another, it's seen as stock-standard, but when women do the same it feels like a much bigger deal. We don't expect that combative, competitive behaviour from women and so we award the conflict greater weight than it actually deserves, because we think it's unusual. The occurrence embeds in our memories because it feels atypical; it goes against what we consider normal feminine behaviour. This means our memories of women engaging in conflict behaviour are stronger than our memories of men doing the same thing.

Women don't treat each other any worse than men do. It's just that our *expectations* of how women should treat one another are much higher. So when a woman fails to meet those expectations, the gap between expectation and reality is greater than it would have been if she were a man. One 2008 study found that 'women working under female supervisors reported more symptoms of physical and psychological stress than did those working under male supervisors'. I can't help but wonder if that was because men supervisors were more supportive, or whether it was because when women supervisors were *less than* supportive it came as more of a shock. We expect better treatment from other women at work. We expect friendship and kindness and empathy from women in a way that we don't from men. When that positive treatment doesn't come, our shock is greater and our pain more intense.

This isn't to say that shitty treatment at the hands of another woman doesn't happen. I do not, by any means, want to invalidate the pain or hurt you've experienced at work because of a woman colleague. When someone treats you badly, they treat you badly. You're entitled to be sad, angry or annoyed. It is, however, worth considering whether you're more upset simply because you've been treated badly by a *woman*. Try this hypothetical on for size: imagine you are returning to work after maternity leave and you'd like more flexible arrangements. Your boss is a woman and she's not having a bar of it. It's awful. You've got raging hormones, there is milk leaking out of you, it's a lifetime since you've had a full night's sleep, and now this? Next, reimagine the scenario but pretend you work for a man. It's still awful. But perhaps the hurt you feel is marginally less? Perhaps you feel angry, but not emotionally betrayed. Now reimagine the scenario a third time and give your hypothetical woman boss some small children of her own. Wow. Suddenly she's not just awful – she's an unfeeling *monster*. A fellow mum who won't empathise with what you're going through.

Double standards work both ways.

Expecting women to behave better than men – simply because they are women – is a form of sexism. In any workplace you're going to come across good colleagues and bad colleagues, good bosses and bad bosses. Chances are the good and bad will be pretty evenly split between genders. The problem is that we've been conditioned to assess women and men against different standards. We have higher expectations for how a woman will treat us at work because she is a woman. We expect her to be kinder, fairer and more compassionate. And we punish her more harshly when she is not.

Beware the powerful woman. She doesn't have your back.

To help out other women is part of an unwritten social pact. When Madeleine Albright famously said, 'There's a special place in hell for women who don't support other women', feminists everywhere responded with a 'hell yes'. Yet women employees keep reporting negative experiences of working with other women, particularly when there is hierarchy involved. All of these experiences can't *only* be the result of unfair expectations and gendered perceptions. While a sexist double standard may have exacerbated our view of the behaviour, that doesn't eliminate the fact that it was poor behaviour in the first place. This suggests that there are a bunch of women who have made it to the top of workplaces who have done so – at least in part – by treating other women badly. So why do we do it?

This behaviour has a lot to do with the context women are operating in. Let me throw you another hypothetical. Imagine you've gone to work at a big engineering firm that employs more than 1000 people. Engineering is a field dominated by men; only 15 per cent of the workforce are women. You look to the executive suite in search of a role model and the options are pretty bleak if your preference is for a hero of the same gender. The same is true of middle management. In your area there are 27 men, but only two women at the same level. When your immediate manager resigns there is an announcement: the firm is having a restructure. Your team is too big and will be split into two. A manager will be appointed to lead each of the new groups. There is a pair of promotions on offer and they'll be filled from within your ranks. Six people apply: four men, the other woman and you. Who is your biggest competition?

Most of us instinctively look to the other woman candidate as the main source of competition. Not because we have any information to suggest she's more talented than the other candidates.

Not because she brings a similar set of skills or because she has the most experience. The reason is both structural and contextual. If you're operating in an environment where few women rise to the top, then you assume there will *only ever be* a few women at the top. Once your brain assumes there are only a limited number of positions available for women – another woman automatically falls into the role of competitor. Put another way, if there are only a handful of seats at the table for women and you'd like one of those seats for yourself, other talented women pose a threat.

The principle of scarcity is at play here. It's the same idea that makes reality-television shows like *The Bachelor* so successful. On that program, a large number of women compete to win the affections of a single, good-looking man. The audience watches on, somewhat baffled by the intensity of these women's desire to be victorious. They really, really, really want this (often quite boring) stranger to fall in love with them. Dr Lauren Rosewarne explains it like this:

> They may not love him yet, hell, they may not even know him yet. But if there's only one of him and every other woman wants a piece, surely he's worth throwing one's panties into the ring for. And thus, we have women – gorgeous, neurotic, insufficiently self-reflective – plotting and scheming and grooming-within-an-inch-of-their-life in the hope of being chosen. To have one's existence validated by a chap whose worth has become alarmingly inflated based purely on each contestant's willingness to grovel for his table scraps.

While *The Bachelor* is undeniably sexist, sexism isn't the fuelling premise of the show. It's scarcity. Each of those women is attractive and engaging; some are smart, some are funny, some are kind, some are artistic and some have enormously successful professional lives. By popular measure, each of these women is a 'catch'. They would have no trouble meeting a partner outside the concocted world of reality television. Inside that world, however, they aren't special. They're one of 20 competing for only *one* of him. *The Bachelor* is a scarce quantity and that – not his six pack or well-tailored suits – is what makes him so desirable.

The scarcity of promotional opportunities for women fosters this same kind of competition. Men compete for jobs too, but for women the competition is more urgent and more fraught because the available number of positions is perceived as more scarce. Susan Shapiro Barash interviewed 500 women for her book *Tripping the Prom Queen: The Truth about Women and Rivalry*. She found that '90 per cent of women in diverse jobs report that competition in the workplace is primarily between women, rather than between women and men'. The reason, she explains, is because women assume that they can do nothing about the success of men. Men have always been successful at work because they built the place. They dominate the top jobs today and probably will for some time to come. Attempting to upset that status quo would be enormously difficult. So women begin competing with one another for what they believe are a limited number of positions for women. What we *should* be doing is working together to boost the number of positions held by women as a whole. What we *should* be doing is looking for opportunities to help women who don't share our privilege and power to succeed, including those women who are locked out of workplaces all together.

Let's return to the hypothetical engineering firm. There were two open managerial positions available. There were two women applicants. Logically, the principle of scarcity doesn't apply. There is no legitimate reason why both positions can't be filled by women. However, the two women applying for the roles will probably assume only one of them has a chance. And, sadly, that's also likely to be the assumption of the people making the decision.

'Women are awful. Gosh, it's lucky I'm not like them.'

Internalised sexism can cause women to behave contrary to the interests of the sisterhood. For example, social distancing involves a woman actively denying her femaleness because she considers it a career drawback. By deliberately setting themselves apart from others of the same gender, women who do this are hoping to avoid the trappings of negative stereotypes. For example, there's a (bullshit) stereotype that women are too emotional to be stable leaders. When a woman becomes a leader in an organisation, she may actively dissociate herself from other women so that people don't apply the stereotype to her.

Perhaps you've come across a woman who does this, or perhaps you are her. She might crack rude or sexual jokes about women. Or make loud pronouncements to the men that she's 'not like other women'. Or complain about other women at work being crazy, emotional or even 'on their periods'. She might gravitate socially to men in the workplace, not because of genuine lack of interest in the women's company but because she is curating a 'one of the boys' image. Social distancing isn't exclusive to women. It's quite common among lower-status groups and has been observed in gay men and people of colour, too. Individuals who belong to a group that has been marginalised may see social distancing as their only path to the top. Pushing back against the negative stereotype of their group is too difficult. Instead, they focus their efforts on differentiating themselves from that group in order to succeed.

Internalised sexism also manifests in the way women display aggression or deal with conflict at work. Have you ever had a disagreement with a woman co-worker and then been frosty towards one another for months afterwards? Did you sigh and think to yourself that this could all be dealt with easily and more cleanly if it were out in the open? Because women aren't expected to engage in conflict at work, that conflict often becomes covert. The dispute goes underground. Women engage in more indirect forms of aggression than men do; they use emotional rather than physical or verbal means to resolve conflict. It's rarely effective.

The kind of behaviour we associate with women's aggression – the bitchiness, the emotional manipulation and the social ostracisation – is indirect. This behaviour isn't a product of femininity. It's a product of powerlessness. Women are punished socially when they're directly aggressive. Indirect aggression is less detectable and less likely to draw ire from onlookers. So women tend to express their anger or frustration towards co-workers in this way instead. It may ultimately be more harmful, but it's more socially acceptable.

Why do we compete? Why do we compare?

Men are schooled so as to be more comfortable competing with one another than women. From their youth, boys are taught to enjoy and excel in friendly competition. They're taught that it's okay to have a wrestle, to really want to win that race, and that being ambitious is a good thing. In adulthood, this translates to workplaces where friendly one-upmanship between blokes is celebrated. Two men will happily apply for the same job, knowing one of them is certain to miss out. They'll even joke about it, teasing one another and making trifling wagers on the outcome. Two of my girlfriends once worked together and both wanted the same promotion. After a fortnight of fraught and flurried phone calls – not to one another but to the rest of our friendship circle – one of them unilaterally decided not to put her name forward. It wasn't worth it, she reasoned. The friendship was more important.

Girls are taught that being open and confident about their ambition to win is a bad thing. So as adult women we tuck our competitiveness away, suppressing a healthy expression of the perfectly normal desire to succeed. What's left is muffled jealousy of others. When we can't openly compete, we silently compare instead. Adults reinforce this behaviour during girlhood through comments like, 'Don't worry about her, she's just jealous of you,' and 'Come on girls, don't fight, that's not nice.' When we arrive in the workplace and competition is expected from us, we're not sure how to go about it. Often we resort to clique behaviour or what the researchers call 'zinging', which is making personal digs at other women that appear humorous on the surface but are designed to cause hurt. Bridget Jones describes it as jelly-fishing.

Humans are relational creatures and we approach the workplace in a social way. Some scientists argue that the female brain is actually hard-wired for connection with other human beings in a way the male brain isn't. As the carers and nurturers back in cave-person days, it was our relationships with others that kept women alive. Research suggests that the higher concentration of oestrogen in female brains means we're more likely to respond to that stress with relationship-focused activities, like building social networks. Women fall back on this when faced with stressful situations at work. It's why women are more likely to see our workmates as potential friends, not just people we sit beside. It may also be why we respond to conflict with one colleague by seeking out other colleagues to befriend instead. We're comforted by the action of rallying a squad around us. This kind of clique-building response can create 'us and them' attitudes among women at work. Anyone who isn't a friend becomes an enemy. And naturally, allies become more important when an enemy has been established.

Have you ever felt wronged by someone at work and then caught yourself talking about it to another person at work who has *absolutely nothing* to do with the whole saga? Did the way you presented what went down just *happen* to paint you in a positive light? Did you get the sympathy and the intimate camaraderie that you were looking for? Did you feel more secure because you had someone on your side who understood? Yes. Yes. Yes. And yes. Allies and enemies, my friend.

Comparison is another evil that can inhibit camaraderie among work colleagues, particularly women. In my experience, men tend to 'run their own race' and assess themselves against objective criteria, like reaching the top of a workplace hierarchy or winning a pay rise. Women are more likely to assess their success against the yardstick of the women around them. We compare ourselves in order to examine ourselves. The rise and rise and rise of social media – with its shiny, glossy version of everyone's lives projected minute by minute – hasn't helped this at all. Comparison made a lot of women's lives a misery even before the Valencia filter was invented. Now it's even worse.

In order to understand why women compare ourselves to one another, we need a crash course in social comparison theory. It goes like this: when we lack objective feedback about ourselves, human beings determine our social and personal worth based on how we 'stack up' against others. Modern living is pretty much devoid of objective feedback. We're excessively polite to one another and rarely talk honestly about one another's flaws. Instead we gloss over things, we put on a face, we flatter, we self-deprecate and we cover up the truth with flowery language and compliments. This means comparison has become the primary source of human's self-assessment. In the ongoing pursuit of likeability, women are even more likely to sugarcoat the things we say. We are gentle with one another's feelings and shy away from delivering direct reproaches because that's not *nice*. We aren't able to rely on our friends or colleagues to tell us honestly how we're going. So we make comparisons instead.

Women are also more likely to be 'alterocenterist', meaning that we make other people the focus of our emotional state. This is again linked to those expectations that women should put the needs of others before their own. It can be a good thing because it means we're more likely to exhibit kind or caring behaviours. It can also be a bad thing because other people *indirectly* affect our emotional states. Other people, just by living their lives and doing their ordinary thing, can have a profound effect on how we feel about ourselves. One little throwaway comment from our colleague becomes an enormously big deal. A perceived slight from our boss becomes an ongoing cause of stress. We are so worried about other people and what they're doing and thinking that we struggle to gain objectivity. By contrast, men tend to be more egocentric and aren't affected by social comparison in the same way.

Remember how I told my husband that I couldn't bear to think there was a person out there, existing in the world that thought badly of me? Remember how he thought I was weird? That.

So what the hell do we do about it?

Hopefully all this information has helped you understand that the conflicts that happen between women at work are no different to any other conflict. We simply notice them, interpret them and react to them differently. Just like men, women are shaped by the sexist environment we live in.

The challenge for each of us is to rise above our own conditioning. We can stop, we can take pause and we can deliberately choose to alter course. We can choose to be better. We can choose to applaud when another woman wins instead of looking away in contempt. We can voice our vulnerabilities, support women who express ambition and hold our bosses to a single standard, regardless of their gender.

Here are a few suggestions to get you started:

1. **Admit when you're jealous.**

   Jealousy is normal. Hiding it doesn't help any of us, most particularly the person doing the harbouring. Next time a friend or colleague excels or is promoted and you're not, try admitting the feelings of envy at the same time as offering your congratulations. It sounds a little trite, but saying, 'Congratulations, that is such an enormous achievement, and I am really happy for you but right now also a little jealous' can actually make you feel better. Recognise envy for what it is. Name it. Articulate it. Then focus on what's next for you personally.

2. **Don't expect more from a woman boss than a man.**

   When you have a woman boss it's easy to assume that your shared anatomy means you'll be buddies. Be aware that this may not happen and that that's okay. Your boss's primary role isn't to be your mate. It's to be your champion and mentor. Your boss is there to make you a better employee, and that means saying things to you (usually critical things) that a friend probably can't. Next time a woman manager appears to be behaving unreasonably, pause and reimagine her as a man. Check your own gender bias.

3. **If you're going to compete, then compete against everyone.**
Don't assume that your main competition for advancement is other women. Even if you know that to be the case because of sexist old men in management, do not give in to it – refute it. When you go for a promotion or a raise or a new job, your competition is everyone else who applied. Not just the women. And when a woman does beat you in the race for advancement, don't think that means the only 'woman' spot is full now. Instead, think about the gender stereotypes she will smash, making it easier for you and other women to follow in her wake.

4. **Choose your comparison, don't let it choose you.**
We all need a yardstick to assess ourselves against, but using every woman you ever meet at work as a yardstick is a recipe for self-loathing. Instead, try identifying the dozen or so people in your life whose opinion really matters to you. That list might include your boss or it might not. It's up to you. Make sure those people are close enough to you to be honest, or that they at least know that when you ask them for feedback you genuinely *desire* honesty. And next time you're worried about your own status or career trajectory, don't reach for the closest woman as a point of comparison. Instead, contact one of your predetermined comparators and check in with them.

5. **Quit thinking that because you did it the 'hard way' others should too.**
Some commentators have criticised women who finally break through the upper echelons of management and then

supposedly close the trapdoor behind them. That is, when a woman has battled hard to get where she is, she expects that those who follow her should have to do the same. Otherwise she considers them less deserving. We have to make sure our better angels win in this scenario. Fight the demon that says, 'I did it tough and so should she.' Instead take pride in the fact you made it easier for the women who came next. Remember there are privileges that made your progression possible, which others don't have. Use your success to help make the place you work more equitable.

Working with women is the actual best.

I've made this point a whole section of its own because it is *that important*. If you've tuned out over the past couple of pages to make a cup of tea or play Candy Crush, that is okay. I will not hold it against you, but I need you to listen now: Please do not give in to the stereotype of women hating other women. Don't give in to it at work, at home, in the community or in the media. It is not who we are. Ignore the 'who wore it best' pages of the magazines. Tune out of the mummy wars on daytime television. Don't click on the link that promises the inside gossip on a celebrity catfight. When you have a bad experience with a woman at work, write it off as a bad experience, not a reflection of how all women are. Do not let one or two bad interactions with women you don't get along with taint your view of what working with women is like.

Because working with women is BLOODY MARVELLOUS.

I have spent the past 18 months employed as a freelance writer and presenter. I haven't worked from a busy, bustling office. I no longer manage a team of people. I love my work, I really do. I love the content, the flexibility and the diversity, but I miss the women

I used to work with. I miss their energy, I miss their ideas, I miss their jokes, I miss their insights and I miss their warmth. I even miss the constant requests for 'just five minutes' of my time. I miss them every day. Working with women made me better and it made me smarter. To miss out on that because of a handful of bad experiences would have been a very great shame. Don't let that happen to you.

Be a champion of other women. Be a friend and supporter to the women whose experience of the workforce might not have been as fortunate as your own. Make your feminism inclusive and generous and open and kind. Embrace the women you work with. They are your natural allies in a workplace culture that still says men should be in charge. It is only together that we can conquer the world.

NETWORKING AND MENTORING

Because when you're good to the sisterhood, she'll be good to you.

Prepare yourself, because I need to get a particularly intense and distressing experience off my chest. I need to tell you about the evening I decided to join social networking website LinkedIn. For the new players, LinkedIn is the world's largest professional network and boasts some 300 million users worldwide. It's basically an online destination for three types of people:

1. People who share quotes about war from dead political leaders and think they apply to their job in accounting
2. People who like to write smugly about themselves in the third person
3. People looking for a new job

I'd resisted joining for several years (not because Jamila doesn't enjoy writing in the third person, because she does). When I finally did, it was because I needed to recruit for a new position in the company I was working for. Sitting in the living room watching TV with my housemates, I opened my laptop and selected the 'join' button. Within minutes I had entered my name, my age, uploaded a photo and roadtested various capitalised and not-capitalised versions of my job title to try to make it Maximum Level Fancy.

Next I needed some friends to connect with, and helpfully LinkedIn already knew who my friends were. Click. Then I got a second prompt asking if I wanted to import some more contacts from my email account. Excellent. Where did I go to school? Australian National University. Click. Would I like to join any of these suggested groups? Not right now, thanks. Click. By now I was thinking that I was actually pretty excellent at LinkedIn and was on my way to becoming an expert-level networker. I continued filling in titbits of information for 20 minutes, blissfully unaware of the social catastrophe I was causing.

'Hello, Jamila Rizvi,' said my housemate Josh. 'I would love to connect with you on LinkedIn.' He laughed. 'I too would like to connect with you, Jamila Rizvi,' said Josh's girlfriend, Jess. 'Although perhaps I didn't need to know which primary school you went to or the 12 other updates you've just provided me with.' Shit. I hadn't turned off the option to update my entire 'network' every time I updated my page. I'd saved 20 or so updates already. I started clicking around desperately looking for instructions on how to deactivate the function. Nothing. I did, however, discover that, thanks to one of those new-fangled prompt things, I'd accidentally selected a diploma from the Australian National Beauty School as my key qualification. Anyone who had ever seen me with make-up on would know how not true that is. Double shit.

My anxious search for the 'edit' or 'undo' button continued. Panic growing, I clicked on my messages to let the company know how much trouble I was having . . . and I had 173 new messages. It turned out I had unwittingly sent invitations to 'link' not just to my email contacts but to anyone I had *ever* had email contact with. This included several people I did not particularly like, my dentist, the removalist who broke my bookcase when I moved house and, super unhelpfully, my ex-boyfriend's parents. So I did what any self-respecting person who works with social media every day but has just COMPLETELY FAILED at a new social media platform would do: I turned off my computer. *I'll just never go back there*, I thought. *I will never use the internet or read my emails again. That'll fix it.*

Why networking matters (even if it feels uncomfortable)

My disastrous foray onto LinkedIn aside, networking is an incredibly important part of building a career. Foolishly, it was something I used to pride myself on *not* doing. I reasoned that I was too busy getting on with doing my job to go out for drinks and eat miniature food. While others were wasting time collecting business cards and rubbing shoulders, I was the one getting stuff done. But when I left salaried employment to work for myself, the value of those relationships I'd never really bothered to cultivate became apparent. The prospect of contacting somebody out of the blue to ask for a favour was daunting and distasteful to me. I didn't really have an alternative, though. The responsibility for generating demand for my work was on my shoulders, and that meant relying on my not-so-well-established networks.

I'd unintentionally put myself in a precarious position. My efforts had all been focused internally, on nurturing relationships within the business I was working for. Once outside of that business, my options were limited. Ideally, I should have been putting effort into both. It's an error that lots of women make. We focus on our current employer, our current job and our current task, to the exclusion of the employers, jobs and tasks we may want to have in the future. This limits our networks to the immediate people we interact with day-to-day in our job. So when the future arrives and we're looking for the next opportunity, we have fewer people to turn to for help.

A joint study of almost 120 companies, conducted by McKinsey, found that women tend to have fewer industry relationships than men. Only 10 per cent of senior women said they had the support of several other executives who helped them to advance in their careers. For men, the number was almost double. Women tended to report fewer but stronger connections. They may only enjoy a professionally beneficial relationship with a few people who they genuinely trust. Another study I came across looked at the behaviour and networks of Wall Street analysts. It found that men were far more dependent on their networks – from school, from university and from previous jobs – to get ahead at work. Moreover, those networks were considered to be extremely valuable by their employers. Having an extensive network made these men more attractive employees. They actively relied on their networks to make them more employable in a way that women in the same industry didn't.

The 'old boys' club' is alive and well, yet we hear very little about the 'old girls' club'. Probably because there isn't one.

Why women don't network

If networking is so beneficial then why don't more women do it? Well, there are several reasons. To begin with, some women labour under the same misconception I did – that networking isn't 'real work'. They consider time away from their computer screens a waste. They worry that colleagues might think they're slack if they're not always at their desks. This can harm an employee's future career prospects, but also hurts the organisation they work for. Remember that your networks benefit your employer as well as you. Attending a work function and meeting people in your industry is certainly more beneficial than a lazy hour spent 'checking emails' (aka browsing Facebook). If you fall into this category of non-networkers, it's time to reconceptualise. Stop thinking about networking as a time-wasting exercise and instead embrace it as part of doing your job better. That means it shouldn't always have to be an additional extra that you do for free in your own time. Talk to your employer about how networking opportunities can be carved out within working hours so that you're paid for them.

There are women who want to network but can't. The expectation that employees can make time outside of their standard working hours for networking is intrinsically classist. That is, it assumes employees don't have significant responsibilities, time pressures or even second jobs. Women tend to miss out on informal networking opportunities because those events often take place outside of standard work hours. The majority of caring and domestic work in Australia still falls on the shoulders of women, so women are more likely to be committed during those times. Men are less likely to have immovable commitments in the evenings and so they can go for an extra beer, or catch up on work they missed because they were at a long lunch. Networking is easier to do when you have more flexible time in your day. Have you ever wondered why 'women's' events are held at breakfast time? It's because this is supposed to make it easier for mothers to attend. Although anyone who has ever discussed cereal choices with a toddler knows this to be a false assumption.

Women often assume that working hard and getting the job done is the fastest way to get noticed. While that certainly should be the case, workplaces are imperfect institutions. Generally it takes more than just hard work to win a promotion within your workplace or positive attention from outside it. In an earlier chapter I talked about the importance of communicating to your boss how good a job you're doing as well as doing a good job in the first place. Networking is the external equivalent of that. Networking is about communicating how good a job you're doing to people who you *don't* work with on a daily basis. That includes people who are outside the organisation you currently work in but employed in the same or a related industry.

And then there is the wanker factor. Many women object to networking because it feels forced and distasteful. I get it. I hear the word networking and I immediately see popped-collar, Ralph Lauren polo shirt–wearing, young gents that talk at the top of their voices about their obscene annual bonuses. They're not exactly the kind of people I'd want to spend an afternoon with. For women from religious backgrounds in which modesty is highly valued, for example Hindu and Muslim women, networking may be particularly uncomfortable. Flagrant self-promotion is the opposite of modesty, and cuts directly against their values. Networking can feel a lot like bragging and a little bit like using other people to get ahead. Neither of those things is enjoyable to do or be around, and women, in particular, often won't be comfortable operating in that kind of environment.

The Old Boys' Club is in session and, no, you're not invited.

On Tuesday nights parliament sits late. By 8 p.m. the bulk of our work as political staffers was done, but the minister was required to remain in the building in case of a vote. Kate Ellis used to insist that there was no point in everyone working late. One of us would be rostered on to stick around until 10 p.m. when business finished up in the House of Representatives, but everyone else was told to go home. Kate could not have been more generous in urging us to leave, and yet I would inevitably remain at my desk late into the night, usually shopping online. My brain had decided it was going home even if my body hadn't. My childless women colleagues tended to do the same. There was no explicit pressure on us to stay late, but somehow we still felt like we should.

My men colleagues would bail out early. Instead of heading home they'd be at the bar, building professional capital with every beer that was poured. The young men, in particular, sought out the kind of informal environment where workplace hierarchies get broken down. Everyone is equal after a few drinks. Everyone gets a say because you're not on the clock. Being at the bar allowed these young men to shine in front of potential future employers and become a known entity outside their immediate working circle. They could introduce themselves to senior colleagues with whom they would never otherwise interact. They became mates with men twice their age for whom they'd be front of mind when a job came up for some bright ambitious kid. Their time was far better spent than mine, and their careers thrived because of it.

That women are 'bad' networkers is a widely accepted fiction in the corporate world. But, as you will know by now, that isn't actually the case. Connection and forming relationships is a key motivator for the female brain. Networking is something women can and should be excellent at. What women are bad at – or what they avoid – is the kind of networking that is constructed for and by men. And because men have dominated workplaces and work-related spaces for so long, most of us can't actually tell the difference. We associate networking with the old boys' club.

The too-many-drinks-at-the-pub-and-let's-organise-a-stripper-or-go-to-the-casino-later version of networking. By its very definition, this is an activity that excludes us.

But what if networking didn't have to be arrogant and bragging? What if networking didn't happen in the same places, in the same style and with the same purpose it has previously? Imagine if women then prioritised forging and nurturing our industry connections in the same way that men do. Imagine if we carved out new spaces for networking to happen, spaces where we felt accepted and welcomed. Imagine if we stopped feeling guilty when we attended an industry event or had that one-on-one with a client or a mentor. Imagine if we forged new professional alliances and friendships and working relationships that weren't based on who has the most bragger and swagger, but because we bonded over the content of our work and our passion for it. Imagine if we prioritised our working and industry relationships over that extra hour slaving away in the office after 5 p.m. and not being paid overtime. Imagine if we fought past the awkward and the uncomfortable and the wanker-factor and the 'this has to be done out of hours' anxiety and Did. It. Anyway.

How to network without being a bragger

Networking is a fancy word for talking to people. Calling it 'networking' makes it sound formal, important and intimidating, but it doesn't need to be. It's just people. It's just talking. The fastest and easiest way to network is by inviting someone you've met and connected with to have a cup of coffee or tea or to share your lunch on a park bench. It might be a client or it might be a colleague or even someone who is connected to your industry only tangentially. Suggesting that you stay in touch doesn't have to be done in a confected or conceited way. Just be you. Do it your way. If you really enjoyed talking to someone, then tell them that. If you admire someone's career path and want to know more about it, tell them that too. If you think they work for a fascinating company and you are hanging out for more stories, tell them. If you've faced common barriers to succeeding or being accepted at work, tell them. If you're looking for new work opportunities, tell them. A little bit of honesty can get you a long way.

If you're up for even more networking, then try attending an industry event. There is usually information about these sorts of events available in workplaces, but, otherwise, have a look online for what's happening in your city or check in with your union or industry association. It's easy to assume that these sorts of functions only exist for lawyers and stock market types, but actually they happen in most industries. You might be surprised by how much is actually going on. Then instead of thinking, *I am setting out to network tonight*, focus on simply having a good time and meeting some new people. That's all you have to do. Don't worry about who is going to get what from whom and when. Worrying about that will inhibit your ability to build a relationship. Be cordial, be generous, be kind and be yourself. If you're feeling nervous or at risk of falling into the wanker trap, then try using these additional tips to help you get by.

1. **Don't think about what networking will do for you, think about what you can do for others.**

   I am pretty sure if former US president John F. Kennedy had been alive in the 2010s he would have said it that way himself. Approaching a networking opportunity focused on what you personally are going to get out of it and who might be able to help you further your career is a recipe for disaster.

It's also a really arsehole-level thing to do. Instead, think about
how you can help the person or people you are talking to.
Be generous with yourself, with your time, your expertise
and your contacts, and eventually the same will come back
to you in turn.

2. **Everybody is important. Every relationship deserves attention.**
   Whether you're meeting someone for the first time over coffee
   or standing in a room full of people, try to give them your full
   attention. You're not a teenager at a One Direction concert
   desperately trying to get a selfie with one of the band. Don't be
   a fan girl over the most important person in the room. Instead,
   give everyone a chance and don't dismiss people who you
   might think unworthy of your time. Everyone is important
   and everyone has something to offer, not just the people you're
   hoping might employ you one day. In fact, why not specifically
   seek out people who seem left out? You can bond over feeling
   uncomfortable and it will give you something to talk about.

3. **Don't obstruct the conversation before it starts –
   aka put the damn phone away.**
   Often when you're in a self-conscious situation, you'll use your
   smart phone as a safety blanket. Burying your head in your
   phone is a subconscious attempt to look busy. You're trying
   to telegraph to the room that while you may not have anyone
   to talk to here, there are *definitely* people elsewhere who want
   to talk to you. The problem is, being on your phone all the
   time *does* make you look busy. It also makes you seem distant,
   unapproachable and uninterested. So put it in your pocket
   or your handbag. Buy a drink at the bar and use the glass to
   occupy your hands if you're desperate to be holding on to
   something. Be brave.

4. **Networking is about listening more than talking. Everyone's favourite topic is themselves.**
The purpose of networking isn't for everyone to leave the event with your resumé embedded in their brain. Avoid blatant self-promotion and focus on making conversation the same way you would at a mate's barbecue. Ask lots of questions and actually listen to the answers, no matter how boring. Resist the temptation to talk about yourself the whole time and concentrate on what is being said to you. Listen. Then demonstrate the fact that you've listened by pulling out the key points, quoting them or rephrasing. Remember that people *are* interesting, especially when they're in the same field as you. Talk for long enough and you'll find common ground.

5. **Have a short 30-second spiel about yourself down pat.**
There are going to be some points when you need to talk about yourself. So have an elevator pitch ready to go – a quick summary of who you are and what you do that can be conveyed in the time it takes to ride a lift next to someone. Once you've said that, shut up and go back to talking about something else. Remember, you aren't trying to sell yourself – this isn't a job interview. If you're an introvert it can also be helpful to have some small goals set. That way you aren't putting extreme pressure on yourself to go outside your comfort zone and transform into the life of the party. For example, 'I will talk to two people I haven't met before,' or 'I will go home after I introduce myself to one group of strangers.'

For the love of Oprah, please quit asking strangers to be your mentor.

Mentoring has been hailed as the almighty solution to the lack of women in leadership roles. The theory is that by connecting bright young women with successful, experienced women, the younger women will get to see how it's done. Together these pairs will create mutually beneficial relationships of care, advice and career coaching before dancing off into the sunset with big corporate bonuses in their pockets. Many large companies now have formal mentoring programs to help facilitate these relationships. Awkward first-date-type scenarios happen where two people with very little in common are expected to form a firm friendship. The younger woman is usually anxious about what to say and how to connect with someone senior whom she barely knows. The more experienced woman is frustrated that she has to take time away from her job to invest in someone who doesn't work for her, and that her men colleagues don't have to do the same.

If you can't tell already, I'm not a fan of excessively formal mentoring programs. While they may have worked for others, I've never found them to be effective in the long term. They can create a manufactured relationship between two people who might have no actual meaningful connection. Sure, a one-off meeting with someone senior who shares advice and experience can be really useful. However, a genuine mentor—mentee relationship is one that lasts. It must be a relationship of trust and authentic investment in one another's careers. The less experienced person has to not just admire but also sincerely respect the more experienced person – and respect takes time to build. The more experienced person has to actually care about their junior's career. Mentorship that is mandated can absolutely work. However, it can also create resentment and frustration, while mentorship that is freely and generously given is more likely to be rewarding.

In my experience, the best mentoring relationships tend to come about by accident. They're not concocted by an organisational hierarchy that wants to tick the 'gender equity' box on their annual report. If you're looking for more guidance in your work and you'd like to be mentored, then begin by considering people already in your circle. They might be friends of your parents, or parents of your friends. They might be a former boss or colleague. They might be a man. I'm not sure when the world decided that the advancement of women through the ranks was the exclusive responsibility of other women. Men have a role to play in nurturing the early careers of women, too. We have to move past the idea that it is only our responsibility to support and nurture the careers of people who are *the same as us*. That kind of thinking will only reinforce workplace structures that disadvantage women and minorities. Remember also that mentoring happens at all levels. A mentor doesn't have to be someone with 20 or 30 years more life or professional experience. Mentoring happens at the beginning of a career, in the middle, and even at the most senior ranks. We can all learn something from someone else; we all have something we've never done before and could use a hand with. That means you can *be* a mentor as well as having one. There are enormous rewards that flow from mentoring someone. It is unquestionably a mutually beneficial relationship. It's a seriously great feeling seeing young women or women who have been shut out of success previously, whose talents you've nurtured and whose fears you've settled, begin to thrive.

Mentors are good but sponsors are even better.

To move up in the world of work you need two things: a push and a pull. The push comes from within, it's the thing inside you that looks to the upper ranks of your organisation and thinks, *I'd like to do that one day*. The push is your motivation, your drive, your talents and your abilities that propel you upwards. A mentor might be a part of this too, because they'll help you make strategic decisions about how to get that push happening. The pull comes from above. The pull is where sponsors matter.

In most workplaces, promotions are not decided according to an objective measure. Unless you're a 100-metre sprinter who runs your way into the next level of achievement by beating everyone else to the finish line, then it is another *person* making the decision about your promotion. That decision is necessarily going to be subjective. While a boss or your boss's boss is the one making that decision, there will be other senior people in the organisation whose views carry weight. And just like a mentor helps with the pushing, a sponsor leans over and assists with the pulling.

A sponsor is someone who advocates for you to get a particular job or promotion from *above*. This means that they are actively helping you to advance. A mentor, by contrast, actively helps you to help *yourself* to advance. A sponsor might not have a long-term emotional investment in your career, but their help on a single occasion will often be the difference between you getting or missing out on a promotion. The Center for Talent Innovation in the US conducted an extensive survey of more than 12 000 white-collar workers and they found that:

> Women are 46 percent more likely than men to be absent the senior-level advocacy that propels top performers into top jobs.

They don't have, as men do, someone in the C suite who will put their name forward and go to bat for them. When they do, our data show, they punch through: women with sponsors are 27 percent more likely than their unsponsored female peers to ask for a raise. They're 22 percent more likely to ask for those all-important stretch assignments, the projects that put them on the radar of the higher-ups. The more progress they make, the more satisfied they are, and the likelier they are to lean in – a 'sponsor effect' on career advancement that we've quantified at 19 percent.'

When I was a student, my sponsor arrived in the unlikely form of the vice-chancellor, an intimidating man called Ian Chubb. On the scale of relative importance and influence within the university, Ian was number one, and I was several thousand notches further down. My student council colleagues and I had spent most of the year working on a paper about how education could be improved at the university. We had a humble 42 recommendations for how the university could improve teaching and learning for the undergraduate students. Some of the recommendations were significant changes to how things had always been done.

Sitting in the meeting where we would present our paper, I remember reaching across to hold the hand of my friend and fellow student Madeleine under the table. It was really daunting. We were about to tell a room of academics and senior university staff – the people who marked our essays – what they could do better. Talk about telling truth to power. At that moment, Ian strode into the room and took a seat at the head of the table. The meeting hadn't even started, but everyone seemed to sit up straighter. Some of the staff began shuffling their papers around, trying to look important.

The vice-chancellor didn't normally attend this meeting. When Ian stood up to speak, he was holding a bound copy of our paper in his right hand.

'I want you all to know that I've read this,' he said in his deep, booming voice. 'And that this meeting will start from the presumption that all the recommendations should be accepted. You can rebut that presumption. You can argue all you want, but the starting point is that we're doing all of this.' He smiled at me and walked out of the room, not even waiting for the rest of the staff to respond. With just two minutes of his time, Ian had increased my level of influence significantly. He had effectively gifted me his power in a meeting where I possessed little of my own. I hadn't even opened my mouth to speak and yet my arguments were already more persuasive than they would otherwise have been. In that moment, Ian had been my sponsor. He set me up for success.

Sponsors can take varied and often unlikely forms. So if you're sitting there panicking that you don't have any, chill. You probably do. By working hard, putting your hand up for new challenges and making the effort to network and meet people in your industry, you'll have impressed potential sponsors without even knowing it. They might look out for opportunities that would suit you and then influence their own networks in your favour. They might promote your ideas in meetings and ensure you're getting public credit for your good work. They might argue against someone who talks down your contribution. They might mention your name when one of their senior colleagues asks them to recommend someone for a role. Or they might grasp you kindly by the arm, walk you across the room and introduce you to the Big Boss as someone who deserves more than a cursory glance.

Shine theory (or 'building an old girls' club where we all shall live')

I read an article in *New York* magazine about former US president Barack Obama's women staff. As political aides at the highest level of government, they struggled just like the rest of us to have their voices heard. In meetings they would be talked over, interrupted, or even ignored. Mansplaining was a regular event. Often one of them would make a great point only to have it passed over until it was subsequently made by a man and applauded. But instead of retreating into themselves and giving up, the women formed a pact. Every time one of them made a particularly significant point in a meeting, one of the others would reaffirm it, paying credit to the woman whose idea it was. Then another would reinforce the point again, backing her woman colleague. The point would be repeated, rephrased and its original source noted until eventually the group acknowledged it. Over time their voices became louder and stronger. They were far more powerful together than they ever could have been alone. They became one another's sponsors by helping one another to shine.

Earlier I said that the role of a sponsor is to pull someone up. Well, sometimes a sponsor can do that important work while sitting alongside someone in the workplace hierarchy. That is, sponsors don't always have to be the most senior people in an organisation. You can choose to sponsor another woman at work by dedicating yourself to making sure her voice is heard and her contribution is valued. Instead of seeing other women as competitors at work, see them as comrades. Remember that success is not finite. There isn't a limited quantity of success to go around. When success comes to another clever, talented woman at work, it doesn't mean you are any less clever or talented. It doesn't mean you are any less worthy of or likely to achieve success.

Writer Ann Friedman and Aminatou Sow call this method of women supporting one another to improve the lot of women 'shine theory'. Friedman advises:

> When you meet a woman who is intimidatingly witty, stylish, beautiful, and professionally accomplished, *befriend her.* Surrounding yourself with the best people doesn't make you look worse by comparison. It makes you better.

I would go further than Friedman. Don't only surround yourself with women whose success and recognition intimidates you. Also try to reach out to women who are deserving of success and recognition but may not be receiving it. You can use your opportunities and your success to help foster opportunities and success for others. That includes women who may not be as privileged as you or who are facing multiple forms of disadvantage at work. As former First Lady Michelle Obama puts it:

> When you've worked hard, and done well, and walked through that doorway of opportunity . . . you do not slam it shut behind you . . . you reach back, and you give other folks the same chances that helped you succeed.

We've already talked about the stereotype that women see one another as enemies at work. That we take pleasure in one another's failures, giggling behind backs and bitching beneath cupped hands. Once we gain power we're depicted with devil horns and pitchforks, crushing other women beneath our pointy high heels. This stereotype is so pervasive that many of us give in to it. We do not have to. We can be better than that. We can laugh at that stereotype for the bullshit concoction that it is. We can be one another's greatest allies and greatest supporters. We can quit worrying about being liked by the Old Boys' Club and instead link arms with our sisters, fighting for a better deal together. We can ensure that our feminism is inclusive and intersectional, even when it can be all too easy to forget the struggles of others that we do not share. We can take the time to recognise that some of our sisters face challenges we do not and that we may never fully understand. Nonetheless we can hold each other up and coax one another to hold on. We can stop calling ourselves lucky and help other women by passing on and sharing the things we've learned along the way. We can be sponsors who give one another the chance to shine.

Women working together can and have changed the course of history. They will again if we so choose, because when women support women everyone wins.

CONCLUSION

Because that'll do, pig, that'll do.

I'm back at the Australian National University for a speech and this time I'm absolutely going to keep my shit together. The sky is clear and the weather is a balmy 31 degrees; a makeshift stage has been constructed outdoors to take advantage of the sunshine. The casual slouching of the students contrasts with the neat plastic lawn chairs that are lined up in orderly rows as far as the eye can see. Coloured flags hang from luscious green trees, which reach over us from either side of University Avenue, meeting in the middle to form a shady canopy. You can smell the eucalypt in the air of Australia's bush capital. It really is beautiful. We're here to celebrate the start of the academic calendar, not to mark the end. So there are no assessments or exams, no papers to grade or unwritten theses to worry about today. The atmosphere is relaxed and happy and so am I. Despite my shaky presentation a few years earlier, this morning I'm nerve-free and eager to begin.

This time, I'm confident. I know exactly what I want to say.

At the start of this book I told you about a famous piece of research that showed men apply for jobs when they meet just

60 per cent of the criteria. Women, on the other hand, won't apply until they're confident they meet the whole 100 per cent. We wait to tick every single box. We wait to be perfect. Well, it's taken me the better part of 30 years to figure it out, but I've decided to stop bothering with perfect and settle for good enough. Why? Because men aren't going to stop applying for jobs when they meet 60 per cent of the criteria. While you and I are sitting there thinking, *Oh but I couldn't possibly do that job, I don't have enough experience, or expertise, or qualifications, or talent,* there is a pretty average bloke who is applying anyway. And he's probably getting the gig. The world can't afford to keep waiting for women to be perfect. To make our workplaces better, our economies stronger and our world a kinder, more inclusive place, we're going to need every little bit of humanity's collective knowledge. We can't do that without women participating in workplaces to a greater degree – and at a higher decision-making level – than we do now.

Yes, women are imperfect creatures. Sometimes you will be the most qualified, the most talented and the most articulate person in the room. Sometimes you won't be. And that's okay too because you still have just as much to offer workplaces – and the world – as the men who run them today. You simply have to find the confidence to have a go. There is already systemic discrimination that makes it inherently harder for women and girls to succeed. Women can't accept any additional obstacles in the race; we're already starting from several metres behind. Many of those obstacles lie outside our immediate control as individuals, but confidence is not one of them. Confidence is ours to control. It is ours to master and ours to conquer. The ability to overcome our conditioning, our fear of failure, our self-doubt and our incessant desire to be liked is something women already possess. Like Dorothy in *The Wizard of Oz,* we've had the power to be confident all along – we just have to find it for ourselves.

Start with the confidence to stop calling yourself lucky.

You may be a privileged person and you may have lived a fortunate life. Acknowledging that is a good thing, an important thing, to do. But do not mistake your hard-fought achievements as the product of luck. The success that comes from working hard, honing your talent and perfecting your skills is not luck. The self-described greatest tennis player of all time, Serena Williams says, 'Luck has nothing to do with it, because I have spent many, many hours, countless hours, on the court working for my one moment in time, not knowing when it would come.'

Every working woman I know struggles with confidence. It holds many of them back from the glittering careers they would otherwise be pursuing. It holds them back from helping others, from looking after their families, from making a difference and from exercising power. It also holds them back from claiming credit for what they achieve. 'Luck' is a substitute for women's lack of confidence and our desire to be liked. It is one of the many ways we twist and turn ourselves inside out to please other people. To seem less powerful, less threatening, less likely to take up space that would otherwise be occupied by a man. By falling back on 'luck' as the explanation for our successes, we reaffirm our lack of confidence again and again and again. And so it remains, lurking behind every barrier, tripping women ahead of each new challenge.

When we call our success 'lucky', we are not being humble. We are not being self-effacing. We are not making ourselves any more likeable. Worse still, we are depriving other women of the opportunity to learn from us. After all, luck can't be imitated or copied. So when we describe our successes as luck, we inadvertently hold the secrets of that success close to our chests. We diminish our own achievements while at the same time making it harder for those women who wish to emulate us. Instead, we should be sharing that experience with others, to give a boost to the next generation by being open and generous with what we've learned. If women are going to lay a greater claim to workplace success, then we have to have each other's backs.

I know it sounds hard. It sounds hard because it is hard. You and I were born into a world where the work of feminism is not done yet. Girls are still taught to look nice, play nice and be nice, and adult women earn less, are heard less and hurt more. For women who face multiple forms of disadvantage, there is more acute intersecting discrimination lurking on worksites, in office cubicles and behind cash registers. A man with zero qualifications can beat a woman with exemplary ones for the most powerful job in the world and that's just how it goes.

But never forget that as hard as things might seem, it was harder for the women who came before us. And if we do our job right it will be less hard for the women who come after us. Our generation is better placed to achieve gender equality than any other in the history of humanity. This is our opportunity to grasp, our campaign to join and it is our fight to be won. So get out there. Show the world your best, be confident and claim your achievements as your own. I'll be right here, cheering you on from the sidelines.

Because you're not just lucky, you're brilliant.

ACKNOWLEDGEMENTS

This book would have been absolute rubbish without the care, guidance and wizardry of the team at Penguin Random House in Melbourne. To Cate Blake, this wasn't your biological book baby but you were the best damn adopted parent she could have had. To Louise Ryan, your fierce belief in *Not Just Lucky* – even before you'd read a word – helped bridge my own confidence gap. To Arwen Summers, you are mighty, magical, and your magnificent editing is a marvel to behold. Thank you also to Sarah Fairhall, Chloe Davies, Jackie Money, Adam Laszczuk and Amanda Martin: your talents and expertise are the reason people who are not my mum might actually buy this book.

To Erin O'Neill, your tremendous support during the research phase was tremendous. Let us never again speak of the chapter that became 'Defining the Double Standard'. To Dr Jennifer Stapledon and Dr Catherine McMahon, I so appreciated your time, care and expertise in making sure I didn't lie about science. It's super handy having such clever aunts. To my manager, Tania Petsinis, thank you for putting up with incessant emails, constant worrying and an excess of political ranting – may you always vote Labor from this day forward. To Laura Bell, thank you for your painstaking work on the references. And thank you to Gaida Cirulis for generously welcoming me into your home when I had too much left to write and too few days to do it in.

While writing *Not Just Lucky* I took shameless advantage of the free wi-fi and excellent coffee at cafes in my neighbourhood. I owe a particularly great debt to Claire and Libby at *Short Round* and to Liam and the baristas/counsellors at *Ampersand*. To my writing buddy Sari Braithwaite, thank you for listening and laughing with me through the hard bits. Thank you to the women I have worked with who generously allowed me to share stories that were theirs as well as my own. I particularly want to thank those women whose stories appear in the 'Sexism and Sexual Harassment' chapter. Each of you is brave and brilliant; I am so sorry for what you went through.

I have been fortunate to work closely with some tremendous operators in my career. To Kate Ellis, Mia Freedman and Ian Chubb, I will always be grateful for your guidance and mentorship; it was a privilege to learn from you. To my friends and heroes who generously provided quotes of endorsement for *Not Just Lucky*. It is a deeply unedifying exercise to approach the people you admire most and ask them to say nice things about you. To Julia Gillard, Lisa Wilkinson, Zoë Foster Blake, Rosie Waterland and Clementine Ford, thank you for being so kind and, also, so worthy of admiration in the first place.

It takes a village to raise a child and it takes an even bigger village to raise a child while writing a book. To Monica, Mum and Dad, thank you for keeping Rafi entertained while I holed myself away in the study with a laptop. To the Thornbury Family, thank you for park trips, emergency babysitting, BBQs, early morning coffees and late(ish) afternoon beers. To 'The Mamas', discovering each of you has been one of the unexpected delights of parenthood. Thank you for your unflinching belief in this book. To the women who work so that other women can work, Australia owes you an enormous debt. Thank you specifically to my toddler's early childhood educators and carers: Paige Lindsay, Dimity Kirkwood and India Bailey, you saved the day – and my sanity – more than a couple of times over the past 12 months. To the staff at Kool Kidz in Preston, you're all glorious. Special thanks goes to Adriana Cosma, Debra Budge and Crystal Beale for cuddling Rafi when I couldn't.

A bundle of love and appreciation goes to my sister, Miriam Rizvi, and dear friend Alys Gagnon who both read hideous early drafts of *Not Just Lucky*. Thank you for being the very first audience and not laughing at me too much. To my girlfriends Marielle Smith, Lucy Ormonde and Anika Wells, thank you for your support, your humour and the careful consideration you gave the title of this book; it's funny how we ended up right back where we started. To 'The Girls' who were my original sisterhood, your forensic analysis of the hand model used on the cover was much appreciated. To Laura Fitzpatrick and Fran Vavallo, your names are here because you're both rad and also because Fran insisted she be included. To Clare Bowditch, I would never have been brave enough to try without your prodding and praise. Now it's your turn.

And finally, thank you to my family. I may be relinquishing the right to call myself 'lucky' at work but I most certainly won the lottery of love. To Mum, Dad, Mim, Jeremy and Rafi: you are my everything. Thank you.

ENDNOTES

Some stories included in this book have previously appeared in columns published on Mamamia. These are reproduced with permission.

Introduction

3   **Even the women who . . .** Workplace Gender Equality Agency, Graduate Statistics – Starting Salary, February 2016, https://www.wgea.gov.au/sites/default/files/GradStats_factsheet_2016.pdf

4   **Flagged down by *Access Hollywood* . . .** https://www.accesshollywood.com/videos/oscars-cate-blanchett-feeling-lucky-over-extraordinary-win-44368/

4   **Television host and former . . .** http://profilemag.com.au/lisa-wilkinson-queen-of-hearts/

4   **Just before Gail Kelly became CEO . . .** http://www.abc.net.au/news/2014-11-17/verrender-above-all,-gail-kelly-was-the-master-of-good-timing/5896068

4   **Oh, I was just lucky . . .** https://www.lawyersweekly.com.au/news/15703-women-need-to-be-kinder-to-each-other

5   **The formidable Lady Justice . . .** http://www.city.ac.uk/news/2016/march/an-audience-with-a-law-lord

5   **Reflecting on her career . . .** https://www.theatlantic.com/technology/archive/2012/02/in-the-new-york-times-sheryl-sandberg-is-lucky-men-are-good/252686/

5   **The late Princess Diana . . .** http://www.bbc.co.uk/news/special/politics97/diana/panorama.html

5   **PepsiCo CEO Indra Nooyi . . .** http://millieleung.com/top-40-inspirational-quotes-for-women-entrepreneurs/

5   **Olympic judo champion . . .** https://www.brainyquote.com/quotes/quotes/r/rondarouse541452.html

5   **And what helped Ursula Burns . . .** https://www.progressivewomensleadership.com/inside-the-c-suite-meet-ursula-burns-ceo-xerox/

11 **They read in the newspaper . . .** As reported by *The Guardian* and others, March 2017. http://www.theguardian.com/sustainable-business/2017/mar/02/australian-women-at-work-underpaid-discriminated-against-told-to-be-more-confident

12 **But the question we ask . . .** Institute for State and Local Governance Report, research conducted by the CUNY Institute, September 2016, http://islg.cuny.edu/sites/2016/09/26/who-runs-our-cities-new-report-on-political-gender-gap/

12   Men, on the other hand . . . Internal Hewlett Packard study, as reported in 'Why women don't apply for jobs unless they're 100 percent qualified' in the *Harvard Business Review*. https://hbr.org/2014/08/why-women-dont-apply-for-jobs-unless-theyre-100-qualified

Forget about nature versus nurture

16   Modern science has repeatedly . . . Colom R, Karama S, Jung R and Haier R, 'Human intelligence and brain networks', *Dialogues in Clinical Neuroscience*, 4(12), December 2010.

16   Some research indicates . . . Colom R, Karama S, Jung R and Haier R, 'Human intelligence and brain networks', *Dialogues in Clinical Neuroscience*, 4(12), December 2010.

17   That's why baby girls . . . McClure 2000, McClure, E.B. (2000). 'A meta-analytic review of sex differences in facial expression processing and their development in infants, children, and adolescents' *Psychological Bulletin*, 126(3), 424–453.

17   While baby boys . . . Marie Ellis, 'Female intuition comes from lower testosterone exposure in womb', *Medical News Today*, 25 April 2014.

17   However, that hypothesis . . . 'Male/female brain differences? Big data says not so much.' *ScienceDaily*, 29 October 2015. <www.sciencedaily.com/releases/2015/10/151029185544. htm>.

17   Male brains have been found . . . Giedd, JN, 'Structural Magnetic Resonance Imaging of the Adolescent Brain', *Annals of the New York Academy of Sciences*, 2014, 1021: 77–85. doi:10.1196/annals.1308.009

18   But, again, more recent studies . . . Ruben C. Gur, Faith Gunning-Dixon, Warren B. Bilker, Raquel E. Gur, 'Sex Differences in Temporo-limbic and Frontal Brain Volumes of Healthy Adults'. *Cereb Cortex* 2002; 12 (9).

18   More recently, researchers . . . *Children Families and Communities*, 5th edition, R Grace, K Hodge and C McMahon, 2016 Oxford University Press.

18   The key takeaway here . . . Cordelia Fine, *Delusions of Gender*, WW Norton and Company Publishing, 2011.

18   In fact, the *total* genomic . . . Jenny Graves, 'Differences between men and women are more than the sum of their genes', *The Conversation*, July 2015: https://theconversation. com/differences-between-men-and-women-are-more-than-the-sum-of-their-genes-39490

18   While every human being . . . *Brain and Culture: Neurobiology, Ideology, and Social Change* (MIT Press), Bruce E Wexler, 2006.

18   Many of the attributes . . . Paul A. Boghossian, 'What is Social Construction', New York University: http://philosophy.fas.nyu.edu/docs/IO/1153/socialconstruction.pdf.

18   The emerging field of epigenetics . . . DP Keating, 'Transformative Role of Epigenetics in Child Development Research: Commentary on the Special Section.' *Child Development*, 2016 Jan-Feb, 87(1): https://www.ncbi.nlm.nih.gov/pubmed/26822449.

19   Lise Eliot, associate profession . . . As quoted in Robin McKie, 'Male and female ability differences down to socialisation, not genetics', *The Guardian*, 15 August 2010: https:// www.theguardian.com/world/2010/aug/15/girls-boys-think-same-way

20   The impact of gender roles . . . Cordelia Fine, *Delusions of Gender*, WW Norton and Company Publishing, 2011.

22   Did you know that mothers . . . Schoppe-Sullivan, Diener, Mangelsdorf, Brown, McHale and Frosch, 'Attachment and sensitivity in family context the roles of parent and infant gender', *Infant and Child Development*, (2006).

22 **Some studies show that a mother** . . . Halpern, DF 2012, *Sex Differences in Cognitive Abilities*, 4th ed, Psychology Press, New York.

22 **For example, baby boys are more likely** . . . Judith E. Owen Blakemore; Sheri A Berenbaum; Lynn S Liben, *Gender Development*, Psychology Press, 2013.

22 **Mothers of sons routinely** . . . Mondschein ER, Adolph KE, Tamis-LeMonda CS, 'Gender bias in mothers' expectations about infant crawling', *Journal of Experimental Child Psychology*, December 2000, 77(4).

22 **While girls and boys spend** . . . Halpern, DF 2012, *Sex Differences in Cognitive Abilities*, 4th ed, Psychology Press, New York.

23 **In one study, researchers observed** . . . B Morrongiello, T Dawber, 'Parental Influences on Toddlers' Injury-Risk Behaviours: Are Sons and Daughters Socialized Differently?' *Journal of Applied Developmental Psychology*, June 199, 20(2).

24 **Girls' conditioned nervousness** . . . Elizabeth E. O'Neal, BAJ odie M. Plumert, PhD Carole Peterson, PhD 'Parent–Child Injury Prevention Conversations Following a Trip to the Emergency Department', *Journal of Pediatric Psychology* (2016) 41(2).

25 **Instead of showing** . . . Reshma Saujani, TED Talk: http://www.ted.com/talks/reshma_saujani_teach_girls_bravery_not_perfection/

25 **A whopping 90 per cent** . . . Sheridan, M. D. *From birth to five years: Children's developmental progress*, (1998) ACER Press.

25 **Babies are born with** . . . *Children Families and Communities*, 5th edition, R Grace, K Hodge and C McMahon, 2016 Oxford University Press

27 **This means that their observation** . . . Linda Babcock & Sara Laschever, *Women don't ask: Negotiation and the Gender Divide*, Princeton University Press (2003).

28 **This is well before** . . . Jae Curtis, 'Reducing Gender Stereotypes in Your Home, March 2012: http://www.education.com/magazine/article/gender-stereotypes-kids/

29 **The praise or censure** . . . Bussey, K. Gender identity development. In S.J. Schwartz, Luyckx, K., & Vignoles, V. L. (Eds.) *Handbook of identity theory and research* (2011) Springer.

Sugar, spice and all things nice

32 **Why? Because 'everybody likes her'** . . . Starr CR and Ferguson GM, 'Sexy Dolls, Sexy Grade-Schoolers? Media & Maternal Influences on Young Girls' Self-Sexualization' *Sex Roles* (2012) 67.

32 **Physical beauty, being dressed up** . . . Chadwick, Dara, *You'd be so pretty if . . . : Teaching our daughters to love their bodies – even when we don't love our own*, DaCapo Press (2009).

33 **Research shows that parents** . . . Laura D. Hanish, Richard A. Fabes, 'Peer socialization of gender in young boys and girls' *T. Denny Sanford School of Social and Family Dynamics*, Arizona State University, August 2014.

33 **Teachers also tend** . . . Judith E. Owen Blakemore; Sheri A Berenbaum; Lynn S Liben, *Gender Development*, Psychology Press, 2013.

33 **Behaving in this so-called** . . . Allan, Alexandra Jane, 2009. The importance of being a 'lady': hyper-femininity and heterosexuality in the private, single-sex primary school.

34 **They're expected to be less** . . . UNICEF Educational Resources, Early Gender Socialisation: https://www.unicef.org/earlychildhood/index_40749.html

34 **Publishers know this** . . . Janice McCabe, Emily Fairchild, Liz Grauerholz, Bernice A. Pescosolido, Daniel Tope, 'Gender in 20th Century Children's Books: Patterns of Disparity in Title and Central Characters', *Gender and Society*, April 2011.

35   **For girls from Indian . . .** Chris Kinkaid, 'Gender Roles of Women in Modern Japan', *Japan Powered*, (June 2014): http://www.japanpowered.com/japan-culture/gender-roles-women-modern-japan

35   **One study found this to be a causal . . .** Paechter, Carrie and Clark, 'Being "nice" or being "normal": girls resisting discourses of "coolness."' (2016) *Discourse: Studies in the Cultural Politics of Education*, 37(3).

36   **A study of toy catalogues . . .** Auster, C.J. & Mansbach, C.S. 'The Gender Marketing of Toys: An Analysis of Color and Type of Toy on the Disney Store Website', *Sex Roles* (2012).

37   **In family films – those . . .** See research conducted for the Geena Davis Institute on Gender in Media (2012): https://seejane.org/research-informs-empowers/

37   **Here in Australia the workforce . . .** Workplace Gender Equality Agency, Statistics at a Glance Fact Sheet: https://www.wgea.gov.au/sites/default/files/Stats_at_a_Glance.pdf

37   **That psychological ceiling . . .** As quoted in press release for the Geena Davis Institute on Gender in Media: https://seejane.org/

38   **Actress Emily Blunt . . .** As reported on *Jezebel*: http://jezebel.com/the-girl-on-the-trains-emily-blunt-likable-is-my-least-1787199735

39   **Anea Bogue, creator of . . .** As quoted in *Forbes* (2012): http://www.forbes.com/sites/learnvest/2012/06/28/7-ways-youre-hurting-your-daughters-future/#109facf633bf

Defining the double standard

44   **Psychologist Carol Dweck . . .** Carol Dweck, *Mindset: The New Psychology of Success*.

44   **NAPLAN results show . . .** Australia's NAPLAN results 2015, national report available here: http://www.nap.edu.au/verve/_resources/2015_NAPLAN_national_report.pdf

44   **Average university admission . . .** See for example: NSW/ACT ATAR averages, 2015: http://uac.edu.au/documents/atar/2015_Prelim_ScalingReport.pdf

45   **Successive studies have shown . . .** Professor Margaret Vickers, as told to Geoff Maslen for the *Sydney Morning Herald* in November 2013: http://www.smh.com.au/national/education/degrees-of-separation-more-women-enrolling-at-universities-20131124-2y46e.html

45   **Similar patterns are . . .** Hannah Rosin, *The End of Men*, Riverhead Books (2012).

45   **Add into the mix . . .** As told to John Tierney, 'The perils of being a male teacher at an all girls school' *The Atlantic*, March 2013: https://www.theatlantic.com/sexes/archive/2013/03/the-perils-of-being-a-male-teacher-at-an-all-girls-school/274411/

46   **For example, women are . . .** Sean Coughlan, 'Men 'outperformed at university", *BBC World News* June 2009: http://news.bbc.co.uk/2/hi/uk_news/education/8085011.stm

46   **There were almost 80 000 . . .** As reported by *The Australian*, http://www.theaustralian.com.au/higher-education/gender-gap-widens-as-women-graduates-outpace-the-men/news-story/654602edef0f1d3ee230fa82cc58a798

46   **Of students graduating . . .** Sean Coughlan, 'Men 'outperformed at university", *BBC World News* June 2009: http://news.bbc.co.uk/2/hi/uk_news/education/8085011.stm

48   **Being nice and behaving nicely . . .** Linda Babcock & Sara Laschever, *Women don't ask: Negotiation and the Gender Divide*, Princeton University Press (2003).

48   **Some research suggests that competing . . .** Hibbard DR & Buhrmester D. Competitiveness, gender, and adjustment among adolescents. *Sex Roles* (2010).

49   **What could have been healthy . . .** Margolies, L. (2016). Competition Among Women: Myth and Reality. *Psych Central*. Retrieved on April 28, 2017, from https://psychcentral.com/lib/competition-among-women-myth-and-reality/

50 **In order to be taken more seriously** . . . See for example Sophia Amoruso, *Girl Boss*, (2015) Penguin.

50 **Other supposedly problematic behaviours** . . . See for example Lois P. Frankel, *Nice Girls Don't Get the Corner Office*, (2014), Little, Brown and Company.

51 **In one study, researchers** . . .Rudman, L. A. 'Self-promotion as a risk factor for women: The costs and benefits of counter-stereotypical impression management' (1998) *Journal of Personality and Social Psychology*, 74(3).

52 **Yet when they do** . . . Rudman, L. A. 'Self-promotion as a risk factor for women: The costs and benefits of counter-stereotypical impression management' (1998) *Journal of Personality and Social Psychology*, 74(3).

52 **These negative stereotypes** . . . Linda Babcock & Sara Laschever, *Women don't ask: Negotiation and the Gender Divide*, Princeton University Press (2003).

52 **Women university graduates** . . . Workplace Gender Equality Agency, Graduate Statistics – Starting Salary, February 2016, https://www.wgea.gov.au/sites/default/files/ GradStats_factsheet_2016.pdf

53 **While men's salary earnings** . . . Westpac International Women's Day Report 2016 as reported in March 2016 by Sophie Elsworth for *NewsCorp Australia*: http://www.news. com.au/finance/work/careers/gender-pay-gap-new-push-for-parity-as-womens-salaries-start-lower-peak-earlier/

53 **The increasing casualisation** . . . Veronica Sheen, 'Labour in vain: casualisation presents a precarious future for workers', *The Conversation* July 2012: http://theconversation.com/ labour-in-vain-casualisation-presents-a-precarious-future-for-workers-8181

53 **As the overwhelming majority** . . . Workplace Gender Equality Agency, Gender Composition of the Workforce by Industry: https://www.wgea.gov.au/sites/default/ files/2014-04-04-Gender%20composition-of-the-workforce-by-industry.pdf

53 **Women are more likely** . . . As told to Anna Patty for *The Sydney Morning* Herald on February 2017: http://www.smh.com.au/business/workplace-relations/sunday-penalty-rates-women-to-bare-the-brunt-of-cuts-experts-say-20170224-gukj9u.html

53 **When duties around the home** . . . Belinda Hewitt, Janeen Baxter, Sharon Givans, Michael Murphy, Paul Myers and Cameron, Meiklejohn for the Office for Women, 'Men's engagement in shared care and domestic work in Australia' (2012): https://www.dss.gov.au/ sites/default/files/documents/05_2012/men_engaged_in_shared_care_1.pdf

53 **In households where women** . . . Belinda Hewitt, Janeen Baxter, Sharon Givans, Michael Murphy, Paul Myers and Cameron, Meiklejohn for the Office for Women, 'Men's engagement in shared care and domestic work in Australia' (2012): https://www.dss.gov.au/ sites/default/files/documents/05_2012/men_engaged_in_shared_care_1.pdf

54 **The achievement and earnings** . . . The Gender Equity Insights 2017: Inside Australia's Gender Pay Gap, Bankwest Curtin Economics Centre in collaboration with the Workplace Gender Equality Agency: http://news.curtin.edu.au/events/gender-equity-insights-2017-inside-australias-gender-pay-gap/

54 **Ninety per cent of senior** . . . Westpac International Women's Day Report 2016 as reported in March 2016 by Sophie Elsworth for NewsCorp Australia: http://www.news. com.au/finance/work/careers/gender-pay-gap-new-push-for-parity-as-womens-salaries-start-lower-peak-earlier/

54 **The 'stupid curve' refers** . . . The 'Stupid Curve' is a term coined by former Deloitte USA Chairman Mike Cook.

55 **Holding just 20 jobs** . . . As reported by Caroline Fairchild in Fortune, July 2014: http://fortune.com/2014/07/08/women-ceos-fortune-500-1000/

55 **Here at home, women** . . . Workplace Gender Equality Agency, Stats at a Glance: https://www.wgea.gov.au/sites/default/files/Stats_at_a_Glance.pdf

55 **But, still, there are more CEOs** . . . As reported by Matt Liddy and Catherine Hanrahan for the ABC in March 2017: http://www.abc.net.au/news/2017-03-08/fewer-women-ceos-than-men-named-john/8327938

55 **Australian women hold 23.6** . . . As reported by Matt Liddy and Catherine Hanrahan for the ABC in March 2017: http://www.abc.net.au/news/2017-03-08/fewer-women-ceos-than-men-named-john/8327938

55 **Women are also significantly** . . . Workplace Gender Equality Agency, Stats at a Glance: https://www.wgea.gov.au/sites/default/files/Stats_at_a_Glance.pdf

56 **The World Health Organization says** . . . World Health organisation recommendations as recorded by the Australian Human Rights Commission factsheet on Valuing Parenthood: https://www.humanrights.gov.au/publications/valuing-parenthood-part-d

56 **Casual and part-time employees** . . . Workplace Gender Equality Agency, Stats at a Glance: https://www.wgea.gov.au/sites/default/files/Stats_at_a_Glance.pdf

57 **Australian women with young children** . . . As reported by Elizabeth Hill for ABC News in May 2016: http://www.abc.net.au/news/2016-05-08/the-best-mothers-day-gift-paid-parental-leave/7389564

57 **Childcare costs rose 8.3 per cent** . . . *Child Care Affordability in Australia*, NATSEM report, University of Canberra (2016): http://www.natsem.canberra.edu.au/storage/AMP_NATSEM_35.pdf

58 **Labour participation rates for women** . . . Labour force participation rates as reported by the Australian Human Rights Commission factsheet on Valuing Parenthood: https://www.humanrights.gov.au/publications/valuing-parenthood-part-d

58 **Yet the presence of children** . . . As reported by the Australian Human Rights Commission factsheet on Valuing Parenthood: https://www.humanrights.gov.au/publications/valuing-parenthood-part-d

58 **Women spend twice as much** . . . Australian Bureau of Statistics, 2012 Census results, caring for children: http://www.abs.gov.au/ausstats/abs@.nsf/Lookup/by+Subject/4125.0-Jan+2012~Main+Features~Caring+for+children~4120

58 **Even when children are** . . . Australian Bureau of Statistics, 2012 Census results, caring for children: http://www.abs.gov.au/ausstats/abs@.nsf/Lookup/by+Subject/4125.0-Jan+2012~Main+Features~Caring+for+children~4120

58 **In 2011, only 51.2 per cent** . . . Australian Bureau of Statistics labour force participation data: http://www.abs.gov.au/ausstats/abs@.nsf/Lookup/4102.0main+features72014

58 **The unemployment rate for Indigenous** . . . Australian Bureau of Statistics labour force participation data: http://www.abs.gov.au/ausstats/abs@.nsf/Lookup/4102.0main+features72014

58 **It is debilitating to people** . . . As told to Beau Donelly and reported in *The Age* in November 2011: http://www.theage.com.au/victoria/aborigines-face-systemic-racial-discrimination-report-20151104-gkqlii.html

59 **The unemployment rate among women** . . . An Overview of the Status of Women With Disabilities in Australia, Women with Disabilities Australia data, accessed 20 October 2016: http://wwda.org.au/about/snapshot/

59 **Damned if you do, damned if you don't . . .** Stella Young, 'We're damned by discrimination not the DSP' *Ramp Up*, May 2014: http://www.abc.net.au/rampup/articles/2014/05/14/4004628.htm

59 **Women are overwhelmingly more . . .** Australian Bureau of Statistics, 2015 data on caring responsibilities: http://www.abs.gov.au/ausstats/abs@.nsf/Lookup/4125.0Feature+Article10009Feb%202015

59 **Over 70 per cent of . . .** Australian Bureau of Statistics, 2015 data on caring responsibilities: http://www.abs.gov.au/ausstats/abs@.nsf/Lookup/4125.0Feature+Article10009Feb%202015

59 **Twenty-three per cent of primary carers . . .** *The economic value of informal care in Australia*, Report by Access Economics for Carers Australia, 2015: http://www.carersaustralia.com.au/storage/access-economics-report-2015.pdf

60 **For example, there are deeply . . .** Helen Gow, 'Why Chinese women still can't get a break', *New York Times,* October 2016: http://www.nytimes.com/2016/10/16/opinion/why-chinese-women-still-cant-get-a-break.html

60 **These factors, coupled with . . .** Andre Chamberlain, 'Demystifying the Gender Pay Gap: Evidence from Glassdoor Salary Data' Glass Door, March 2016: https://www.glassdoor.com/research/studies/gender-pay-gap/

60 **Typically, an Australian woman . . .** Australian Human Rights Commission, fact sheet on gender pay gap and retirement savings: https://www.humanrights.gov.au/publications/gender-gap-retirement-savings

60 **A massive 40 per cent of retired . . .** Industry Super Australia Report as reported by Tracy Bowden, ABC 7.30, April 2016: http://www.abc.net.au/news/2016-04-21/super-gender-gap-leaves-australian-women-struggling/7346764

60 **Academic and writer Anne-Marie Slaughter . . .** Slaughter, Anne-Marie *Unfinished Business: Women, Men, Work, Family* (2015) Penguin Random House.

61 **In a recent report it found . . .** 'Barriers and Bias: The Status of Women in Leadership', *American Association of University Women,* March 2016: http://www.aauw.org/aauw_check/pdf_download/show_pdf

61 **Australian journalist and author Annabel Crabb . . .** Crabb, Annabel, *The Wife Drought,* (2015) Penguin Random House Australia.

The confidence deficit

64 **But did you know that . . .** Gilovich, Thomas; Kerr, Margaret; Medvec, Victoria H 'Effect of temporal perspective on subjective confidence', *Journal of Personality and Social Psychology*, 64(4), Apr 1993.

65 **They aren't *consciously trying* . . .** Katty Kay and Claire Shipman, 'The Confidence Gap', *The Atlantic* May 2014: http://www.theatlantic.com/magazine/archive/2014/05/the-confidence-gap/359815/

65 **People who are confident . . .** Ehrlinger and Dunning, *How Chronic Self-Views Influences (and Potentially Mislead) Estimates of Performance* (2003).

65 **Doing an action and . . .** Nanditha Ram, 'Visualize your success and sure enough it's yours' *Mind Body Science,* March 2016: http://www.mindbodyscience.news/2016-03-01-visualize-your-success-and-sure-enough-its-yours.html

65 **Research shows women tend . . .** Ehrlinger and Dunning, *How Chronic Self-Views Influences (and Potentially Mislead) Estimates of Performance* (2003).

66 **Self-advocacy is a big . . .** Amy Giddon as told to Naomi Woolf for 'Young women give up the vocal fry and reclaim your strong female voice', *The* Guardian July 2015: http://www.theguardian.com/commentisfree/2015/jul/24/vocal-fry-strong-female-voice

67 **Researchers at Columbia Business . . .** Reuben, E, Rey-Biel, P, Sapienza, P, Zingales, L 'The emergence of male leadership in competitive environments', *Journal of Economic Behaviour and Organisation* 83(1) June 2012.

67 **It was confidence that dictated . . .** Reuben, E, Rey-Biel, P, Sapienza, P, Zingales, L 'The emergence of male leadership in competitive environments', *Journal of Economic Behaviour and Organisation* 83(1) June 2012.

67 **The researchers concluded . . .** Reuben, E, Rey-Biel, P, Sapienza, P, Zingales, L 'The emergence of male leadership in competitive environments', *Journal of Economic Behaviour and Organisation* 83(1) June 2012.

What confidence sounds like

73 **It takes a grand total . . .** David DiSalvo, 'Your brain detected confidences in voices faster than you can blink' *Forbes*, March 2015: http://www.forbes.com/sites/daviddisalvo/2015/03/31/your-brain-detects-confidence-in-voices-faster-than-you-can-blink/#65aacf81522b

73 **The brain assesses voices . . .** Bonnie Gross as told to Leah eichler for 'Vocal fry is not a feminist issue' published in *The Globe and Mail* August 2015: http://www.theglobeandmail.com/report-on-business/careers/career-advice/life-at-work/vocal-fry-is-not-a-feminist-issue/article25880800/

73 **On the other hand . . .** Wolk, L, Abdelli-Beruh, NB, 'Habitual use of vocal fry in young adult female' *Journal of Voice*, 26(3) May 2012.

73 **In one study, researchers . . .** Research by *Quantified Impressions* as reported by Sue Shellenbarger, 'Is this how you really talk?' and published in *The Wall Street Journal* April 2013: https://www.wsj.com/articles/SB10001424127887323735604578440851083674898

74 **Nobody is really sure . . .** Amanda Marcotte 'The war on female voices is just another way of telling women to shut up' *Daily Dot*, July 2015: http://www.dailydot.com/via/vocal-fry-99-percent-invisible-womens-voices/

74 **Alicia Silverstone's character Cher . . .** Similarities noted by Caroline Winter, 'What does how you talk have to do with how you get ahead' Bloomberg April 2014: http://www.bloomberg.com/news/articles/2014-04-24/upspeaks-use-by-smart-men-and-women-and-what-it-means

75 **The upward inflection has been incorporated . . .** Hank Davis, 'The Uptalk Epidemic' *Psychology Today* October 2010: https://www.psychologytoday.com/blog/caveman-logic/201010/the-uptalk-epidemic/

75 **By retaining a sense of uncertainty . . .** Caroline Winter, 'What does how you talk have to do with how you get ahead' Bloomberg April 2014: http://www.bloomberg.com/news/articles/2014-04-24/upspeaks-use-by-smart-men-and-women-and-what-it-means

75 **Unfortunately, upspeak can . . .** Hank Davis, 'The Uptalk Epidemic' *Psychology Today* October 2010: https://www.psychologytoday.com/blog/caveman-logic/201010/the-uptalk-epidemic/

75 **Upspeak can undercut . . .** John Baldoni, 'Will upspeak you're your career?' *Forbes*, July 2015: http://www.forbes.com/sites/johnbaldoni/2015/07/30/will-upspeak-hurt-your-career/#6af9d8047a47

75 **One study of 700 bosses . . .** Internal study by UK Publisher Pearson as reported by Lydia Dallet in 'This communication quirk could cost you a promotion' for *Business Insider*, January 2014: http://www.businessinsider.com.au/how-uptalk-could-cost-you-a-promotion-2014-1

75 **A further 70 per cent found . . .** Internal study by UK Publisher Pearson as reported by Lydia Dallet in 'This communication quirk could cost you a promotion' for *Business Insider*, January 2014: http://www.businessinsider.com.au/how-uptalk-could-cost-you-a-promotion-2014-1

77 **While the prevalence of vocal fry . . .** Wolk, L, Abdelli-Beruh, NB, 'Habitual use of vocal fry in young adult female' *Journal of Voice*, 26(3) May 2012.

77 **One 2011 study found . . .** Anderson RC, Klofstad CA, Mayew WJ, Venkatachalam M 'Vocal Fry May Undermine the Success of Young Women in the Labor Market' *PLoS One* (2014): http://journals.plos.org/plosone/article/file?id=10.1371/journal.pone.0097506&type=printable

77 **In fact, among younger people . . .** Anderson RC, Klofstad CA, Mayew WJ, Venkatachalam M 'Vocal Fry May Undermine the Success of Young Women in the Labor Market' *PLoS One* (2014): http://journals.plos.org/plosone/article/file?id=10.1371/journal.pone.0097506&type=printable

77 **Among older people of both genders . . .** Anderson RC, Klofstad CA, Mayew WJ, Venkatachalam M 'Vocal Fry May Undermine the Success of Young Women in the Labor Market' *PLoS One* (2014): http://journals.plos.org/plosone/article/file?id=10.1371/journal.pone.0097506&type=printable

77 **While men's vocal fry . . .** See for example Amanda Marcotte 'The war on female voices is just another way of telling women to shut up' *Daily Dot*, July 2015: http://www.dailydot.com/via/vocal-fry-99-percent-invisible-womens-voices/

78 **Like with upspeak . . .** John Baldoni, 'Will upspeak you're your career?' *Forbes*, July 2015: http://www.forbes.com/sites/johnbaldoni/2015/07/30/will-upspeak-hurt-your-career/#6af9d8047a47

78 **Studies show that when a person . . .** As reported by Olga Khazan, 'Vocal fry may hurt women's job prospects', *The Atlantic*, May 2015: http://www.theatlantic.com/business/archive/2014/05/employers-look-down-on-women-with-vocal-fry/371811/

78 **However, the negative perceptions . . .** As reported by Olga Khazan, 'Vocal fry may hurt women's job prospects', *The Atlantic*, May 2015: http://www.theatlantic.com/business/archive/2014/05/employers-look-down-on-women-with-vocal-fry/371811/

79 **Studies show that when English . . .** Shiri Lev-Ari, Boaz Keysar, 'Why don't we believe no native speakers? The influence of accent on credibility' *Journal of Experimental Psychology*, 46, 2010: https://mdl.uchicago.edu/sites/keysarlab.uchicago.edu/files/uploads/Lev%20Ari%202010.pdf

82 **Comedian and writer Sarah Cooper . . .** Sarah Cooper, 'Non Threatening Leadership Strategies for Women', *The Cooper Review:* http://thecooperreview.com/non-threatening-leadership-strategies-for-women/

83 **Hillary Clinton was the first . . .** Transcript of Clinton 2016 presidential concession speech, as recorded by CNN November 2016: http://edition.cnn.com/2016/11/09/politics/hillary-clinton-concession-speech/

85 **Tara Mohr, author of *Playing Big* . . .** Tara Mohr, author of *Playing Big*, as told to *Goop:* http://goop.com/how-women-undermine-themselves-with-words/

85 **Of course, there are men** . . . Tara Mohr author of *Playing Big* as told to *Goop:* http://
goop.com/how-women-undermine-themselves-with-words/

86 **All I hear and see all day** . . . Jennifer Lawrence as told to Lena Dunham, *Lenny Letter*
and reported by Alexandra Petri, 'Famous quotes, the way women have to say them in a
meeting', *The Washington Post,* October 2015: https://www.washingtonpost.com/blogs/
compost/wp/2015/10/13/jennifer-lawrence-has-a-point-famous-quotes-the-way-a-woman-
would-have-to-say-them-during-a-meeting/

87 **But only in the sense that** . . . Ann Friedman, 'Can we just get over the way women talk?'
New York Magazine July 2015: http://nymag.com/thecut/2015/07/can-we-just-like-get-
over-the-way-women-talk.html#

88 **The often bandied-about claim** . . . James W Penebreaker, 'Do women really talk
more than men', study conducted by the University of Texas, 2007: https://news.utexas.
edu/2007/07/05/psychology

88 **In fact, a woman barrister** . . . Daniel Reynolds and George Williams, 'Gender Equality
Among Barristers Before the High Court', *Australian Law Journal* 91(6), 2017.

88 **Women actually tend to talk** *less* . . . Tali Mendelberg and Christopher Karpowitz discuss
this research in, 'More women but not nearly enough', *New York Times,* November 2012:
https://campaignstops.blogs.nytimes.com/2012/11/08/more-women-but-not-nearly-enough/

89 **The review explained that** . . . 'Women underrepresented on Q and A: report' *SBS
Online,* December 2015: http://www.sbs.com.au/news/article/2015/12/17/women-under-
represented-qa-report

89 **How much an individual speaks** . . . Katty Kay and Claire Shipman, 'The Confidence
Gap', *The Atlantic* May 2014: http://www.theatlantic.com/magazine/archive/2014/05/the-
confidence-gap/359815/

89 **In a Yale School of Management** . . . Victoria Brescoll, '*Who Takes the Floor and Why:
Gender, Power and Volubility in Organisations' Administrative Science Quarterly (2011).*

89 **Brescoll's study concluded that** . . . Victoria Brescoll, '*Who Takes the Floor and Why:
Gender, Power and Volubility in Organisations' Administrative Science Quarterly (2011).*

90 **Brescoll says that society expects** . . . Victoria Brescoll, '*Who Takes the Floor and Why:
Gender, Power and Volubility in Organisations' Administrative Science Quarterly (2011).*

What confidence looks like

93 **One study found that women** . . .Study published in the Australian Economic Review as
reported by Ty Kiisel in 'You are judged by your appearance' for *Forbes* 2013: http://www.
forbes.com/sites/tykiisel/2013/03/20/you-are-judged-by-your-appearance/#7e2cf84d30f0

93 **Another discovered that people** . . .The George Washington University Study utilised data
from the National Longitudinal Survey of Youth 2004 and was widely reported, including
by Angela Llyuk, 'Dress for Success', *USA Today* February 2015; https://www.usatoday.com/
story/money/business/blogs/innovation/2015/02/04/dress-for-success/22882545/

93 **Women with observable disabilities** . . . An Overview of the Status of Women With
Disabilities in Australia, Women with Disabilities Australia data, accessed 20 October
2016: http://wwda.org.au/about/snapshot/

93 **On average, a woman who is five** . . . Journal of Applied Psychology study by Timothy
Judge and Daniel Cable as reported in "Think looks don't matter', *Forbes* December 2009:
https://www.forbes.com/2009/12/05/appearance-work-pay-forbes-woman-leadership-
body-weight.html

93   **Chief executives are usually . . .** Kristie M. Engemann, Michael T. Owyang, 'So Much for That Merit Raise: The Link between Wages and Appearance' The Regional Economist, April 2005.

93   **One American study found . . .** Emma Mishel, 'Discrimination against Queer Women in the U.S. Workforce: A Resume Audit Study' *Socius: Sociological Research for a Dynamic World*, (2016), 2: http://gap.hks.harvard.edu/discrimination-against-queer-women-us-workforce-resume-audit-study.

93   **Another study of 13 000 . . .** Queensland University of Technology study as reported by Vivien Iove, 'Blondes have more funds: study shows', *ABC Online*, April 2010: http://www.abc.net.au/news/2010-04-09/blondes-have-more-funds/2577976

93   **While the exact figures vary . . .** Kristie M. Engemann, Michael T. Owyang, 'So Much for That Merit Raise: The Link between Wages and Appearance' *The Regional Economist*, April 2005.

93   **Some studies suggest beautiful . . .** Kristie M. Engemann, Michael T. Owyang, 'So Much for That Merit Raise: The Link between Wages and Appearance' *The Regional Economist*, April 2014.

93   **And other studies conclude that beautiful . . .** Ruffle, Bradley J. and Shtudiner, Ze'ev, 'Are Good-Looking People More Employable?' (February 2014). Available at SSRN: https://ssrn.com/abstract=1705244

95   **In our perception of people . . .** Leonard Mlodinow, *Subliminal: How your subconscious mind rules your behaviour*, Pantheon Press, 2012.

95   **It's estimated to be somewhere . . .** Lucy Debenham, 'Communication: What percentage is body language?' *The Body Language Expert, July 2016*: http://www.bodylanguageexpert.co.uk/communication-what-percentage-body-language.html

96   **I should note here the double . . .** *Women and Disability, The Double Handicap*, edited by Jo Deegan and Nancy A Brooks, Transaction Books, 1985.

99   **Imagine a long, rectangular boardroom table . . .** Bernardo Tirado, 'The Power Seat: Where you sit matters', *Psychology Today*, October 2012: https://www.psychologytoday.com/blog/digital-leaders/201210/the-power-seat-where-you-sit-matters

100   **Tata Chemicals is an American company . . .** Tata Chemicals internal experience as told to Carol Kinsey Gorman for 'Watch where you sit if you want collaboration', as published in *Forbes*, April 2012: http://www.forbes.com/sites/carolkinseygoman/2012/04/02/want-collaboration-watch-where-you-sit/#17b38f2561c5

100   **Social psychologist Amy Cuddy . . .** Amy Cuddy, *Presence*, Orion Publishing Group, 2016.

100   **Power posing is based on the idea . . .** *TED Talk*, June 2012: https://www.ted.com/talks/amy_cuddy_your_body_language_shapes_who_you_are

101   **The 'pride' gesture . . .** Jessica Tracy and David Matsumoto, 'The spontaneous expression of pride and shame: Evidence for biologically innate nonverbal displays' *Proceedings of the National Academy of Sciences for the United States of America*, June 2008: http://www.pnas.org/content/105/33/11655.full

101   **Sometimes we do it intentionally . . .** Vanessa Van Edwards, *Captivate: The Science of Succeeding with People* Penguin Publishing, 2017.

101   **Interestingly, non-threatening body . . .** Rugsaken, K. (2006). *Body speaks: Body language around the world*. Retrieved from *NACADA Clearinghouse of Academic Advising Resources*: http://www.nacada.ksu.edu/Resources/Clearinghouse/View-Articles/body-speaks.aspx.

104 Human beings can read . . . Schupp HT, Öhman AO, Junghöfer M, Weike AI, Stockburger J, Hamm AO. 'The facilitated processing of threatening faces: an ERP analysis. Emotion' 2004.

104 We subconsciously attach . . . Adrian Furnham, *The psychology of physical attraction*, Routledge, 2007.

104 Simply looking at a photograph . . . M Bradley, P Lang, 'The international affective picture system in the study of emotion and attention *Handbook of Emotion Elicitation and Assessment*, Oxford University Press, 2007.

104 Research shows that men . . . Audrey Nelson, Susan Golant, You Don't Say: Navigating Nonverbal Communication Between the Sexes, Prentice Hall Press, 2004.

105 A key exception is in . . . Rugsaken, K. (2006). *Body speaks: Body language around the world.* Retrieved from *NACADA Clearinghouse of Academic Advising Resources*: http://www. nacada.ksu.edu/Resources/Clearinghouse/View-Articles/body-speaks.aspx

105 Lack of eye contact . . . Fischler, M.A. and Firschein, O., *Intelligence, Eye Contact and The Brain*, Addison Wesley Publishing, 1987.

105 Whereas steady eye contact is . . . Adrian Furnham, *The psychology of physical attraction*, Routledge, 2007.

105 When initiating conversation . . . Shogo Kajimura and Michio Nomura, 'When we cannot speak: Eye contact disrupts resources available to cognitive control processes during verb generation' *Cognition*, October 2016.

105 Looking at the audience . . . Fischler, M.A. and Firschein, O., *Intelligence, Eye Contact and The Brain*, Addison Wesley Publishing, 1987.

106 Today's outfit is particularly . . . Lisa Wilkinson, Andrew Olle Lecture October 2013, transcript as published by *ABC Online*: http://www.abc.net.au/local/ stories/2013/10/25/3876439.htm

106 In some cultures it was men . . . Sue Gerrard, 'The Working Wardrobe: Perceptions of women's clothing at work', unpublished thesis for the University of Kent: https://www. cs.kent.ac.uk/people/staff/saf/scaffolding/second-workshop/pubfiles/GerrardThesis.pdf

106 In other cultures, women's dress . . . Sue Gerrard, 'The Working Wardrobe: Perceptions of women's clothing at work', unpublished thesis for the University of Kent: https://www. cs.kent.ac.uk/people/staff/saf/scaffolding/second-workshop/pubfiles/GerrardThesis.pdf

107 It wasn't until the end . . . Sandra M. Forsythe, 'Effect of Clothing Masculinity on Perceptions of Managerial Traits: Does Gender of the Perceiver Make a Difference?' *Clothing and Textiles Research Journal*, 6(2), July 2016.

107 Those who rejected more . . . DiPaolo, Brian. 'Flappers' *Issues & Controversies in American History*, Infobase Publishing, July 2007.

107 The resurgence of ultra-feminine . . . Vanessa Martins Lamb. 'The 1950's and the 1960's and the American Woman: the transition from the "housewife" to the feminist'. *History* (2011): https://dumas.ccsd.cnrs.fr/dumas-00680821/document

107 While the sexual revolution . . . Vanessa Martins Lamb. 'The 1950's and the 1960's and the American Woman: the transition from the "housewife" to the feminist'. *History* (2011): https://dumas.ccsd.cnrs.fr/dumas-00680821/document

107 She just needs to be perfectly . . . Hadley Freeman, 'How should Hillary Clinton dress? However she goddamn pleases', *The Guardian*, June 2016: https://www.theguardian.com/ us-news/2016/jun/13/how-should-hillary-clinton-dress-however-she-goddamn-pleases

108 Caitlin Moran explains . . . Caitlin Moran, *How to be a Woman*, Ebury Press, 2012.

What confidence feels like

112 Forty per cent of women . . . Anne Kreamer, *It's Always Personal: Navigating Emotion in the New Workplace*, Random House 2013.

113 The number of men who . . . Anne Kreamer, *It's Always Personal: Navigating Emotion in the New Workplace*, Random House 2013.

113 The average woman cries . . . Referencing the research of William H. Frey II, biochemist in Kopecky G and Tynan D, *'Have a good cry'* Redbook, May 1992, 179(1).

113 There is a hormone called prolactin . . . Lorna Collier, 'Why we cry', American Psychological Association, February 2014, Vol 45, No. 2: http://www.apa.org/monitor/2014/02/cry.aspx

113 Men also have larger tear ducts . . . Richard Post, 'Tear duct size differences of age, sex and race', University of Michigan Medical School: https://deepblue.lib.umich.edu/bitstream/handle/2027.42/37483/1330300109/

114 She has discovered that there are certain . . . Jenna Goudreau, 'Crying at work is a woman's burden', *Forbes*, January 2011: http://www.forbes.com/sites/jennagoudreau/2011/01/11/crying-at-work-a-womans-burden-study-men-sex-testosterone-tears-arousal/#498f5dcc4e54

115 Crying women are rarely viewed positively . . . Jenna Goudreau, 'Crying at work is a woman's burden', *Forbes*, January 2011: http://www.forbes.com/sites/jennagoudreau/2011/01/11/crying-at-work-a-womans-burden-study-men-sex-testosterone-tears-arousal/#498f5dcc4e54

115 Crying in response . . . Jenna Goudreau, 'Crying at work is a woman's burden', *Forbes*, January 2011: http://www.forbes.com/sites/jennagoudreau/2011/01/11/crying-at-work-a-womans-burden-study-men-sex-testosterone-tears-arousal/#498f5dcc4e54

115 Interestingly, it's women themselves . . . Anne Kreamer, It's Always Personal: Navigating Emotion in the New Workplace, Random House 2013.

115 Ardent Leisure CEO Deborah Thomas . . . See for example Glenda Korporaal, 'Can we accept CEOs who don't cry?' *The Australian*, November 2016: http://www.theaustralian.com.au/business/opinion/dreamworld-tragedy-can-we-accept-ceos-who-cry/

116 But too much crying . . . Dodai Stewart, 'Can a woman cry and be taken seriously', *Jezebel*, October 2007: http://jezebel.com/315114/can-a-woman-cry--be-taken-seriously

116 Five million of Australia's . . . Australian Bureau of Statistics Labour Force Figures August 2014 as reported by Peter Martin for the *Sydney Morning Herald*, January 2015: http://www.smh.com.au/business/workplace-relations/the-38hour-week-a-rarity-among-fulltime-workers-new-data-shows-20151027-gkk1r6.html

116 Of those, 1.4 million . . . Australian Bureau of Statistics Labour Force Figures August 2014 as reported by Peter Martin for the *Sydney Morning Herald*, January 2015: http://www.smh.com.au/business/workplace-relations/the-38hour-week-a-rarity-among-fulltime-workers-new-data-shows-20151027-gkk1r6.html

116 Around 270 000 will work for more than 70 hours . . . Australian Bureau of Statistics Labour Force Figures August 2014 as reported by Peter Martin for the *Sydney Morning Herald*, January 2015: http://www.smh.com.au/business/workplace-relations/the-38hour-week-a-rarity-among-fulltime-workers-new-data-shows-20151027-gkk1r6.html

117 Where boys are encouraged . . . By Richardson, Deborah C.; Bernstein, Sandy; Taylor, Stuart P 'The effect of situational contingencies of female retaliative behaviour' *Journal of Personality and Social Psychology*, Vol 37(11), Nov 1979.

118 **Women also more often cite** . . . Ad Vingerhoets, 'Why only humans weep: unravelling the mysteries of tears' Oxford University Press, 2013.

118 **In one American study, 51 per cent** . . . Virginia Eatough Jonathan A. Smith Rachel Shaw, 'Women, Anger, and Aggression: An Interpretative Phenomenological Analysis' *Journal of Interpersonal Violence*, vol. 23, 12, 2008.

118 **Women have been taught** . . . Virginia Eatough Jonathan A. Smith Rachel Shaw, 'Women, Anger, and Aggression: An Interpretative Phenomenological Analysis', *Journal of Interpersonal Violence*, vol. 23, 12, 2008.

118 **Women aren't sad or distressed** . . . Steven Laurent, *The Anger Fallacy: Uncovering the Irrationality of the Angry Mindset*, Australian Academic Press, 2013.

119 **Brené Brown, an expert on social** . . . *Brene Brown, Daring Greatly, Avery, 2015.*

121 **In basic terms** . . . Friedman H, Martin L. *The Longevity Project: Surprising Discoveries for Health and Long Life from the Landmark Eight-Decade Study*. 2011. Plume.

122 **At any one time, women** . . . Amen, D, Trujillo, M, Keator, D, et al. 'Gender differences in CBF in a healthy and psychiatric cohort of 46034 SPECT scans.' *Amen Clinics*. 2013.

122 **This is what makes women** . . . Amen, D, Trujillo, M, Keator, D, et al. 'Gender differences in CBF in a healthy and psychiatric cohort of 46034 SPECT scans.' *Amen Clinics*. 2013.

122 **Researchers have found** . . . Amen, D, Trujillo, M, Keator, D, et al. 'Gender differences in CBF in a healthy and psychiatric cohort of 46034 SPECT scans.' *Amen Clinics*. 2013.

122 **Some scientists even believe** . . . Friedman H, Martin L. 'The Longevity Project: Surprising Discoveries for Health and Long Life from the Landmark Eight-Decade Study.' 2011. Plume.

122 **Some scientists think brain** . . . Pujol J1, López A, Deus J, Cardoner N, Vallejo J, Capdevila A, Paus T, 'Anatomical variability of the anterior cingulate gyrus and basic dimensions of human personality', *Neuroimage* (April 2002).

122 **There is a small part** . . . Pujol J1, López A, Deus J, Cardoner N, Vallejo J, Capdevila A, Paus T, 'Anatomical variability of the anterior cingulate gyrus and basic dimensions of human personality', *Neuroimage* (April 2002).

123 **One corporate finance study** . . . Brad M. Barber, Terrance Odean; Boys will be Boys: Gender, Overconfidence, and Common Stock Investment. *Quarterly Journal of Economics* (2001), 116(1).

123 **Men tended to suffer** . . . Brad M. Barber, Terrance Odean; Boys will be Boys: Gender, Overconfidence, and Common Stock Investment. *Quarterly Journal of Economics* (2001), 116(1).

123 **Similarly, inpatients treated** . . . Tsugawa Y, Jena AB, Figueroa JF, Orav EJ, Blumenthal DM, Jha AK. Comparison of Hospital Mortality and Readmission Rates for Medicare Patients Treated by Male vs Female Physicians. *JAMA Intern Med.* 2017;177(2).

123 **Companies with a higher proportion** . . . 'Women in Business: The Value of Diversity', Grant Thornton Internal Report: https://www.grantthornton.global/globalassets/wib_value_of_diversity.pdf

123 **These kinds of studies** . . . See for example Harbey Deutschendorf, '7 reasons why emotional intelligence is one of the fastest growing job skills', *Fast Company*, May 2016: http://www.fastcompany.com/3059481/7-reasons-why-emotional-intelligence-is-one-of-the-fastest-growing-job-skills

123 **Increasingly, it is considered vital . . .** Friedman H, Martin L. 'The Longevity Project: Surprising Discoveries for Health and Long Life from the Landmark Eight-Decade Study.' 2011. Plume.

123 **Research by the universities . . .** Korb S, With S, Niedenthal P, Kaiser S, Grandjean D (2014) 'The Perception and Mimicry of Facial Movements Predict Judgments of Smile Authenticity'. *PLoS* ONE 9(6)

124 **Emotionally intelligent managers . . .** Barbuto, J.E., & Wheeler, D.W. (2006). Scale development and construct clarification of servant leadership. *Group & Organization Management*, 31.

124 **This is defined as values-based . . .** Barbuto, J.E., & Wheeler, D.W. (2006). Scale development and construct clarification of servant leadership. Group & Organization Management, 31.

125 **The effort it takes to fake . . .** *Stylist UK* article summarising the advice of Dr Sandi Mann, senior lecturer in occupational psychology at the University of Lancashire: http://www.stylist.co.uk/stylist-network/big-girls-dont-cry

128 **Because there is a lot . . .** Excerpted from the prepared Commencement Address to the graduates of *Pitzer College* in Claremont, California, by John Lovett, *May 2013*, as reported *in The Atlantic*, also in May 2013: http://www.theatlantic.com/politics/archive/2013/05/life-lessons-in-fighting-the-culture-of-bullshit/276030/

Taming your fear of failure

131 **Women tend to have a more . . .** Shelly Correll, 'Constraints into preferences: gender, status and emerging career aspirations', *American Sociological Review,* February 2004, 69.

131 **This has been documented . . .** See for example: https://hbr.org/2013/09/women-rising-the-unseen-barriers; http://www.elle.com/life-love/a36828/why-women-are-afraid-of-failure/; https://www.nytimes.com/2016/02/21/opinion/sunday/why-do-we-teach-girls-that-its-cute-to-be-scared.html

131 **After analysing students' results . . .** Claudia Goldin, *Notes on the Undergraduate Economics Major at a Highly Selective Liberal Arts College*, Department of Economics Harvard University: http://scholar.harvard.edu/files/goldin/files/claudia_gender_paper.pdf?m=1429198526

132 **Men who were outstanding . . .** Claudia Goldin, *Notes on the Undergraduate Economics Major at a Highly Selective Liberal Arts College*, Department of Economics Harvard University: http://scholar.harvard.edu/files/goldin/files/claudia_gender_paper.pdf?m=1429198526

132 **Women tend to view . . .** Arianna Huffington in conversation with Issie *Lapowsky.*, 'Arianna Huffington's Rule for Success: Dare to Fail', *Inc 5000,*: https://www.inc.com/magazine/201302/rules-for-success/arianna-huffington-dare-to-fail.html

132 **We consider failure a perpetual . . .** Christy Wright, 'The only fix for your fear of failure', Propel Women, retrieved 17 September 2017: http://www.propelwomen.org/content/the-only-fix-for-your-fear-of-failure/gjeb3t

132 **Former Obama adviser . . .** Valerie Jarrett as quoted in '26 things every woman should know about success', *The Huffington Post,* June 2013: http://www.huffingtonpost.com.au/entry/26-things-every-woman-should-know-about-success_n_3404523

133 **Some scientists have argued . . .** Lungo, O, Potvin, S, Tikasz, A, Mendrek, A, 'Sex differences in effective fronto-limbic connectivity during negative emotion processing', *Psychoneuroendocrinology*, December 2015, 62.

133 In other words, women . . . Moheb Costandi, *50 Human Brain Ideas You Really Need to Know (50 Ideas You Really Need to Know series)*, Quercus, 2013.

134 Procrastination is motivated by fear . . . Maria Konnikova, 'Getting over procrastination', *The New Yorker*, July 2014. http://www.newyorker.com/science/maria-konnikova/a-procrastination-gene

134 Researcher Piers Steel . . . Katrin B. Klingsieck, Axel Grund, Sebastian Schmid, Stefan Fries, 'Why Students Procrastinate: A Qualitative Approach' *Journal of College Student Development*, Volume 54, Number 4, July/August 2013.

134 Procrastinators are not unintelligent . . . Katrin B. Klingsieck, Axel Grund, Sebastian Schmid, Stefan Fries, 'Why Students Procrastinate: A Qualitative Approach' *Journal of College Student Development*, Volume 54, Number 4, July/August 2013.

134 Research shows that the first 15 minutes . . . Katrin B. Klingsieck, Axel Grund, Sebastian Schmid, Stefan Fries, 'Why Students Procrastinate: A Qualitative Approach' *Journal of College Student Development*, Volume 54, Number 4, July/August 2013.

135 As Elizabeth Gilbert, creative guru . . . Elizabeth Gilbert, *Big Magic*, Riverhead Books, 2013.

135 Excessive self-criticism . . . Dr. Mandeep Kaur, Inderbir Kaur, 'Dysfunctional Attitude and Self-Blame: Effect on Self-Esteem and Self-Conscious Emotions among Adolescents', *The International Journal of Indian Psychology*, 2015 (3)1.

135 Researcher Timothy A. Judge . . . Timothy A Judge, Core Self-Evaluations and Work Success', *Current Directions in Psychological Science*, 2001, 18(1).

135 They're also less likely . . . Timothy A Judge, Core Self-Evaluations and Work Success', *Current Directions in Psychological Science*, 2001, 18(1).

136 Chronic sufferers of low self-esteem . . . Timothy A Judge, Core Self-Evaluations and Work Success', *Current Directions in Psychological Science*, 2001, 18(1).

136 Much like other self-sabotaging . . . Katty Kay and Claire Shipman, 'The Confidence Gap', *The Atlantic* May 2014: http://www.theatlantic.com/magazine/archive/2014/05/the-confidence-gap/359815/

136 Perfectionism is often mischaracterised . . . David Burns, 'The Perfectionist's Script for Self-Defeat', *Psychology Today*, 1980.

137 This can particularly be the case among women . . . Martin M. Smith, Donald H. Saklofske, Gonggu Yan, and Simon B. Sherry, 'Cultural Similarities in Perfectionism: Perfectionistic strivings and concerns generalize across Chinese and Canadian groups', *Measurement and Evaluation in Counselling and Development*, 2015.

137 In its most extreme form . . . Eating Disorders Victoria Perfectionism Fact Sheet, retrieved 18 December 2016: https://www.eatingdisorders.org.au/eating-disorders/what-is-an-eating-disorder/risk-factors/perfectionism

137 For example, perfectionism . . . Flett, Gordon L, Hewitt, Paul L, Heisel, Marnin J, 'The destructiveness of perfectionism revisited: Implications for the assessment of suicide risk and the prevention of suicide' *Review of General Psychology*, 18(3) 2014.

140 As the late actress Carrie Fisher said . . . Quote as collated by staff writers for *The Cut NY Mag*, '15 of Carrie Fisher's Best, Most Honest Feminist Quotes', December 2016: http://nymag.com/thecut/2016/12/15-of-carrie-fishers-best-most-honest-feminist-quotes.html

141 Imposter syndrome is when . . . Pauline Rose Clance & Suzanne Imes, 'The Imposter Phenomenon in High Achieving Women: Dynamics and Therapeutic Intervention', *Psychotherapy Theory, Research and Practice* Volume 15(3), 1973.

141 They are scared of being . . . Scott Berinato, 'The Personality Traits That Make Us Feel Like Frauds', *Harvard Business Review*, October 2015: https://hbr.org/2015/10/the-personality-traits-that-make-us-feel-like-frauds/

142 Imposter syndrome is so much more . . . Pauline Rose Clance & Suzanne Imes, 'The Imposter Phenomenon in High Achieving Women: Dynamics and Therapeutic Intervention', Psychotherapy Theory, Research and Practice Volume 15(3), 1973.

142 While the syndrome . . . Jaruwan Sakulku, James Alexander, 'The Imposter Phenomenon'. *Journal pf Behavioural Science*, 2011, (6)1.

142 Imposter syndrome is even more common . . . Jaruwan Sakulku, James Alexander, 'The Imposter Phenomenon'. *Journal pf Behavioural Science*, 2011, (6)1.

142 People are susceptible . . . Jaruwan Sakulku, James Alexander, 'The Imposter Phenomenon'. *Journal pf Behavioural Science*, 2011, (6)1.

143 Overcoming imposter syndrome . . . Scott Berinato, 'The Personality Traits That Make Us Feel Like Frauds', *Harvard Business Review*, October 2015: https://hbr.org/2015/10/the-personality-traits-that-make-us-feel-like-frauds/

143 They don't feel at all like frauds . . . Jessica Collett as told to Oliver Burkeman, 'This column will change your life: Do you feel a fraud?' *The Guardian* November 2013: https://www.theguardian.com/lifeandstyle/2013/nov/09/impostor-syndrome-oliver-burkeman

144 Meryl Streep, Tina Fey and Oprah Winfrey have all . . . As reported by: https://www.theguardian.com/film/2006/sep/23/awardsandprizes; http://www.forbes.com/sites/jennagoudreau/2011/10/19/women-feel-like-frauds-failures-tina-fey-sheryl-sandberg/; http://www.news.com.au/finance/highachievers-suffering-from-imposter-syndrome/

144 There's literally nothing else to do . . . Leigh Sales, as told to Shannon Molloy and published by News Corp, September 2015: http://www.dailytelegraph.com.au/entertainment/tv-presenter-leigh-sales-opens-up-about-near-death-heated-criticism-and-her-nagging-selfdoubt/

Coping with setbacks

145 A dozen editors rejected . . . Maev Kennedy, 'JK Rowling posts letters of rejection on Twitter to help budding authors', *The Guardian, March 2016:* https://www.theguardian.com/books/2016/mar/25/jk-rowling-harry-potter-posts-letters-of-rejection-on-twitter

145 Oprah Winfrey was fired . . . Oprah Winfrey, as told to David Rubenstein for 'The David Rubenstein Show: Peer-to-Peer Conversations' on *Bloomberg Television*. Video link: https://www.youtube.com/watch?v=9DyYV44yDbc

146 Vera Wang was a figure skater . . . As told to Jennifer Vineyard for 'Vera Wang Says: Know When to Walk Away . . . and Start Something New', as publish in NY Mag, June 2015: http://nymag.com/thecut/2015/06/vera-wang-says-know-when-to-walk-away.html

146 Julia Child didn't release . . . Richard Feloni, '20 people who became highly successful after age 40', *Business Insider,* September 2014: https://www.businessinsider.com.au/people-who-became-successful-after-age-40

149 This makes recovering from it harder . . . Gender Differences in Persuasive Communication and Attribution of Success – Patricia Hayes Andrews (*Human Communication Research*, vol. 13, no. 3, 1987)

149 Men, on the other hand . . . Michelle C. Haynes, Madeline E. Heilman 'It Had to Be You (Not Me)! Women's Attributional Rationalization of Their Contribution to Successful Joint Work Outcomes', Personality and Social Psychology Bulletin, 2013, 39(7).

149 As part of a famous Indiana University experiment . . . Michelle C. Haynes, Madeline E. Heilman 'It Had to Be You (Not Me)! Women's Attributional Rationalization of Their Contribution to Successful Joint Work Outcomes', Personality and Social Psychology Bulletin, 2013, 39(7).

150 Some people – particularly the hypersensitive . . . Deborah Ward 'Coping with setback in a meaningful way' *Psychology Today* January 2014: https://www.psychologytoday.com/blog/sense-and-sensitivity/201401/coping-setback-the-sensitive-way

152 A brave face is . . . Deborah Ward 'Coping with setback in a meaningful way' *Psychology Today* January 2014: https://www.psychologytoday.com/blog/sense-and-sensitivity/201401/coping-setback-the-sensitive-way

152 If you need a crying jag . . . Hillary Rettig as told to Michael Koh in '11 People Reveal The Best Way To Handle Rejection In Life' *Thought Catalogue* March 2014: http://thoughtcatalog.com/michael-koh/2014/03/11-people-reveal-the-best-way-to-handle-rejection-in-life/7/

154 Resentment has even been compared . . . Steven Stosny 'Overcoming chronic resentment and the abuse it causes' *Psychology Today* August 2011: https://www.psychologytoday.com/blog/anger-in-the-age-entitlement/201108/overcoming-chronic-resentment-and-the-abuse-it-causes

155 Women in particular . . . See for example, Jennifer Weiner, 'The Pressure to look good', The New York Times, May 2015: https://www.nytimes.com/2015/05/31/opinion/sunday/jennifer-weiner-the-pressure-to-look-good

156 And it's all supposed to come easy . . . Mika Brzezinski in conversation with *The Huffington Post Live*, June 2013: http://www.huffingtonpost.com.au/entry/career-failure-women_n_3690668

156 Of those five, four . . . Karl Albrecht, *Practical Intelligence: The Art and Science of Common Sense*, Phieffer, 2007.

157 Ego death is basically . . . Karl Albrecht, *Practical Intelligence: The Art and Science of Common Sense*, Phieffer, 2007.

157 It's a fear everyone . . . Karl Albrecht, *Practical Intelligence: The Art and Science of Common Sense*, Phieffer, 2007.

158 Negativity bias means we . . . Jonathan Haidt, as quoted by Tony Schwartz, 'Overcoming your negativity bias', *The New York Times*, June 2013: http://nytimes.com/2013/06/14/overcoming-your-negativity-bias/

158 The human brain has systems . . . Roy Baumeister, as quoted by Tony Schwartz, 'Overcoming your negativity bias', *The New York Times*, June 2013: http://nytimes.com/2013/06/14/overcoming-your-negativity-bias/

Managing up like a boss

162 As many as one in two . . . The Deloitte Millenial Survey 2017: https://www2.deloitte.com/global/en/pages/about-deloitte/articles/millennialsurvey.html

163 Postgraduates, women in middle management . . . See for example: Nona Y. Glazer 'Overlooked, Overworked: Women's Unpaid and Paid Work in the Health Services' "Cost Crisis"' *International Journal of Health Services*, 1988 and *Significance of the gender divide in financial services*, August 2012, FINSIA: https://finsia.com/docs/default-source/industry-reports-diversity-in-financial-services/significance-of-the-gender-divide-in-financial-services-2012.pdf

163 Carol Frohlinger and Deborah Kolb, the founders . . . Carol Frohlinger, Deborah Kolb and Judith Williams, *Her Place at the Table: A Woman's Guide to Negotiating Five Key Challenges to Leadership Success,* Jossey-Bass, 2010.

168 White hot and passionate . . . Sophie Gadd '12 Inspiring Roald Dahl Quotes', *The Mirro,* September 2014: http://www.mirror.co.uk/news/uk-news/12-inspiring-roald-dahl-quotes-4210456

175 Workplaces are made stronger . . . Whitney Johnston, 'Managing up without sucking up', *Harvard Business Review,* December 2014: https://hbr.org/2014/12/managing-up-without-sucking-up

How to ask for more

175 It was way back in February . . . Tiffany K Wayne, *Women's Rights in the United States: A Comprehensive Encyclopedia of Issues, Events, and People: A Comprehensive Encyclopedia of Issues, Events, and People,* ABC-CLIO, December 2014.

175 This gap has remained . . . Workplace Gender Equality Agency, Gender Equity Scorecard 2015-16: https://www.wgea.gov.au/sites/default.files.80653_2015-16-gender-equality-scorecard.pdf

175 Even Hollywood actresses . . . Maddie Berg, 'Everything you need to know about the Hollywood pay gap', *Forbes* November 2015: https://www.forbes.com/sites/maddieberg/2015/11/12/everything-you-need-to-know-about-the-hollywood-pay-gap/

179 One in five Australian women . . . Ross-Smith, A., & Chesterman, C. (2009). 'Girl disease': Women managers' reticence and ambivalence towards organizational advancement. *Journal of Management and Organization,* 15(5),

179 Researcher Linda C. Babcock . . . Linda Babcock & Sara Laschever, *Women don't ask: Negotiation and the Gender Divide,* Princeton University Press (2003).

179 Women are 2.5 times more likely . . . Liz Doherty, Simonetta Manfredi, (2006) 'Women's progression to senior positions in English universities', *Employee Relations,* 28(6).

179 This reluctance to negotiate . . . Ian Ayres and Peter Siegelman 'Race and gender discrimination in bargaining for a new car', *The American Economic Review,* June 1995 85(3).

179 One study comparing students . . . Linda Babcock & Sara Laschever, *Women don't ask: Negotiation and the Gender Divide,* Princeton University Press (2003).

180 When asked, American men . . . Probert, B. (2005), 'I Just Couldn't Fit It In': Gender and Unequal Outcomes in Academic Careers. *Gender, Work & Organization,* 12: 50–72.

180 It's why men initiate . . . Linda Babcock & Sara Laschever, *Women don't ask: Negotiation and the Gender Divide,* Princeton University Press (2003).

180 Studies estimate that by not negotiating . . . Ross-Smith, A., & Chesterman, C. (2009). 'Girl disease': Women managers' reticence and ambivalence towards organizational advancement. *Journal of Management and Organization,* 15(5), 582-595

181 This messaging is so powerful . . . Lyons, BD & McArthur, C, 2007, 'Gender's unspoken role in leadership evaluations', *Human Resource Planning,* 30(3).

181 For example, women with disabilities . . . 'Double Disadvantage' – Barriers Facing Women With Disabilities in Accessing Employment, Education and Training Opportunities: A Discussion Paper', research conducted for *Women With Disabilities Australia,* paper written by Natalie Thomas (1991), retrieved on 12 January 2017: http://wwda.org.au/issues/employment/employm1995/double/

181 **Disability advocate Carly Findlay** . . . See for example stories from women as told to *Women With Disabilities Australia:* http://wwda.org.au/poems/personalstories/womdis/womdis4/

181 **Part of women's anxiety** . . . Linda Babcock & Sara Laschever, *Women don't ask: Negotiation and the Gender Divide,* Princeton University Press (2003).

182 **Researchers Bowles and Babcock** . . . Hannah Riley Bowles and Linda Babcock, 'Why Women Don't Negotiate their Job Offers' *Harvard Business Review* June 2014: https://hbr.org/2014/06/why-women-dont-negotiate-their-job-offers

183 **Young women, in particular** . . . Linda Babcock & Sara Laschever, *Women don't ask: Negotiation and the Gender Divide,* Princeton University Press (2003).

184 **Studies show that women** . . . Carol Frohlinger, Deborah Kolb and Judith Williams, *Her Place at the Table: A Woman's Guide to Negotiating Five Key Challenges to Leadership Success,* Jossey-Bass, 2010.

184 **Women tend to be more focused** . . . Carol Frohlinger, Deborah Kolb and Judith Williams, *Her Place at the Table: A Woman's Guide to Negotiating Five Key Challenges to Leadership Success,* Jossey-Bass, 2010.

184 **Men – having been raised** . . . Hannah Riley and Kathleen L. McGinn 'When Does Gender Matter in Negotiation?' Kennedy School of Government, unpublished, September 2002.

184 **Once adulthood is reached** . . . Sara Laschever as quoted by Babcock, Laschaver, Gelfand and Small in 'Nice Girls Don't Ask' *Harvard Business Review* October 2003: https://hbr.org/2003/10/nice-girls-dont-ask/

184 **For many women, the chief** . . . Andreas Leibbrandt, John List, 'Do women avoid salary negotiations? Evidence from a large scale natural field experiment' *National Bureau of Economic Research Working Paper Series* 2012: http://s3.amazonaws.com/fieldexperiments-papers/papers/00201.pdf

185 **Bosses expect women to** . . . Linda Babcock & Sara Laschever, *Women don't ask: Negotiation and the Gender Divide,* Princeton University Press (2003).

185 **Research shows that when negotiating** . . . Constraints and triggers: Situational mechanics of gender in negotiation. Bowles, Hannah Riley; Babcock, Linda; McGinn, Kathleen L. *Journal of Personality and Social Psychology,* 89(6), December 2005.

185 **Women are more likely to succeed** . . . Carol Frohlinger, Deborah Kolb and Judith Williams, *Her Place at the Table: A Woman's Guide to Negotiating Five Key Challenges to Leadership Success,* Jossey-Bass, 2010.

185 **Research shows that women's** . . . Linda Babcock & Sara Laschever, *Women don't ask: Negotiation and the Gender Divide,* Princeton University Press (2003).

186 **And the gap between** . . . Linda Babcock & Sara Laschever, *Women don't ask: Negotiation and the Gender Divide,* Princeton University Press (2003).

186 **One of my favourite** . . . Pam Young, *The Hatpin – A Weapon: Women and the 1912 Brisbane General Strike,* published in Hecate, (1988).

186 **Emma Miller, a seamstress** . . . Pam Young, *Proud to be a Rebel – The Life and Times of Emma Miller,* University of Queensland Press, 1991.

187 **Unions have played** . . . *Australian Council of Trade Unions 75th Anniversary Commemorative Booklet:* http://www.actu.org.au/media/349395/actu-75th-anniversary-commemorative-booklet.pdf

193 **So if you've got** . . . Jenny Foss, '4 Times to Negotiate Your Salary (and 3 Times Not To)' *The Muse:* https://www.themuse.com/advice/4-times-to-negotiate-your-salary-and-3-times-not-to

194 Linda Babcock and Sara Lashever . . . Linda Babcock & Sara Laschever, *Women don't ask: Negotiation and the Gender Divide,* Princeton University Press (2003).

194 Some studies suggest . . . Charles B. Craver, 'Negotiation Styles: The Impact on Bargaining Transactions', *GW Law Faculty Publications & Other Works,* (2003).

How to be a manager of people

197 Standing soberly with the . . . Michael Gordon, 'Gillard and the question of gender', *Sydney Morning Herald,* September 2014: http://www.smh.com.au/federal-politics/political-news/gillard-and-the-question-of-gender-20140923-10kts4.html

197 Women leaders can be . . . Sheryl Sandberg, *Lean In: Women, work and the will to lead,* Knopf, 2013.

198 If you're not familiar . . . 'Heidi vs Howard' study, 2003 as cited by Sheryl Sandberg, *Lean In: Women, work and the will to lead,* Knopf, 2013.

199 Whereas when we think . . . Therese Huston, *How Women Decide – What's True, What's Not, and What Strategies Spark the Best Choices.*

200 Gender researcher Associate Professor . . . Farida Jalalzai as told to Sharmilla Ganesan in 'What Do Women Leaders Have in Common?' for *The Atlantic* August 2016: https://www.theatlantic.com/business/archive/2016/08/what-do-women-leaders-have-in-common/492656/

200 This refers to the fact . . . Susanne Bruckmüller and Nyla R. Branscombe, 'How women end up on the 'glass cliff" *Harvard Business Review* January 2011: https://hbr.org/2011/01/how-women-end-up-on-the-glass-cliff

200 For example, Marissa Mayer . . . Rachel Sklar, 'The Glass Cliff Is Real & Marissa Mayer Is About To Fall Off Of It 'Refinery 29,* February 2016: http://www.refinery29.com/2016/02/102369/marissa-mayer-sexism

200 The glass cliff phenomenon . . . Julia Yates, 'Are women party leaders set up to fail? What business tells us about the 'glass cliff" *The Conversation* July 2016: https://theconversation.com/are-women-party-leaders-set-up-to-fail-what-business-tells-us-about-the-glass-cliff-62242

201 It's related to not having support . . . Michelle Ryan as told to Melissa Davey, 'Women start out as ambitious as men but it erodes over time says researcher', *The Guardian,* November 2015: https://www.theguardian.com/australia-news/2015/nov/19/women-start-out-as-ambitious-as-men-but-it-erodes-over-time-says-researcher

201 The concept of 'women's leadership' . . . http://www.hbs.edu/faculty/conferences/2013-w50-research-symposium/Documents/eagly.pdf

202 Research suggests that women . . . 'Women Leadership Styles', *Forbes,* May 2010, retrieved 16 August 2016: http://www.forbes.com/sites/work-in-progress/2010/05/26/women-leadership-styles/#1f7290d06b98

202 This difference is more pronounced . . . Sue Shellenbarger, 'The XX Factor: What's Holding Women Back?' *Wall Street Journal,* May 2012: http://www.wsj.com/articles/SB10001424052702304746604577381953238775784

202 Some researchers have found . . . Alice H. Eagly, Gender and Work: Challenging Conventional Wisdom, *Harvard Business School Research Symposium 2013*: http://www.hbs.edu/faculty/conferences/2013-w50-research-symposium/Documents/eagly.pdf

202 That is, women are . . . Reinert, Regina M. and Weigert, Florian and Winnefeld, Christoph H., 'Does Female Management Influence Firm Performance? Evidence from Luxembourg Banks' (March 31, 2016). *Financial Markets and Portfolio Management* (2016); University of St. Gallen, School of Finance Research Paper No. 2015/01.

202 General Motors CEO . . . Daniel Akerson as quoted by Sue Shellenbarger, The XX Factor: What's Holding Women Back?' *Wall Street Journal,* May 2012: http://www.wsj.com/articles/SB10001424052702304746604577381953238775784

202 Mamatha Chamarthi, now VP . . . Mamatha Chamarthi as quoted by Sue Shellenbarger, The XX Factor: What's Holding Women Back?' *Wall Street Journal,* May 2012: http://www.wsj.com/articles/SB10001424052702304746604577381951953238775784

203 They are team players . . . Neelie Kroes told to Reinert, Regina M. and Weigert, Florian and Winnefeld, Christoph H., 'Does Female Management Influence Firm Performance? Evidence from Luxembourg Banks' (March 31, 2016). *Financial Markets and Portfolio Management* (2016); University of St. Gallen, School of Finance Research Paper No. 2015/01.

203 The view that women leaders . . . Reinert, Regina M. and Weigert, Florian and Winnefeld, Christoph H., 'Does Female Management Influence Firm Performance? Evidence from Luxembourg Banks' (March 31, 2016). *Financial Markets and Portfolio Management* (2016); University of St. Gallen, School of Finance Research Paper No. 2015/01.

203 Again, while this sounds . . . Cordelia Fine, 'Business as usual: The confused case for corporate gender equality' *The Monthly,* March 2017 https://www.themonthly.com.au/issue/2017/march/1488286800/cordelia-fine/business-usual

204 Worse still, whether . . . Jennifer Wheelan, 'Let's Stop Talking Up the Feminine Leadership Style', *Daily Life,* March 2016: http://www.dailylife.com.au/life-and-love/work-and-money/lets-stop-talking-up-the-feminine-leadership-style-20160321-gnni06.html

205 Research from the Human Rights Commission . . . *Leading for Change: A blueprint for cultural diversity and inclusive leadership,* Australian Human Rights Commission, 2016: https://www.humanrights.gov.au/our-work/race-discrimination/publications/leading-change-blueprint-cultural-diversity-and-inclusive

205 I think there is an assumption . . . Ming Long speaking to Danuta Kozaki, 'Bamboo ceiling keeping non-Anglo Australians from leadership roles, Rights Commission finds', *ABC Online,* July 2017: http://www.abc.net.au/news/2016-07-28/human-rights-commission-finds-lack-of-diversity-among-leaders/7666094

205 Women tend to mix . . . Eagly, A. H., Johannesen-Schmidt, M. C., and van Engen, M. (2003). Transformational, transactional, and laissez-faire leadership styles: A meta-analysis comparing women and men. *Psychological Bulletin,* 95.

206 Human beings are inwardly focused . . . Adrian F. Ward, 'The Neuroscience of Everybody's Favorite Topic', *The Scientific American,* July 2013: http://www.scientificamerican.com/article/the-neuroscience-of-everybody-favorite-topic-themselves/

206 In an average conversation . . . Dunbar, Marriot, Duncan, 'Human conversational behaviour', *Human Nature,* 8(3) 1997: http://www.medisch-fitness.com/documents/75procentdagelijksegesprekkenbestedenweaanroddelen.pdf

207 A Templeton Foundation study . . . Emiliana R. Simon-Thomas, Jeremy Adam Smith, 'How Grateful are Americans', *Templeton Foundation Report, January 2013:* http://greatergood.berkeley.edu/article/item/how_grateful_are_americans

207 Increased loyalty, productivity . . . Tony Schwartz, 'Why appreciation matters so much', *Harvard Business Review,* 2012: https://hbr.org/2012/01/why-appreciation-matters-so-mu.html

208 Your team members need . . . Harter, J.K., Schmidt, F.L., & Killham, E.A. *Employee engagement, satisfaction, and business-unit-level outcomes: a meta-analysis.* Washington DC: The Gallup Organization, 2003

210 While no personality test . . . 'The problem with using personality tests for hiring' *Harvard Business Review* August 2014: https://hbr.org/2014/08/the-problem-with-using-personality-tests-for-hiring

212 They discovered that employees . . . As reported by Emily Peck, 'Google Has Discovered The 5 Key Traits Employees Need To Succeed' *The Huffington Post*, November 2015: http://www.huffingtonpost.com.au/entry/google-employee-success-traits_us_564cd621e4b031745cef50fe?section=australia

213 Having friends at work . . . 'We all need friends at work', *Harvard Business Review*, August 2013: https://hbr.org/2013/07/we-all-need-friends-at-work

215 And like they do at home . . . Rose Hackman, 'Women are just better at this stuff': is emotional labor feminism's next frontier?' *The Guardian*, November 2015: https://www.theguardian.com/world/2015/nov/08/women-gender-roles-sexism-emotional-labor-feminism

215 Women managers are assumed . . . Rebecca Erickson, 'Why Emotion Work Matters: Sex, Gender, and the Division of Household Labor', *Journal of Marriage and Family*, 67(2) (May, 2005).

Exhaustion and burnout

221 Everybody you work with . . . Liz Ryan, 'Five ways your loyalty to your job can hurt you' *Forbes*, May 2016: http://www.forbes.com/sites/lizryan/2016/05/04/five-ways-your-loyalty-to-your-job-can-hurt-you/

222 I do not know of . . . Sheryl Sandberg, *Lean In: Women, work and the will to lead*, Knopf, 2013.

224 While 60 per cent of . . . Australian Bureau of statistics labourforce data, 2014, as noted by Annabel Crabb, *The Wife Drought*, (2015) Penguin Random House Australia.

224 In *The Wife Drought* . . . Annabel Crabb, *The Wife Drought*, (2015) Penguin Random House Australia.

227 If you think about . . . 'Relax, you have 168 hours this week', *Harvard Business Review* August 2014: https://hbr.org/2014/08/relax-you-have-168-hours-this-week

227 This refers to a scheduled . . . As told to Jeremiah Dillon, 'This Google Employee Has A Brilliant Time Management Strategy' *Huffington Post*, December 2015: http://www.huffingtonpost.com/entry/google-time-management_5671f55de4b0dfd4bcc0969f

227 This approach results in . . . As told to Jeremiah Dillon, 'This Google Employee Has A Brilliant Time Management Strategy' *Huffington Post*, December 2015: http://www.huffingtonpost.com/entry/google-time-management_5671f55de4b0dfd4bcc0969f

230 Career coach Jenn DeWall . . . Jen DeWall as told to Allana Akhtar for '8 Career Tips for Young Women Who Want to Be the Boss', *US News* July 2015: http://money.usnews.com/money/careers/articles/2015/07/30/8-career-tips-for-young-women-who-want-to-be-the-boss/

230 By contrast, DeWall says . . . Jen DeWall as told to Allana Akhtar for '8 Career Tips for Young Women Who Want to Be the Boss', *US News* July 2015: http://money.usnews.com/money/careers/articles/2015/07/30/8-career-tips-for-young-women-who-want-to-be-the-boss/

232 Linda A. Hill, professor . . . Linda A. Hill as told to *Harvard Business Review* for 'How to work for a workaholic', March 2016: https://hbr.org/2016/03/how-to-work-for-a-workaholic

234 More than 50 per cent . . . 'The state of mental health in Australian workplaces', report for *Beyond Blue* 2014, available at: https://www.headsup.org.au/docs/default-source/resources/bl1270-report---tns-the-state-of-mental-health-in-australian-workplaces-hr.pdf

234 One in five people . . .'The state of mental health in Australian workplaces', report for *Beyond Blue* 2014, available at: https://www.headsup.org.au/docs/default-source/resources/bl1270-report---tns-the-state-of-mental-health-in-australian-workplaces-hr.pdf

234 Psychologist David W. Ballard . . . David Ballard of the American Psychological Association as quoted by Sharie Bourg Carter, *High Octane Women: How Superachievers Can Avoid Burnout* (2011, Prometheus Books).

234 Burnout has been observed . . . Sharie Bourg Carter, *High Octane Women: How Superachievers Can Avoid Burnout* (2011, Prometheus Books).

234 Burnout is caused when . . . Sharie Bourg Carter, *High Octane Women: How Superachievers Can Avoid Burnout* (2011, Prometheus Books).

235 There are several warning . . . Sharie Bourg Carter, *High Octane Women: How Superachievers Can Avoid Burnout* (2011, Prometheus Books).

Sexism and sexual harassment

238 Documented sexism in Australia . . . *The World Upside Down: Australia 1788-1830*, National Library of Australia 2000.

238 Eight thousand five hundred women . . . *The World Upside Down: Australia 1788-1830*, National Library of Australia 2000.

238 Author and political commentator . . . George Megalogenis, 'Australia's second chance', 2015, Penguin Random House.

239 Women who did work . . . *The World Upside Down: Australia 1788-1830*, National Library of Australia 2000.

239 The first women workers' . . . *The World Upside Down: Australia 1788-1830*, National Library of Australia 2000.

239 Women protested against . . . *The World Upside Down: Australia 1788-1830*, National Library of Australia 2000.

239 The Australian Suffrage Society . . . 'The Australian Women's Suffrage Society. (1888-1898)' 2009. *Trove*.

239 White women were given . . . The Australian Women's Suffrage Society. (1888-1898)' 2009. *Trove*.

239 Indigenous women weren't extended . . . *History of the Indigenous Vote*, Australian Electoral Commission, August 2006: http://www.aec.gov.au/indigenous/files/history_indigenous_vote.pdf

239 The contraceptive pill arrived . . . 'Family Formation: Family planning', *Australian Bureau of Statistics Social Trends* 1998: http://www.abs.gov.au/AUSSTATS/abs@.nsf/2f762f95845417aeca25706c00834efa/e50a5b60e048fc07ca2570ec001909

240 The determination of the . . . Equal Pay Case 1969, (1969) *Commonwealth Arbitration Reports*, vol. 127, p.1142+. (To be phased in over 4 years, culminating in 1972)

240 And in 1983 Australia signed . . . *Sex Discrimination Act 1984* (Cth)

242 She was overwhelmed by . . . *The Saturday Paper,* October 2016: https://www. thesaturdaypaper.com.au/2016/10/22/the-ubiquity-sexual-harassment/14770548003886

242 In fact, research shows . . . Hannah Fingerhut 'In both parties, men and women differ over whether women still face obstacles to progress' *Pew Research Centre,* August 2016: http://www.pewresearch.org/fact-tank/2016/08/16/in-both-parties-men-and-women-differ-over-whether-women-still-face-obstacles-to-progress/

242 When the questionnaire probed . . . Lauren Ahn and Michelle Ruiz, 'Survey: 1 in 3 Women Has Been Sexually Harassed at Work' *Cosmopolitan March 2015:* http://www. cosmopolitan.com/career/news/a36453/cosmopolitan-sexual-harassment-survey/

242 Eighty-one per cent . . . Lauren Ahn and Michelle Ruiz, 'Survey: 1 in 3 Women Has Been Sexually Harassed at Work' *Cosmopolitan March 2015:* http://www.cosmopolitan. com/career/news/a36453/cosmopolitan-sexual-harassment-survey/

243 Forty-four per cent . . . Lauren Ahn and Michelle Ruiz, 'Survey: 1 in 3 Women Has Been Sexually Harassed at Work' *Cosmopolitan March 2015:* http://www.cosmopolitan.com/career/news/a36453/cosmopolitan-sexual-harassment-survey/

243 Twenty-five per cent had . . . Lauren Ahn and Michelle Ruiz, 'Survey: 1 in 3 Women Has Been Sexually Harassed at Work' *Cosmopolitan March 2015:* http://www.cosmopolitan. com/career/news/a36453/cosmopolitan-sexual-harassment-survey/

243 Of all the women . . . Lauren Ahn and Michelle Ruiz, 'Survey: 1 in 3 Women Has Been Sexually Harassed at Work' *Cosmopolitan March 2015:* http://www.cosmopolitan.com/career/news/a36453/cosmopolitan-sexual-harassment-survey/

243 The Sex Discrimination Act . . . *The Sex Discrimination Act 1984* (Cth), Section 28A.

Working with mean girls

252 The idea that women . . . Alana Jayne Piper, 'Woman's Special Enemy: Female Enmity in Criminal Discourse during the Long Nineteenth Century', *Journal of Social History* 2016; 49 (3).

252 Rather than enjoying . . . Alana Jayne Piper, 'Woman's Special Enemy: Female Enmity in Criminal Discourse during the Long Nineteenth Century', *Journal of Social History* 2016; 49 (3).

252 Women – as natural rivals . . . Alana Jayne Piper; 'Woman's Special Enemy: Female Enmity in Criminal Discourse during the Long Nineteenth Century', *Journal of Social History* 2016; 49 (3).

253 The media's casting . . . Rebecca Traister, 'True, new, female friendship', *Salon,* April 2012: http://www.salon.com/2012/04/12/true_new_female_friendship/

254 A 2011 study found . . . As cited by Peggy Drexler, 'The tyranny of the queen bee', *Wall Street Journal,* March 2013: http://www.wsj.com/news/articles/SB10001424127887 323884304578328271526080496

255 This means our memories . . . Sheppard, Leah D., and Karl Aquino. 'Much Ado About Nothing? Observers' Problematization of Women's Same-Sex Conflict at Work', *Academy of Management Perspectives,* vol. 27, no. 1, 2013.

255 One 2008 study found . . . Scott Schieman and Taralyn McMullen. Relational Demography in the Workplace and Health: An Analysis of Gender and the Subordinate-Superordinate Role-Set. *Journal of Health and Social Behavior,* September 2008.

257 **When Madeleine Albright famously . . .** Madeleine Albright, as quoted by Tom McCarthy 'Albright: 'special place in hell' for women who don't support Clinton', *The Guardian*, February 2016.

258 **To have one's existence . . .** Lauren Rosewarne, 'Scarcity and sexism: does watching The Bachelor make you a bad feminist?' *The Conversation*, https://theconversation.com/scarcity-and-sexism-does-watching-the-bachelor-make-you-a-bad-feminist-47417

259 **She found that '90 per cent . . .** Susan Shapiro Barash, Tripping the Prom Queen: The Truth about Women and Rivalry' *St Martin's Griffin*, 2007.

260 **By deliberately setting themselves . . .** Sheryl Sandberg and Adam Grant, 'Sheryl Sandberg on the myth of catty women' *The New York Times*, June 2016: http://www.nytimes.com/2016/06/23/opinion/sunday/sheryl-sandberg-on-the-myth-of-the-catty-woman.html

260 **It's quite common among . . .** Marianne Cooper 'Why women sometimes don't help other women' *The Atlantic*, July 2016: https://www.theatlantic.com/business/archive/2016/06/queen-bee/488144/

261 **Women engage in more . . .** Sibylle Artz, Wassilis Kassis, Stephanie Moldenhauer, 'Rethinking Indirect Aggression: The End of the Mean Girl Myth' *Victims & Offenders*, 8(3), 2013.

261 **Women are punished socially . . .** 'Powerlessness and the use of indirect aggression in friendships' Duncan, L. & Owen-Smith, A. *Sex Roles* (2006) 55: 493.

261 **In adulthood, this translates . . .** Doyle, H. S., & Mcloughlin, C. S. (2010). Do Science and Common Wisdom Collide or Coincide in their Understanding of Relational Aggression? *Frontiers in Psychology*, 1, 179.

262 **So as adult women . . .** Doyle, H. S., & Mcloughlin, C. S. (2010). 'Do Science and Common Wisdom Collide or Coincide in their Understanding of Relational Aggression?' *Frontiers in Psychology*, 1, 179.

262 **Often we resort to clique behaviour . . .** Susan Shapiro Barash, Tripping the Prom Queen: The Truth about Women and Rivalry' *St Martin's Griffin*, 2007.

262 **Research suggests that the higher . . .** Louann Brizendine, *The Female Brain*, Harmony Press, 2007.

262 **Women fall back on this . . .** Louann Brizendine, *The Female Brain*, Harmony Press, 2007.

263 **In order to understand why . . .** Festinger, Leon. (1954).*A Theory of Social Comparison Processes*, Retrieved September 12, 2007

264 **Women are also more likely . . .** White, J.B., Langer, E.J., Yariv, L. et al. 'Frequent Social Comparisons and Destructive Emotions and Behaviors: The Dark Side of Social Comparisons' *Journal of Adult Development* (2006) 13(36).

264 **By contrast, men tend . . .** Guimond, S., Chatard, A., Martinot, D., Crisp, R. J., & Redersdorff, S. 'Social comparison, self-stereotyping, and gender differences in self-construals'. *Journal of Personality and Social Psychology*, (2006), 90(2).

266 **Some commentators have criticized . . .** Howard J Morgan and Joelle K Jay, *The New Advantage: How Women in Leadership Can Create Win-Wins for Their Companies and Themselves*, Praeger Press, 2016.

Networking and mentoring

272 A joint study . . . *Women in the Workplace 2015*, Lean In and McKinsey & Company: https://womenintheworkplace.com/

272 They may only enjoy a professionally . . . *Women in the Workplace 2015*, Lean In and McKinsey & Company: https://womenintheworkplace.com/

272 Another study I came across . . . Lily Fang and Sterling Huang, 'Gender and connections among Wall Street analysts', INSEAD Faculty and Research Working Paper, retrieved 18 August 2016: http://sites.insead.edu/facultyresearch/research/doc.cfm?did=48816

272 To begin with, some women . . . See for example Daniëlle van de Kemenade, 'Sisterhood 2.0: why traditional networking isn't working for women', *The Guardian*, November 2015: https://www.theguardian.com/women-in-leadership/2015/nov/12/sisterhood-20-why-traditional-networking-isnt-working-for-women

273 The majority of caring and domestic . . . 'Parenting, work and the gender pay gap', *Different Gender, Different Lives*, Workplace Gender Equality Agency, 2014: https://www.wgea.gov.au/sites/default/files/2014-03-04_PP_Pay_Gap_and_Parenting.pdf

280 Mentoring has been hailed . . . Sylvia Ann Hewlett, 'Forget about mentors, women need sponsors' *TIME Magazine*, March 2013: http://ideas.time.com/2013/03/07/forget-about-mentors-women-need-sponsors/

283 The more progress they make . . . Sylvia Ann Hewlett, 'Forget about mentors, women need sponsors' *TIME Magazine*, March 2013: http://ideas.time.com/2013/03/07/forget-about-mentors-women-need-sponsors/

285 I read an article in New York magazine . . . Ann Friedman in Claire Landsbaum's article 'How Obama's female staffers made their voices heard', *NY Mag, The Cut*, 2013: http://nymag.com/thecut/2016/09/heres-how-obamas-female-staffers-made-their-voices-heard.html

286 When you've worked hard . . . Michelle Obama as quoted in 'Michelle Obama's 16 most powerful quotes about women' *The Telegraph*, December 2016: http://www.telegraph.co.uk/women/life/michelle-obamas-12-most-powerful-quotes-about-women/when-youve-worked-hard-and-done-well-and-walked-through-that-doo/

Conclusion

290 The self-described greatest tennis . . . Serena Williams as interviewed by Common, *ESPN*, air date 19 December 2016: http://www.espn.com/espnw/quote/6391571/223/luck-do-i-spent-many-many-hours-countless-hours-court-working-my-one-moment-not-knowing-come

Discover a
new favourite

Visit **penguin.com.au/readmore**